STUDIES IN MARXISM, Vol. 4
Papers from the Third Midwest Marxist Scholars Conference

The United States in Crisis: Marxist Analyses

Lajos Biro and Marc J. Cohen, Editors

MARXIST EDUCATIONAL PRESS
Minneapolis

Copyright 1979 Marxist Educational Press

First printing 1979

Library of Congress
Midwest Marxist Scholars Conference, 3rd,
University of Illinois, 1978
The United States in Crisis
(Studies in Marxism, Vol. 4)

1. United States - Social Conditions - 1960 -- Congresses. 2. United States - Economic Conditions - 1961 - -- Congresses. 3. United States -- Foreign Relations -- Congresses. 4. Social Conflicts -- Congresses 5. Capitalism -- Congresses.

I. Biro, Lajos, 1927- II. Cohen, Marc J., 1952- III.Title IV. Series: Studies in Marxism (Minneapolis) v.4

HN65.M49, 1978   309.1'73'092   78-61686

ISBN 930656-56-08-3 hardcover
ISBN 0-930656-07-5 paperback
ISBN 0-930656-00-8 series
Printed in the United States of America

Marxist Educational Press
c/o Department of Anthropology
University of Minnesota
224 Church Street SE
Minneapolis, MN   55455

CONTENTS

Preface
Lajos Biro, Marc J. Cohen 9

Introduction
Herbert Aptheker 15

**Part I: Welfare and Labor:
Contradictions Under State Monopoly Capitalism**

1: Capitalism and Social Welfare:
Structures and Oppositions
Arline Prigoff 31

2: Black Workers and the Labor Movement:
Recent Transformations
Philip S. Foner 47

3: The Impact of Mexican Immigration:
A Panel Discussion
John Womack, John Coatsworth,
Marc Zimmerman, Renato Barahona 71

Part II: Class, Race and Education

4: Developmental Education:
A Beleaugured Species
Michael Washington, Sr. 103

5: The Struggle for Desegregated Quality Education:
The Case of Appalachia
    Marvin Berlowitz   109

6: The Developing Parent Movement in Boston:
Dynamics of Change
    Rayleen M. Craig   127

Part III: The Crisis and Consciousness:
    A Debate

7: Late Capitalism and Mental Illness:
Toward a Critical Theory of Psychic Crisis
    Robert B. Sipe   151

8: Alienation and Humanization:
Subjective and Objective Factors
    Irving J. Crain, M.D.   167

9: Pathological Illusions:
and Commodity Fetishism
    Francis H. Bartlett   177

Part IV: Culture, Politics and Technology
    in Capitalist Development

10: Bilingualism and the Limits of the Melting Pot
    Lajos Biro   187

11: The Neutron Bomb
and the Crisis of U.S. Foreign Policy
    Georgia Stevic   205

12: The Ideology of Austerity:
A Critique of Futurism
    David L. Morgan and Dan G. Rebik   221

PREFACE: THIRD MIDWEST MARXIST SCHOLARS CONFERENCE

The Third Midwest Marxist Scholars Conference, sponsored by the Marxist Educational Press, was held at the University of Illinois, Chicago Circle in Chicago, Illinois on March 3-5, 1978. The conference, at which over 200 persons were present, had as its theme, "Crisis and Austerity in the 1970's: Class Struggle in Economics, Politics, and Culture." This fourth volume of *Studies in Marxism* is a selection of papers presented at the conference. Since the number of presentations given far exceeds the publishing capacity of this volume, the editors had to confront the difficult task of selecting a limited sampling able to reflect the wide range of topics covered during those three days in Chicago.

"Crisis and Austerity" is not only a fine-sounding title for an academic conference, but also a signification of the harsh reality of life for millions of people in the U. S. and elsewhere in the capitalist world. At the end of World War II, the United States was unmatched as an economic and military power, and its policy makers set out to remake the world in a fashion that would generate even greater profits for the American ruling class while providing continued strategic dominance. By the 1970's this bubble had burst. It had become clear that the United States was overextended, both in terms of the military aims of its imperialist foreign policy, and in economic terms. The multinational corporations' flight abroad in search of cheap labor and quick profits left unemployment and idle capacity behind. With the collapse of the U. S. position in Indochina before the national liberation movements in 1975, a permanent crisis set in domestically. Vital services were cut back in an effort by the government to continue supporting the military-industrial complex. This crisis has had its greatest impact on oppressed minorities, women, and youth, who have been victimized by "last hired, first fired" policies and the watering down of affirmative action programs.

Whatever the offical ruling class explanations may be — excessive wages, too much social spending, phoney racist and sexist apologetics, or the alleged military threat from the Soviet Union — one factor that never emerges is that the root of the crisis is the capitalist system itself. The conference in Chicago proved that the forces of resistance to the institutionalization of the crisis are growing stronger and that Marxism provides an indispensible method of illumination of the underlying features of the crisis, one that is attracting an ever-growing number of concerned individuals interested in meaningful solutions.

The conference brought together a number of nationally known Marxist scholars, including Herbert Aptheker and Philip Foner, together with industrial and social service workers, civil rights, community and labor activists, and academics who are struggling to make the Marxist approach legitimate in the schools and universities.

Aptheker, who has worked for 40 years to promote Marxist scholarship in the U. S., gave the paper included here at the first general session of the conference. Serving as our introduction, the paper suggests certain of the contours of the capitalist crisis by describing its manifestations in several areas of American life.

More detailed treatment of subjects touched on by Aptheker is contained in the other papers comprising this collection. These papers fall into four major categories which constitute the distinct sections of the volume. Section I, "Welfare and Labor: Contradictions under State Monopoly Capitalism," shows how the present socio-economic crisis has affected the lives of working people. Arline Prigoff provides a general theoretical analysis of
U.S. socio-economic transformations resulting in current trends of social welfare and their effect on the poor. Prigoff discusses how social welfare programs involving concessions wrung from the ruling class by prolonged struggle have become the means for maintaining social control over workers and oppressed minorities. The present crisis, however, has stimulated efforts to weaken or eliminate many such programs.The stuggle to maintain social services becomes an important part of the progressive counteroffensive to the austerity drive.

The ways in which members of the working class, particularly Black, Chicano, and other minority workers, have been made to pay the costs of monopoly capitalism's failures at home and abroad are explored by Philip Foner and by the participants in the panel discussion on Mexican Immigration. Foner, who has written extensively on the history of the labor movement in the United States, traces the growth of participation by Black workers in the labor

Preface

force and in the trade union movement. He notes the gains resulting from the civil rights movement of the 1960's, but points out the still-present higher unemployment rates for Blacks at all levels. He examines the role of the labor movement in the struggle against racism including the need for strong labor support for affirmative action programs. The relationship between immigration from Mexico and changing trends in the capitalist system in both the U.S. and Mexico are discussed by John Womack, John Coatsworth, Marc Zimmerman, and Renato Barahona. The participants note the divisive nature of campaigns against undocumented workers and stress the relationship between the struggle for working class unity in the United States and international solidarity with workers elsewhere.

The effects of the overall crisis on education, particularily on the struggle for desegregation and racial unity in the schools, are examined by Michael Washington, Marvin Berlowitz and Rayleen Craig in Section II, "Class, Race and Education." While stressing higher education, Washington provides a brief introduction to the section by pointing to how the crisis has given new impetus to racist practices throughout the entire educational system. He examines the special problems faced by developmental programs which seek to promote equality of educational opportunity in the face of capitalist control of education. Berlowitz examines the struggle for desegregated education and the role of urban Appalacians in this process. He exposes the insufficiency of certain New Left theories which put forward a separatist approach to education. Focussing on the impact of institutional racism as an obstacle to parent unity, Rayleen Craig details aspects of the struggle for school desegregation in Boston, including the role of parents in Court-ordered citizen participation structures.

The insights of Marxism on mental illness and the present psychic crisis in the U.S. are the subject of a discussion by Robert Sipe, Irving Crain and Francis Bartlett, in Section III, "The Crisis and Consciousness: A Debate." Sipe stresses the role of commodity fetishism in creating schizophrenia under the conditions of what he calls "late capitalism." Crain replies by emphasizing the need for working class struggle to overcome the source of alienation (namely, the capitalist mode of production), while holding that Sipe oversimplifies the relationship between capitalism and mental health. Bartlett notes the extreme subtleties in the relations between the individual and society; he points out the need for detailed Marxist analysis of the affects of commodity fetishism on personality traits.

The final section, "Culture, Politics and Technology in Capitalist Development," consists of three papers which exemplify the wide range of perspectives presented at the conference. These papers are also of particular importance in the effort to understand and overcome the capitalist system. A search for unity within a multi-cultural working class is the subject of Lajos Biro's paper on bilingualism. Biro frames his subject in a broad theoretical context which relates the historical roles of bilingualism and bilingual education to those of the U.S. "melting pot" and culture in the struggle against capitalism.

In terms of foreign policy, the United States still seeks to be the chief defender of the world capitalist system, but tries to avoid the huge financial and human losses of the Vietnam-style conflicts with the socialist camp and national liberation movements. Hence, horrid weapons like the neutron bomb represent, from the perspective of the ruling class, a cheaper and more efficient way to maintain capitalism's position on a world scale, as Georgia Stevic shows in her paper.

Finally, David Morgan and Dan Rebik discuss the currently fashionable trend of so-called "futurism" among bourgeois intellectuals. The paper emphasizes the fetishization of technology in this trend which ranges from pictures of leisurely utopias to neo-Malthusianism. For the most part futurists do not see a future without capitalism in which people have overcome capitalist crises and regained control of their lives under socialism.

We would particularly like to thank Wigand Lange, Charles Spencer and Sarah Markham Pietsch of Wisconsin, as well as members of the Minnesota Marxist Scholars and the Marxist Educational Press editorial board (A.A. Aldaraca, Ed Baker, Deb Owen, Bill Rowe, Harold Schwartz, Matt Schub and Bill Simbolov), for their assistance in editing this volume.

Madison, Wisconsin
December, 1978

Lajos Biro
Marc J. Cohen

INTRODUCTION: CRISIS IN THE CAPITALIST WORLD

Herbert Aptheker
American Institute of Marxist Studies

1.

Affirmations of the existance of crisis in the capitalist world abound. A dozen years ago, Nat Hentoff wrote of what he called "The Cold Society" in no less an authoritative voice of that society than *Playboy* magazine. Hentoff was referring to the ubiquitous sense of alienation and futility that pervaded much of that social order. It was a year later that Senator J. William Fullbright wrote of the United States as "A Sick Society" in the *New York Times Magazine* (Aug. 20,1976). Last year, viewing the United States from afar, Australian scholar Andrew Parken, called this country "The Homicidal Nation." Examining the statistics of homicides, which show the U.S. rate to be from two to twelve times higher than that in other capitalist nations, Parken concluded: "The American Dream carries along with it...the Violent Nightmare."[1]

Just a few months ago Gunnar Myrdal wrote of "a worried America" now facing a "multifaceted crisis" marked by "steady deterioration" so that, he warned, "what is at stake...in America is nothing less than the nation's soul."[2]

In addition to such affirmations, it will not be out of place to offer some illustrations. David Herbert Donald, Charles Warren Professor of History at Harvard University, greeted the beginning of the 1977 school year by contributing an essay on "Our Irrelevant History" to the Op-Ed page of the *New York Times* (Sept. 26, 1977). Professor Donald noted: "In a few days college classes will begin again, and I am once more preparing new lectures on American history." Here is his central paragraph:

> What undergraduates want from their history teachers is an understanding of how the American past relates to the present and the future. But if I teach what I believe to be the truth, I can only share with them my sense of the irrelevance of that history and of the

bleakness of the new era we are entering.

Moving down — or up — from Harvard to television, here is how the *New York Times* critic, Les Brown, described the story line of a new comedy series:

> Two middle-aged sisters have married quite differently, one to a wealthy lecher, the other to a blue-collar worker, her second husband, who is sexually impotent. The wealthy sister and her young daughter are separately having affairs with the same tennis pro. . . . The couple also have a puritanical daughter, described in the show as a 'latent nun,' and a son in puberty who is obsessed with pornography. . . the poorer sister has two sons, one a member of the Mafia, the other a homosexual desirous of a sex-change operation who likes to model his mother's gowns.

Mr. Brown concluded by quoting the program chief of the network scheduling this extravaganza: "It is an intelligent show written and produced by intelligent people, and in time will be perceived as a moral show."

Unique in the world's literature, I think, is the genre produced in capitalism's senility depicting the future as distressful, cruel and utterly unwholesome; instead of the utopian works regularly appearing since Bacon coined the term, one has anti-utopian works patterned after *1984*. Additionally, now there is an entire series of best-selling novels in which children are portrayed as monsters, demons, murderers. Children appear not as reflections of innocence, joy and renewal but rather of guilt, terror and the absence of any future at all. I have in mind such recent books — selling by the hundreds of thousands and dramatized often in movies and television — as *The Omen* by David Seltzer, *Suffer the Children* by John Saul, *Julia* by Peter Straub, *It's Alive* by Richard Woodley, *Carrie* by Stephen King and *The Godsend* by Bernard Taylor.[4]

A new development in the United States is the appearance of hundreds of communities wherein landlords bar the presence of children; in whole areas, such as southern California, it is actually becoming very difficult for people with children to find living quarters.

2.

Ideologues of capitalism discover the end of ideology, the exhaustion of Man, the early demise of Civilization — because of over-population, of pollution, of technology, of apathy — of scores of other "Causes." These ideologues confuse the uselessness of their own ideology with the end of ideology, the senility of their system with Civilization's death throes, the Frankenstein quality of technological development, given imperialism, with the liberating capacity of enhanced productivity, given a rational, humane social order.

These ideologues, having exhausted their capacities for persuasive rationalization, repudiate reason, embrace cults of withdrawal and make a profession of cynicism. Actually, the exhaustion of their cherished capitalism is the counterpart of a new burst of energy, creativity and progressive capacity on the part of the gravediggers for the corpse. Those still serving the corpse sense this stirring, cannot understand it and are more terrified by it because of their lack of comprehension.

When colonialism dies, national liberation flourishes; when racism is routed, friendship flowers; when male supremacy is overcome, true adult relationships are possible; when war is prevented, creative living together becomes possible — when the system of monopoly capitalism is in its death throes, the red dawn of a higher civilization has already reached noon.

3.

The techniques of these increasingly desperate ideologues of decay has now descended to transparent levels of deceit, mimicing the worst aspects of the system's security apparatus, from the local sheriff to the FBI chief, from the Red Squad sergeant to the CIA Director. Since the *Communist Manifesto*, anti-communism has been a basic feature of the propaganda of the bourgeoisie; and since the Bolshevik Revolution of 1917, anti-Sovietism has been the central incantation of imperialists, from Churchill to Mussolini, from Franco to Hitler, from Joseph McCarthy to Henry Kissinger. It must be noted, however, that it is necessary to return to the absolute hysteria of the *New York Times* in the three to four years just after the Great October to find the like of the persistent and massive anti-Soviet campaign conducted by that bellwether of Imperialism in the past few years.

Accompanying this rabid anti-communism and anti-Sovietism is a renewed intensity of racist practices and propaganda, from resistance to, and then growing attacks upon, affirmative action to the appearance of still another wave of "scientific" racism in areas of history, psychology, sociology and legal theory.

Here, however, I want to point to the utter bankruptcy of what may be called the methodology of these imperialist propagandists. That is, one observes — even on the "highest levels" — what can only be described as deliberate lying and cheating which display contempt for the public's intelligence.

Here are some illustrations of this policy of outright deception. The official data on unemployment are distorted by excluding about three and a half million so-called "involuntary part-time workers," and by excluding over one million people called "discouraged workers" — these four and a half to five million workers simply are not counted when the government announces seven million unemployed. Nor is there any count made of the millions of potential jobseekers who include, as Professor Helen Ginsburg has recently reminded us, "many forced retirees, physically and mentally handicapped persons"[5] and those who would work — especially women — if jobs were available. Additionally, one has in the United States millions of racially and nationally oppressed young people who have never been allowed to enter the labor market and thus never appear in the official data on unemployment.

Senile capitalism finds people to be pollutants; it finds itself unable to employ increasing millions of workers. That system which feeds on the exploitation of workers, and through that feeding conquered and revolutionized the world, now, in its dotage, finds workers themselves undigestible. This is terminal cancer with a vengeance!

Another illustration of deception: The official figures hide the scandalous rate of actual illiteracy in this country — probably reaching some 30% of the population — by having the Census define illiterates as those who did not complete a fifth-grade education, when as everyone knows, many people have "graduated" high school and are functionally illiterate.

Another illustration is the manner in which the numbers of mentally ill people in this anti-human society are reduced lately: State governments simply turn out tens of thousands of such patients from hospitals — many of whom now live in garages, condemned buildings and chicken coops or wander the streets. That is the way, for example, that former Governor Ronald Reagan reduced the mental hospital population in California from 35,000 in 1963 to 6,500 in 1974![6]

Here is a final example of official sleight-of-hand. The Carter Administration is boasting that it has "reduced" armament expenditures; in fact, however, it has boosted the budget for arms — according to its own figures — by seven billion dollars over last year. And not only is this increase falsely described as a decrease, but the actual increase is even greater than revealed. Thus, while the Carter budget for fiscal 1979 used the figure $126 billions, an additional 2.8 billions for nuclear weapons was put in the budget of the new Department of Energy, and still another 3.6 billions marked for "military aid" was moved from "national defense" into the column for "international affairs." Hence, the Carter budget for arms in fiscal 1979 is not $126 billions — unprecedented as that is — but actually is at least $132 billions.[7]

4.

Propaganda in defense of such a system in today's world tends to be ineffective. Some partisans of the system are blinded by that bias and confess bewilderment at this public relations failure. Former U.S. Army General James M. Gavin, for instance, wrote in *The Saturday Review* a dozen years ago: "At a time when we possess more power than any other nation on earth, we are not very persuasive. It is frustrating and baffling" (July 30, 1966).

Perhaps a Pentagon general may be forgiven for confusing power with persuasiveness. But others of a more civilian — even intellectual cast — express bewilderment at the other side of the coin that baffled the General. George Kennan, for example, from his Princeton University vantage point, confessed in a recent interview published in the CIA-financed magazine, *Encounter*, that it was inexplicable to him that Marxism — with all its crudities and irrelevancies — still was potent and, God help us, was even growing in influence.

Henry Kissinger is being paid one million dollars by the National Broadcasting Company for granting several televised interviews. So far in these interviews the former Secretary of State has emphasized his opinions on Communism and on the C.I.A. As to the former, Dr. Kissinger states he is puzzled, he finds in "paradoxical" that in Western Europe, Communist Parties are powerful and are even "gaining influence," although — as every really sophisticated person in the United States understands and as accepted wisdom has it — Marxism is irrelevant to "advanced" societies.

What is needed, said Kissinger, echoing the line of every Administration since Truman, are governments in Western Europe that would successfully face significant social problems and manifest "compassion" toward their inhabitants; were this true, the deviltry of Marxism and the wizardry of Communism would lose effectiveness. Why it is not true and why afflicted ones should turn to agents of the devil is, of course, beyond Dr. Kissinger's comprehension. Hence, it is "puzzling"; indeed, he adds, "One has to say this is a moral problem and not a material one."

That seems to mean that many of the peoples of Western Europe are suffering from moral defects, and who better than the main architect of Washington's effort in Vietnam may judge the morals of others?

When discussing the C.I.A., Dr. Kissinger also adopted a moralistic tone. He observed, in moving prose, that: "No institution should be asked to be infallible, and I also believe that in common decency the dedicated men and women who have served in intelligence for thirty years do not deserve to be pilloried in the manner which has been the case in recent years."

Dr. Kissinger neglected to make clear who had demanded infallibility. But when he joins "common decency" to the C.I.A., even this Communist is astonished. Of course, it is not a question of an infallible institution, but a criminal one.

The C.I.A. in the last thirty years — according to uncontroverted evidence, mostly from its own files — has maintained brothels, has corrupted trade unions in the interest of bosses, has corrupted the communications industry of the United States and other nations, has overthrown, with mass murder, liberal and progressive governments from Guatamala to Iran to Ghana to Thailand to Chile, has carried out assassinations, has experimented without knowledge or consent upon the bodies and minds of human beings, has bought politicians and kings in order to maintain oppressive regimes in power.

In the interest of "common decency" I shall illustrate the activities of the "dedicated" personnel of the C.I.A. by two instances recently reported by one such employee — now facing serious legal attacks because of his disclosures. Frank Snepp, formerly chief strategic analyst for the C.I.A. in Vietnam, in his *Decent Interval*

(New York: Random House, 1978) tells how he, himself, had had a Communist, Nguyen Van Tai, placed within a refrigerator, and that while the person was thus freezing had "insulted and cajoled" him in order to obtain information — but had failed. At the suggestion of the C.I.A., continues Snepp, a South Vietnamese employee loaded Nguyen Van Tai aboard a plane from whence he was "thrown out at ten thousand feet over the South China Sea."

In this same book, Snepp writes of an "interrogation" he conducted in 1972 of another Communist, Nam Quyet. Comrade Nam Quyet also resisted to the end. Here is Snepp again:

> Whenever I prodded him with leading questions, he would lapse into a fit of coughing thereby tearing open tubercular scars in his lungs and throat. As the interrogation continued, blood would begin oozing from his nose and mouth. He couldn't resist spitting mouthfuls at me.

As stated, Kissinger knows a moral problem when he sees one and he also comprehends "common decency." It is comrades like Nguyen Van Tai and Nam Quyet who puzzle Kissinger and his class, and who spit in the faces of their hirelings. Naturally, in the United States, with a devout President passionately devoted to human rights, it will be the Kissingers who serve as Secretaries of State and who are paid off with a million pieces of silver by a great corporation dedicated to freedom of speech.

5.

Kennan and Kissinger persist in asserting that the strength of Marxism "baffles" them. No doubt their class allegiance does make the modern world a puzzle as well as a menace. But now that the "spectre" of 1848 has become the reality of the twentieth century and now that that reality has endured — despite everything — for over sixty years and has spread through the Western Hemisphere, into Africa and Asia and through Europe in terms of actual state power, now, if one is still puzzled at Marxism's strength it is because one loathes it and fears it and is quite incapable of comprehending it; fear has paralyzed thought.

Others from time to time — including many who were not Marxists and certainly not Communists — have been capable of some objectivity. Thus, here are the words of the late Harold J. Laski, once a leader of the British Labour Party, in one of his last volumes (*Liberty in the Modern State*, New York 1949). The quotation is long, but given the source and its content, it is not too long:

> It has been part of the strategy of the enemies of freedom in part to decry the accomplishment of the Soviet Union's makers, and in part to declare that the price is too heavy for the end. It is vital for those who care for freedom to maintain a proper perspective in this matter. The Soviet Union has been the pioneer of a new civilization. The conditions upon which it began the task of its building were of a magnitued unexampled in our experience. Its leaders came to power in a country accustomed only to bloody tyranny, racked and impoverished by unsuccessful war. Its peoples were overwhelmingly illiterate and untrained in the use of that industrial technology upon which the standards of modern civilization depend. Its task of construction was begun amidst civil war, intervention from without, famine and pestilence. . . . No doubt Lenin and his colleagues were responsible, in the first seven years of the Revolution, for blunders, mistakes, even crimes. It is nevertheless true that, in those years, they accomplished a remarkable work of renovation. They accomplished it, moreover, in such a fashion that, within ten years of the overthrow of the Czar, they were able to proceed to the socialization of the productive system.
>
> In the last decade, the achievements have been immense. The war has been won, unemployment has been abolished; illiteracy has been conquered; the growing productivity of the Soviet Union stands in startling contrast to the deliberate organization of scarcity in the capitalist states.

Introduction: Herbert Aptheker

> In the treatment of criminals, in the scientific handling of backward peoples, in the application of science to industry and agriculture, in the conquest of racial prejudice, and in the provision of opportunity to the individual — in the full sense of the career opened to the talents — the Soviet Union stands today at the forefront of civilization. It is, of course, true that, judged by the standards of Great Britain and the United States, its material levels of life are low; it has not rivalled in twenty years the unimpeded century-long development of the most progressive capitalist states. The true comparison, of course, is with pre-revolutionary Russia; and the gains, both material and spiritual, are immense. In wages, hours of labor, conditions of sanitation and safety, industrial security, and educational opportunity, the comparison is at every point favorable to the new regime.

One might conclude that this remarkable passage is the product of wartime euphoria and the memory of the comradeship in the great struggle against Hitlerism. However, here is the testimony offered almost twenty years later, and offered not by a British Labourite but by a leading U.S. diplomat and "Kremlinologist" — no less a personage than George Kennan, the same one who was the Mr. X of the 1940's, and the same one who announced himself as puzzled with Marxism's strength in 1977. These words from Mr. Kennan in the late 1960's appear no less a prestigious organ of the Establishment than *Foreign Affairs* (Oct. 1967, p.19):

> In creating a new order out of the chaos of 1918-1919; in clinging to power successfully for a half a century in a great and variegated country where the exertion of political power has never been easy; in retaining its own discipline and vitality as a political instrument in the face of the corrupting influence that the exercise of power invariably exerts; in realizing many of its far-reaching social objectives; in carrying to the present

level the industrialization of the country and the development of new technology; in giving firm, determined and in many ways inspired leadership in the struggle against the armies of German fascism; in providing political inspiration and guidance to many of the radical-socialist forces of the world over most of this period; in these achievements, the Communist Party of the Soviet Union has not only stamped itself as the greatest political organization of the century in vigor and will, but has remained faithful to the quality of the Russian Revolution as the century's greatest political event.

6.

We — two hundred of us — are gathered in a Marxist Scholars Conference right here in the center of the United States. This, itself, is some testimony to the strength which puzzles Kissinger.

Scholars are wedded to science, and the consensus among Establishment scholars hold that science must be value-free, hold partisan science to be a contradiction in terms.

Let us see. There are two fundamental commitments to science. One is to truth over falsehood; surely no one will deny that. But preferring truth to falsehood, is that not a value judgement?

Secondly, science is committed to the ennoblement of humanity. Experts who turn their skills and learning in a contrary direction may be skilled and even "learned" in a textbook fashion, but if their commitment is not to such ennoblement they are not scientists.

Science, then, seeks truth and the betterment of humanity. To those who say how can one know what is "better" I reply:

> courtesy is better than vulgarity
> dignity is better than insult
> literacy is better than illiteracy
> fulfilling work is better than enforced idleness
> health is better than sickness
> adequate living conditions are better than improvishment
> life is better than death

If anyone disagrees with these propositions, he or she may be able to get secure appointments in prestigious U.S. universities, but such a person is not worthy of argument. Such a person requires therapy not argument.

7.

Those of us who say we are Marxist scholars mean that our learning is at the service of the oppressed, the insulted and the exploited. We mean that we are partisans to the cause of equality, national liberation, an end to racism, male supremacy, elitism, poverty, unemployment — an end to spending billions for bombs, to threatening world wide conflagration. As I came here by plane from California, I read a one-sentence story taking up half an inch on a back page of the San Francisco *Chronicle* (March 3, 1978). It is datelined Brussels, the NATO headquarters city, and reads in its entirety: "The United States is considering going ahead with the production of the neutron bomb without public support from its NATO allies in Europe, informed Alliance sources said yesterday."

Without "public support." Of course, such a decision must be made surreptitiously in the face of known mass opinion in Europe; and it must be hidden from the public in the United States also by these kinds of half-inch and cryptic notices.

From crematoria to N-bombs, from stationary ovens to mobile ones, from incinerating, a few millions to annihilating all humanity — there is imperialism's "progress" towards a "final solution".

We who think of ourselves as Marxist scholars must — if we are to be worthy of that title — battle against that system and for the victory here in the United States of a rational, humane egalitarian system, of socialism.

Notes

1. See *Politics*, 12 (Flinders University, Australia: May, 1977, 78-88.
2. *Christian Century* (December 14, 1977), pp. 1161-66.
3. I am indebted to the newly reborn *Benjamin Rush Newsletter* (February, 1978), for calling attention to this bit of Americana. The *Newsletter*, published in New York City, speaks for a growing group of Marxist oriented workers in the area of psychology and mental health.
4. See J. S. Gordon, "Demonic Children," in *New York Times Book Review* (September 11, 1977).
5. Helen Ginsburg, "Domestic Issue Number One: Jobs for all the Jobless," in *Christianity & Crisis*, 16 (January, 1978), pp. 325-29. The author is a professor of economics in Brooklyn College in New York City.
6. The Jack Anderson syndicated column dated February 19, 1978 was devoted to an expose of this practice of creating what he called "psychiatric ghettoes" in many cities by simply dismissing mental patients from hospitals.
7. Data supplied by the Friends Committee on National Legislation, Washington, D.C.

I.
WELFARE AND LABOR: CONTRADICTIONS UNDER STATE MONOPOLY CAPITALISM

CAPITALISM AND SOCIAL WELFARE: STRUCTURES AND OPPOSITIONS

Arline Prigoff

1. Introduction

This paper is based on material presented and discussed at a workshop on "Social Welfare and Monopoly Capitalism" during the third annual Midwest Marxist Scholar Conference. The workshop perspective is presented in article form in order to clarify and condense principal concepts. The conceptual framework (part 2) reflects my own thinking as workshop leader, but it also encompasses comments and contradictions highlighted by workshop participants. In this sense, the paper contains an analysis which may not be definitive, but which does constitute a collective effort to establish some of the key features of state monopoly capitalism by a broad range of people attending the conference.

Backgrounds in Marxist Social Welfare Research

The workshop attempted to explore social welfare and social service practice in the U.S. from a Marxist perspective. This topic has not been addressed frequently, despite the clear historical connections between the field of social welfare and the nature of advanced capitalist structures. Although social welfare policy deals with the allocation and distribution of income, goods and services, as well as with the social and material conditions of living, we have had a paucity of Marxist analysis on this subject. Bertha Reynolds, an outstanding social work activist and socialist of the 1930's, edited the journal, *Social Work Today*, which advocated a Marxist orientation. Currently the writings of Jeffry Galper on radical social work,[1] the articles appearing in the journal, *Catalyst*, and materials developed by the Radical Alliance of Social Service Workers in New York are published evidences of Marxist dialogue in the field. But an attempt to introduce a coherent Marxist analysis of social welfare and social service practice remains a novel, exploratory undertaking.

Capitalism, the Context for the Development of Social Welfare

From the historic beginnings of industrialization in England and its North American colonies, social welfare laws and the establishemnt of "social provision" were based on the negative social consequences of capitalist development. The emergence and growth of capitalism demanded the recruitment of a wage labor force of workers and their families whose survival was threatened by low wages and periodic unemployment. The politically ascendant bourgeoisie possessed the power to transfer the social costs of worker survival to the government. The bourgeois state assumed responsibility in providing some benefits to ameliorate social conditions which might have jeopardized the political stability of the socio-economic order. From its origin, then, social welfare has been an arena of conflict between the working class and the owners of the means of production, in which there were concessions made to resolve some of the social consequences of the capitalist system: proletarianization, unemployment, social dependency, health hazards, etc. Social welfare represents the institutionalization of the bourgeois state's reluctant social insurance and transfer payments made in response to working class organization and potential political power.

The major social welfare legislation in the U. S., as in other countries, resulted from workers' economic and political struggle. The Social Security Act, the nation's major social welfare law, came about through working class pressure for social insurance and other benefits during the Great Depression. Internationally, the level of social service benefits generally reflects a country's level of trade union organization and political strength.[2] (Ironically, the correlation between labor's politically organized power and the national level of social welfare and service provision is scarcely noted in social work literature.) The contradictions of social welfare programming within the context of capitalism result in service institutions which, while gained through workers' struggle, operate to contain and pacify labor militancy. In dialectical terms, social welfare benefits contribute to workers' power, yet at the same time may tend to foster economic dependency and passivity.

These are the kinds of dialectical contradictions and dilemmas which exist in the field of social welfare. Social welfare issues are important to the broader socio-economic and political context; inversely, this context is essential to configurations and developments within social welfare. Yet analyses of social welfare matters are marginal to most theoretical studies of capitalism, and analyses of broad economic structures and conflicts tend to be absent in social work literature. It is in an effort to break out of this unproductive circularity that we will attempt to identify and examine some essential features of monopoly capitalism which have massive consequences for social relations in U.S. society. Our goal is to establish a framework which accounts for social welfare as an arena central to capitalist society and the effort to oppose it.

2. Essential Features of State Monopoly Capitalism

Monopolistic Constraints on Production

In the monoplistic phase of capitalism, the productive processes are not fully expanded, but are limited in order to maintain maximum profitability. Competition is curtailed through mergers, and other corporate strategies which manage to gain oligopolistic control of resources and access to markets. Currently, high prices coexistent with high levels of unemployment reflect the level of corporate consolidation in the U. S. Scarcities in commodities often indicate corporate limitations on market supply for maximization of profit rather than any real lack of essential resources. (The national gasoline shortage in 1973 is a relevant example.) As a result of corporate consolidation in basic U. S. industries, types of commodities which now may be artificially limited to maxamize profitability include food products, housing, energy fuels and other products essential to life in an urban environment.

The Domination of Financial Capital over Productive Processes

More ruthlessly than ever, corporations under advanced capitalism are in business not to produce goods which satisfy human wants, but to accumulate capital. The material product is irrelevant, as is quality or utility. Financial considerations and institutions increasingly control corporate decisions and enterprises. Luxury goods of little or no social value are often more profitable than socially useful products, so that the manufacturing process produces attractively packaged but practically worthless items.

Corporate development, in which fiscal numbers alone determine production decisions, has left U. S. labor ever more vulnerable to company lockouts and run-away shops — to operation transfers from union to non-union plants and locations, to large-scale shifts from domestic to "off-shore" manufacturing abroad. The social risks of permanent, industry-wide unemployment and chronic national employment are heightened when not only the product but the worker becomes expendable. Such is the effect of rising financial control in the corporate system.

The Export of Capital as a Feature of Imperialism

The expansion of capital flow from the U. S. to other geographic areas is witnessed by the rapid expansion since World War II of "multi-national" corporations — or more accurately, by the proliferation of foreign subsidies of U. S. corporations around the world. U. S. financial institutions have branched out rapidly all over the globe, tying their lending practices to the enforcement of economic and political guarantees of U. S. access to national resources and markets. Cultural penetration accompanies this flow of U. S. Capital in the "developing countries." Thus the move of capital investment and ownership interest from domestic industries to cheap and exploitable labor colonies is detrimental to U. S. labor as well as to the develoopment of national indigenous industry and oppositional culture abroad. Cuba is one of the few non-industrial nations that has been able to escape the destructive consequences of imperialist penetration through its achievement of socialist revolution.

Although employed U. S. workers benefit as consumers from the imperialist exploitation of foreign labor, the ultimate interests of the U. S. working class are not advanced by imperialism. With the export of capital abroad in pursuit of cheap labor, and with corporate growth which strengthens the hold of the capitalist ruling class, imperialism is detrimental to the political power of organized labor. The "costs of empire" include the livelihoods and lives of workers and the expenditure of their tax dollars in ways which lead to little margin for the social services which their net impoverishment demands.

Concentration of Capitalist Wealth and Power, with Control of the State

Behind the facade of the bourgeois electoral system (which, through independent forms, can sometimes become an arena of genuine political struggle), there is a tremendous concentration of wealth and political control in the U. S.[3] The primary role of the state under capitalism is to guard, preserve and protect private property and the persons of its owners. The protection of persons is secondary to the protection of property, property rights and the social order based on private property. Moreover, since World War II, corporate control of the state aparatus has increased to unparalleled levels. In ever greater numbers, members of the ruling class take a direct role in government as elected and appointed officials, in order to guarantee the ever-growing profitability of monopoly enterprise. For example, the remarkable progress in computer and communications technology, so highly profitable for IBM, ITT and others, was paid for by the governmental space program and not these private interests. In the wake of the Chilean coup, under the influence of ITT, Congress created a public fund which protects U. S. corporate interests against nationalization of their overseas investments. Ever more restrictive anti-labor and racist legislation, such as S1437 sponsored by Senators Kennedy and McClellan, is being developed in national and state legislatures. Social progress in health, education, housing and other areas are denied vital funds while the already bloated military expenditures grow.

To maintain the myth that representative government under capitalism represents the entire community, and not the interests of the bourgeoisie alone, the state provides public services. The state's dual role as agent of capital and its victims creates a contradictory situation in which the formulation of public social policy becomes a matter of class conflict. The working class can engage in battle and at times gain some victories, in spite of the fact that the political system under capitalism is profoundly weighted in favor of the wealthy owners of the means of production, their finanacial institutions and their carefully selected representatives.

At the present time we recognize that both major political parties in the United States are financed by and operate in the service of the finanacial and corporate elite in the United States. The network of corporate power in the United States invests substantial funds in political campaigns, and influences the formulation of national policy, both directly and indirectly. The Business Round-table, a corporate executive council, concerns itself with national economic policy, which includes social welfare policy. In fact, social welfare policy is a vital area of interest for U. S. corporate capitalism. The Democratic Party at times has attempted to package its image as representative of labor and its interests. Fundamentally, party decisions and policies are determined by money, and although the financial contributions of the AFL-CIO have been sizable, the bourgeiosie is the class with capital to invest, and therefore the most influential in the coalition.

Marginalization and Containment of the Working Class

Under monopoly capitalism, ultimately every worker becomes marginal, expendable and vulnerable to displacement by cheaper labor or more capital-intensive equipment. The development of a permanently marginalized working class in the U.S., particularly among nationally oppressed ethnic minorities, is a social phenomenon that has been instrumental in the development of the social welfare system. This system maintains the reserve army of the unemployed and underemployed at subsistence levels; it also functions to contain working class consciousness and action. In U. S. society, persons who lack regular employment are further disadvantaged by social stigma, unsafe housing and all the multiple deficits of poverty in an affluent society. The media depicts them as drains on the economy rather than characteristic bi-products of advanced capitalism; every effort is made to make them feel unworthy and defeated. Public hospitals, mental wards and prisons constitute the alternative human warehouses for the more difficult-to-manage members of this group.

As a result of institutional racism and a dual labor market, Blacks, American Indians and Latinos are more likely to be marginal workers. But increasingly workers of all backgrounds, including workers in basic industries, are beginning to experience their marginality and expendability. Unskilled workers, skilled workers and now professionals face marginality when their skills fail to serve the pursuit of profits.

The most important historic task of labor in the U. S. is the development of a mass political party which represents the interests of the working class. Social service workers should be allies of labor in political organizing efforts, because the quality of public housing, health, education and welfare services are dependent on the strength of politically organized labor. Yet enormous financial and institutional resources of business and government combine to prevent the emergence of a working class political party in this country.

The Ideological and Repressive State Apparatuses

Louis Althusser's analysis of the ideological and repressive apparatuses of the state is very revealing when applied to capitalist social institutions in the U.S.[4]

The ideological state apparatus refers to the health, educational and welfare institutions and the media, which legitimize the state and its governance as operating "in the public interest." These institutions maintain the social structure that Kenneth Boulding has described as "an integrative system."[5] "The public interest" is presented as if it is a singular interest, without class conflict, when, in fact, the maintenance of social concensus in support of the social order perpetuates the existing social and economic stratification, which is uniquely in the interest of the capitalist class. The ideology of U. S. education and the media does not teach conceptual skills which clarify the nature of class structure and conflicting class interests. The culture and ideology presented in U. S. educational institutions reflect the economic control of the ownership class over those social institutions. The function of the ideological state apparatus explains the virtual exclusion in the U. S. of Marxist theoreticians from sensitive teaching positions in which they may pass on to students conceptual tools useful in a critical analysis of social reality.

The repressive state apparatus is based on the instrumental use of force when the ideological apparatuses fail in their task of legitimizing capitalist rule. The repressive institutions, including the police, the military, the courts and the prisons, preserve and protect private property and privilege based on class. When persons do not accept the legitimacy of the rules and regulations under which the system operates, alienation, isolation and deviant behavior are alternatives to collective struggle. To contain the unruly behavior of marginal sectors of the society without altering opportunity structures or property relations, collective action is persecuted, and larger jails are built. Real security for people is unattainable through law and order strategies. Movements for social change may be destroyed by repression, while property rights are preserved, but the causes of unrest and rebellion continue.

3. Social Welfare and the Dialectics of Struggle

Welfare and the Apparatuses

Social welfare plays an important role within the ideological apparatus in legitimizing the state as servant of the people through government-sponsored services. The existence of social problems in the U.S. cannot be denied. Social welfare services conceal the extent to which the state serves the rich and powerful by granting benefits and services to persons whose lives have been adversely affected by capitalism and the materialistic, dehumanized culture which a profit-seeking system generates.

Social welfare also functions within the repressive apparatus to control the oppressed national minorities and other sectors of the working class who are feared to be ungovernable and out of control. The marginal working class, a "difficult to manage" population, is registered, classified and contained by social welfare programs. Program procedures involve rules and regulations for the governance of persons outside the corporate structures and labor marketplace which are the primary economic institutions for control of the U. S. work force.

Moreover, social work as a profession has supported the view that the individual, rather than the structure of the socio-economic system, is the source for social dysfunction. Together with the disciplines of psychology and psychiatry, social work has distorted the nature of social problems in the United States, mystifying the processes of social breakdown. Internalization of negatively stigmatized status is pathogenic, whether it occurs in the individual, family or social group. Socio-economic and political factors have been absent from the social diagnoses of too many social work colleagues. Even now, a narrow perspective holds sway over the field.

The Dialectical Question

Given the role of social welfare programs and institutions in maintaining the social order in the U. S., can social workers be genuine activists in the struggle for socialism and a new socio-economic system? Can social service workers, employed in institutions of social containment, participate in class struggles as workers and allies of the working class?

1: Capitalism and Social Welfare

These are vital questions for social workers and for other human service workers who are concerned about social conditions and social change. As students, many youths concerned about social justice enter the social work field, only to become socialized into a "professional" stance during the course of training and to thereby lose their social commitment.[6] A Marxist analysis is needed, to present a different perspective and to develop strategies for social work participation in working class struggles for significant social reconstruction.

Most existing jobs in the social work area involve delivering crisis intervention to victims of the social system. Although the intermediate interests of social workers lie in the struggle to maintain and expand existing opportunities, this concern should not obscure the long-term interest in a fundamental reorganization of society. A first step in this reorganization involves the coming together of social work professionals and community activists in a common campaign to go beyond mere intervention towards making positive changes in the overall quality of life.

Arenas of Activist Potential

To examine possibilities of an activist role for social workers in class struggle for radical or revolutionary changes in the U.S. socioeconomic system, we need to formulate strategies in each of the following arenas of struggle.

the economic arena
the political arena
the ideological arena
the psychological arena

This framework for analysis includes aspects of social conflict in the United States not usually recognized as areas of class struggle. The positions of social service workers in these arenas of class conflict are often ambivalent, characteristic of the contradictory position in class struggle of professional groups, who may serve either as allies of capital or labor or both simultaneously, with division in the ranks of the profession itself.

The Economic Arena

The wage struggle of workers in the production process is the central arena of class conflict. Service workers are workers, dependent on wages as are other laborers; but unless they are employed in profit-making organizations, human service workers are not part of the proletariat. Unlike the proletariat, their production does not directly contribute to the production of surplus value, and thereby to capital accumulation. In the class structure, service workers are professionals and in some instances crafts people, workers with trained skills and expertise, intellectuals who are members of a composite known as the "middle" class, including the petty bourgeoisie, small producers and individual entrepreneurs, a category which covers private practitioners.

Social service workers who are government employees or on the staff of agencies which provide services purchased by the state, are in a particularly ambiguous and vulnerable position. Since these workers do not contribute directly to capital accumulation, they are not in a strong strategic position to bargain for increased pay and job security in a society not ethically committed to support public services at tax expenses.

Nevertheless, we should not underestimate the potential oppositional contribution of social service workers. Under capitalism, the commodity which they produce is human concern. Capitalism converts both material resources and human labor into commodity production. Attentive listening and therapeutic response are often essential to the maintenance of minimal functionality in an alienated society, where human relationship is mainly available in the form of a commodity.

An important way in which social workers can be more directly involved in economic struggle is through union organization and activity. In the past, the mystique of professional status often misled service workers into identification with management. Community organizational skills possessed by practitioners have not often enough been used to build unity and group action for collective bargaining in the field. But unionization appears to be growing, and social service workers appear more ready to join the ranks of organized labor.

The Political Arena

Social policy is an important area of class struggle in the United States. In social policy formulation and its enactment into law as social welfare legislation, decisions are made about who gets what in the society. Of course, the most fundamental allocations of income, goods and services in the nation are made through the marketplace, and the decisions made in corporate and banking

1: Capitalism and Social Welfare 41

board rooms. But policy battles over taxation, transfer payments, housing, health, education and welfare programs, over the overall allocation of national and state budgets show that the struggle over social legislation has critical consequences for living conditions in the U. S. Public social policy affects all classes and social groups in the society, whether or not they are politically active. Failure to participate in struggles on social policy is to be powerless, indeed. Social workers and professional associations often have been involved in presenting policy statements on social issues, but there is rarely an understanding of social issues as arenas of class struggle, or of the vital importance of alliances with organized labor.

Today, attacks on public service programs by anti-labor forces are part of their attacks on the living standards of American labor. Struggles to maintain community services are struggles for survival in communities of the marginally-employed working class. The jobs and program benefits can mark the difference between life and death for some community residents. Because capitalism is in crisis on an international scale, the struggle over the use of public funds has intensified. The corporations demand that the state be instrumental in keeping corporations afloat at a profit, with cost-plus government contracts and other supports and incentives for investment, while maintaining a military posture and establishment that supports counter-revolutionary forces around the world. Meanwhile, communities in this country need public funds to maintain services which are essential to community survival. That struggle over the allocation of public funds is the essence of class struggle in social legislation.

Social work organizations have noted the advancement of social services in other industrialized nations, in comparison to public service systems in the United States, but these organizations have not recognized the extent to which the expansion and stability of public support for that development is tied to the political strength of organized labor. Professionals in the United States rarely have been allies of the working class, with some memorable exceptions, such as Jane Addams in Chicago. Communities wanting to expand services often have found professional groups hostile to community development projects, unwilling to modify their own service roles and to work as partners in service delivery, accountable to the self-determined needs of the community.

Social service workers who want to fight for better living conditions in poverty communities clearly must identify themselves as allies of local community organizations and local labor councils.

They must be ready to join in the struggle to bring resources into those communities, and to develop in themselves skills which facilitate the process of community resource development. Some courses available in schools of social work can be instructive toward these goals. To provide genuine help to troubled communities, professional practices and role norms need modification; this is an additional area of policy struggle. Contradictions between professional ethics and institutional practices are characteristic in the field of social welfare.

The Ideological Arena

In regard to ideology in the United States, theoretical constructs and conceptual frameworks either clarify or mystify the class nature of our society. The normative perspectives of the social sciences, as taught by most faculty in the nation's universities, assume that the capitalist system is the economic system best suited to technological progress, to human nature, and to political democracy. The extent to which the concentration of economic power under state monopoly capitalism distorts political and productive processes while it commercializes human relationships is little considered. However, there are growing numbers of social critics and researchers in the universities who recognize the destructive and dehumanizing features of this social order, and whose works are evidence of an anti-capitalist critical consciousness in the intellectual community. Their contributions are important to the struggle, because of the vital role of the ideological state apparatus in legitimization of the social order. Among the social critics there are some idealists, whose efforts to define an ideal socialist society lead to ritualistic and somewhat self-congratulatory activity, unrelated to the realities of social struggle. Academic institutions tolerate and even support the practioners of such radical chic. Marxist analysis, in contrast, leads to theory which can produce strategies for collective action and struggle toward socialism, not to the perfection of utopian designs for a future socialist society.

Those of us who identify ourselves as Marxist intellectuals and scholars need to be disciplined in our study and research, in order to produce analytical materials based on concrete historical fact and current information, which illuminate class stratification in the past and present, and can serve to inform present and future action for social change.

Efforts to support academic freedom of thought, as well as

1: Capitalism and Social Welfare

academic employment and tenure based on quality of scholarship and teaching credentials, are aspects of class struggle in the ideological arena, in social work educational institutions and other academic departments. These struggles build critical consciousness.

The Psychological Arena

Another area of struggle in which social service workers can participate is the battlefield of therapy. There is substance to the statement by radical therapists that therapy can be liberating. Typically, therapeutic professional services have fostered adjustment to traditional patterns of role relationships. But when therapy teaches people how to fight against exploitative and oppressive conditions, how to assert their own needs and rights, and to gain control of their own lives, it enables people to regain power and dignity, and brings them into conflict with dehumanizing social institutions. The women's movement, in its consciousness raising groups, has offered this kind of therapeutic process, in which people have supported each other in learning how to fight. Liberating therapy, which helps people to overcome oppression and dehumanization on a personal level, has political implications and potential. It is not surprising that the Human Potential Movement is a favorite target of the far right in the United States. On the other hand, therapy which fosters dependency and submission to the control of others, especially including elite professionals, is counter-revolutionary.

4. Conclusion

At the present time, institutions in the social welfare field are becoming increasingly managerial, controlling and repressive, while the paid jobs in the service field assume allegiance to the existing social order. Social workers, like other workers, need jobs. There are contradictions between the rhetoric of service and the realities of agency operations. To the extent that social service workers analyze, perceive and confront the contradictions in our places of work between the authorization of public care and the meager appropriation of resources, we can struggle in alliance with working class communities. In fact, service workers have the potential to be a revolutionary force for social transformation. In

Chile during the period of the *Unidad Popular*, service workers were among the strongest sectors involved in the development and implementation of new programs for the social transformation of the nation.

In spite of gaps or carefully engineered erasures in class consciousness, the U. S. working class has militancy, organization and the economic and political potential to wipe out the profit margins and nationalize the means of production. The growth of the far right in the United States aims to smash the power of labor and the growing political power of oppressed national minority communities. The growing strength of Blacks and Latinos and the increasing militancy of American Indians, present serious problems in social management for the power elite, who continue to use the dual tactics of cooptation and brutal harrassment as forms of social control.

Despite similarities between the bourgeois political parties in the United States, there have been clear differences. The policies endorsed by Nixon and Ford, representing the Republican Party, are much more repressive in regard to social welfare than the Democratic Party positions. The fascist solution to the existence of social problems in a given population is the genocidal elimination of that population. Republican Party policies are threateningly close to that formula, as are governmental policies in Latin America and South Africa. In the U. S., past governmental management of oppressed national minorities has typically presented two options — super exploitation or the strangulation of life supports. As industry in the U. S. becomes more capital intensive, with cheap labor more available off-shore, as a result of increased multi-national penetration of labor markets and skills development in the Third World, more repressive and genocidal forms of social control of the U. S. working class, especially the marginalized sectors, are to be expected. In this context, struggles to maintain and expand community systems of services, social welfare benefits and civil liberties are struggles for working class survival. In some instances, alliances with politicians within the Democratic Party may be useful, as determined by the actions and platform of the particular candidate. Meanwhile, the control of world resources and markets by U. S. monopoly capitalism is continuously eroding. In the struggles of this critical time in the nation, social service workers are on the front lines. As ever, the crucial question is, "Which side are you on?"

Notes

1. See Jeffry Galper, "What Are Radical Social Services?," *Social Policy* (January/February, 1978), pp. 37-41; also, Galper, *The Politics of Social Services* (Englewood Cliffs, N. J.: Prentice-Hall, Inc., 1975), pp. 65-69.
2. This correlation is presented by Harold L. Wilensky in *The Welfare State and Equality* (Berkeley/Los Angeles: University of California Press, 1975), pp. 65-69.
3. For data on the concentration of wealth and power in the U.S., see: C. Wright Mills, *The Power Elite* (New York: Oxford University Press, 1956); Ferdinand Lundberg, *The Rich and the Super Rich* (New York: Lyle Stuart, Inc., 1968); Morton Mintz, Jerry S. Cohen, *America, Inc.: Who Owns and Operates the United States?* (Englewood Cliffs, N.J.: Prentice-Hall, Inc., 1967).
4. Louis Althusser, "Ideology and Ideological State Apparatuses," in *Lenin and Philosophy and Other Essays* (New York: Monthly Review Press, 1971), pp. 143-153.
5. Kenneth Boulding, "The Boundaries of Social Policy," in *Strategic Perspectives on Social Policy*, ed. by John E. Tooman, Nilan Dluhy, Roger Lind, Wayne Vasey, Tom A. Croxton (New York, Pergamon Press, 1976), p. 15.
6. Arthur G. Cryns, "Social Work Education and Student Ideology: A Multivariate Study of Professional Socialization," *Journal of Education for Social Work*, 13, No. 1 (Winter, 1977), pp. 44-51.

BLACK WORKERS AND THE LABOR MOVEMENT: RECENT TRANSFORMATIONS

Philip S. Foner
Lincoln University

In several ways the 1960's was a period of great promise for black workers. It was a period of comprehensive civil rights legislation, of the longest economic expansion in modern American history, and of gains for Afro-Americans unprecedented in their long, suffering experience. These gains were the result of the economic pump-priming of the Vietnam war, special government programs funded by an expansionist economy, and intense, bitter, and often bloody struggles. As a result of these developments, and particularly of struggles of black workers and their progressive white allies against the trade union bureaucracies, the American labor movement by the end of the 1960's had traveled a far distance from the days when most industries were entirely "lily-white" and many unions excluded blacks from membership by either constitutional provision or initiation rituals, while others prohibited blacks by more subtle devices or permitted only token membership. By 1970 there were not only 2,500,000 and 2,750,000 black trade unionists in America but the percentage of blacks in the unions was a good deal higher than the percentage of blacks in the total population —15 percent as compared with 11 percent.[1]

By 1970 about 9 million black men and women were part of the work force of the United States. In such industries as steel metal fabricating, retail trade, food-processing and meat-packing, railroading, medical services, and communications, blacks numbered one-third to one-half of the basic industry. Carried away by such statistics, social science professors began predicting that the American labor force would soon be mainly darker in color and younger. "By 1980," went one prediction, "the number of young black people entering the work force will be five times that of young workers."[2]

Yet precisely at the time this was written in 1970, the black unemployment rate was still two to three times that of whites, and black unemployment stood at the official figure of 29 percent, while black median family income was only 61 percent that of whites.[3] Moreover, blacks remained grossly over-represented in the low-skill, low-paying jobs and under-represented in the high-paying jobs. Of the 9 million black workers, 2,004,000 were classified as "operatives," or, as it is generally defined, semiskilled. Most of the others were in two classifications below operatives — laborers and service workers. In most industries black workers made up a large proportion of these three categories. In the automobile industry, for example, blacks compromised 13.6 percent of the total work force but 21 percent of the three lowest categories; in steel, where 1.8 percent of the force was black, the percentage in the lowest three categories was 21. In the electrical-equipment industry, where blacks had 6.4 percent of the jobs, their percentage at various levels broke down as follows:

High-level managerial, professional, and sales jobs			0.7%
Clerical jobs			2.4%
Skilled blue-collar jobs			3.8%
Operatives			9.9%
Laborers	11.9%	Service jobs	18.5%

An increasing number of studies have demonstrated that during the 1960's considerable economic gains were made by black workers and that many industries once traditionally closed to blacks were forced to abandon their "lily-white" employment policies. Yet they also reveal that blacks by 1970 were still disproportionately concentrated in unskilled and semi-skilled work, earning the lowest wages, and in a precarious economic situation because, for the most part, they still occupied the lower rungs of seniority. It was clear that any dramatic setbacks in the economy would have immediate impact for black workers, many of whom were only a pink slip away from unemployment.

Writing in *The Black Scholar*, Carl Bloice saw a "triple threat" against black workers: "(1) the challenge...presented by the rapidly expanding scientific and technological revolution; (2) the growing concentration of finance, the growth of multinational or transnational corporations, and the appearance of huge diversified conglomerates; (3) governmental policies designed to preser-

2: Black Workers and the Labor Movement 49

ve a high profit financial system, which acts adversely on black people." Bloice envisaged an increase in the introduction of automated processes in industry, the export of capital and jobs by multi-talented corporations, an increasing government stimulus through tax credits to achieve more rationalization, and to seriously reduce the demands for employees in the unskilled areas in which most black workers were concnetrated. In short, the serious dislocations created for blacks by the mechanization of agriculture were already making themselves felt through this "triple threat" in steel, automobile, meat-packing, and other industries, and this tendency, Bloice contended, was bound to increase enormously.[5]

Yet even Bloice did not forsee the catastrophic developments facing black workers within a few years after this article was published. For one thing, to the "triple threat" to the future of black workers one had to add others. One was the fact that throughout the country industry was moving out of the cities to rural areas or suburban parks, diminishing employment opportunities for blacks, since they could not, in most cases, move to the suburban areas. According to the 1970 census, half of all employment in the nation's fifteen largest metropolitan area was already outside city limits. Indeed, one of the fastest expanding job markets, that of service and retail industries, is increasingly centered in the suburbs.

"It's a nice atmosphere," said one white worker in a suburban plant. But as the National Committee Against Discrimination in Housing observed, this "nice atmosphere" was not for most inner-city black workers, who could not find housing in the suburbs. "They would have to own cars, or take several buses at high fares and long traveling times to get jobs that average from $2.50 to $3 an hour."[6]

In April, 1977 Patricia Roberts Harris, Secretary of Housing and Urban Development in President Carter's Cabinet made it known that she intended to use Federal leverage to provide equal access to housing for poor and racial minorities in the middle-class white suburbs. "When businesses are moving from the central city to the suburbs, it seems to me unjust to say to the black and the poor that they may not live near where you earn your living," she said. "Communities that say we will take the benefit of a good tax base but will not let people who might benefit from that employment live in this community ought to be required to think about the injustices of that."[7]

But talk opened no suburbs to black workers, and by September, 1977, the situation had grown even worse. A major new study prepared for the Department of Housing and Urban Development confirmed the continued economic drift of jobs to the suburbs which still continued to resist successfully housing for black workers.[8] Little wonder the headline in the *Wall Street Journal* read: "To Many Ghetto Blacks A Steady Job Becomes Only A Distant Hope." The article went on to point out that "companies and jobs are moving out of the cities to the suburbs and beyond, where most blacks can't reach them. The importance of this can't be measured. Black unemployment is going to be excessively high as long as present housing patterns continue."[9]

"Troubled Town" was the heading of an article in the financial section of the *New York Times* (October 9, 1977). The town was New Stanton, Pennsylvania, chosen by Volkswagen for its U.S. plant-site to produce the Rabbit. What was troubling the inhabitants of New Stanton was that blacks from the Pittsburgh area would be seeking some of V.W.'s 5,000 promised jobs and would simultaneously seek to find housing in the coomunity. John Reagan, New Stanton's mayor, concede that the community stood fast against blacks living in the town, "There's very, very few blacks around here and people worry about it. I always tell them, hey, they've got to live too, but what can you do?" Volkswagen has met the problem by informing the NAACP in Pittsburgh that "35 miles is a logical commuting distance," not adding of course — for blacks only. Since the NAACP does not seem to be able to convince New Stanton to permit blacks to reside where they work, it has come up with the propsal that Volkswagen "run shuttle buses into Pittsburgh beyond the 35 mile zone," buses which of course would be for blacks only. If adopted, this bus service plan would mean that while white workers who can live in New Stanton would have an eight-hour day, black workers who would be forced to commute between 35 and 50 miles each way would have at least a twelve hour day — for the same wages. The company's position, as reported by its vice president for personnel, F.J. Short, is that Volkswagen is "sincerely concerned" about the situation, but can think of no solution.

These threats to the future of black workers take on added significance when they are coupled with the serious blows these workers have suffered from the recession that got under way in the first quarters of 1974. Today unemployment in the black community is at depression levels. Officially, the unemployment rate

2: Black Workers and the Labor Movement 51

for blacks in the last quarter of 1976 was put at 12.6 percent. The official rate, however, gives only a part of the real extent of joblessness among blacks. Blacks are more likely than whites to be numbered among the discouraged workers who have given up the search for a job or among those who are forced to accept part-time work when they want and need full-time jobs. Thus, just as the real level of overall U.S. unemployment is 10 percent, a more accurate measure would put the black rate at 20 percent or more.[1]

Black workers suffered a double blow from the recession and its aftermath. The recession hit black workers harder and the limited recovery has reached them to a lesser extent. Blacks, who held 10.9 percent of all jobs in September, 1974, endured more than 21.7 percent of the recession-induced employment decline in only the next seven months. In its report the Urban League declared gloomily that "actual Black joblessness has remained at the depression level of one out of every four workers."[11]

As bleak as the unemployment picture is for black men, it is even worse for black women. In 1976, 13 percent of black women heading households were officially listed as being unemployed. It is likely that the real figure was closer to 25 percent. Since about one-third of black families are headed by women, it is clear that millions of black children are reared in families with unemployed heads. In fact, today about one-third of all black children under 18 are in families in which male or female heads are unemployed or not in the labor force.[12]

U.S. News & World Report (December 5, 1977) carried on its front cover the drawing of a bomb whose fuse was burning rapidly. The headline read "Young Blacks Out Of Work. Time Bomb For U.S." The opening paragraphs of the startling story read:

> Drifting further and further out of the American mainstream is a growing army of the unemployed whose intractable joblessness baffles the experts.
>
> Some had jobs but lost them in the recent recession or when urban employers started moving out to the suburbs. Others, however, are well into their 20's and 30's without ever having held a job successfully.

As stated again and again, the unemployment problems of black youth are so severe that a whole generation is growing up without the job experience vital for successful careers. Black youths made almost no progress toward improving their relative economic position during the 1960's — in sharp contrast to white youth. Today the situation is much worse. Officially, two out of every five black teenagers who actively sought work in 1976 were unemployed. However, since unemployment among black youth often takes the form of low labor market participation, some experts judge the real black teenage unemployment rate to be close to 60 percent . (Even the Federal government conceded as early as February 1975 that 41.1 percent of all black teenagers in the country were out of work.) In New York City the unemployed percentage of black youth is officially placed at 86 percent![13]

Bernard W. Anderson of the University of Pennsylvania Wharton School of Economics, who has done considerable work in the field on unemployment among young blacks, declared pessimistically: "Nothing at the moment promises to reverse the 'permanence' of black joblessness."[14]

Two things are clear: (1) blacks have not participated at all in the national recovery from the 1974 recession; (2) the mounting black unemployment makes a mockery of the last decade and a half of affirmative-action programs designed to eliminate racial discrimination in the workplace. Indeed, the United States Commission on Civil Rights conceded the validity of these conclusions in its February, 1977 report entitled, "Last Hired, First Fired — Layoffs and Civil Rights." The Commission's study brought to the fore a **problem** which most white unionists are even unwilling to face **let alone** deal with. It stated that layoffs based solely on **seniority in rec**ession times threatened "to cripple the economic **progress of minor**ities and women, and to erode affirmative-action plans." Again: "The continuing implementing of layoffs by seniority inevitably means the gutting of affirmative action efforts in unemployment...."[15]

One does not have to be an expert in labor relations to understand that the seniority issue is a complex one. To workers in the factory seniority is crucial. Their standing on the seniority roster, which is determined by the date on which they were hired, governs whether, when layoffs come, they will be demoted or perhaps let go altogether. It also determines his/her prospects for advancement into more skilled and higher-paying jobs. Naturally, workers can be expected to defend their seniority fiercely against any move to interfere with it. Still, it is difficult to escape the fact that the use of seniority promotes racial discrimination and black unemployment, since white workers, having obtained their positions in most cases before blacks, have the most jobs with senior status. As the events of the last years have painfully demonstrated, despite all the progress in the field of employment and union membership for black workers, the traditional slogan applied to the black working class since the founding of the nation — "Last Hired, First Fired" — is in full operation after the nation's bicentennial.

Of course, blacks who have entered industires earlier and continued on the job also have seniority rights which they are anxious to protect. But even they confront the seniority issue when they try to move into better-paying categories.

The relation of seniority to black (and female) unemployment has long been recognized but long neglected by the labor movement. Many union leaders argue that to modify the seniority provisions even slightly, especially in a period of unemployment, be discrimination in reverse, in this case against white workers. To this blacks answer that they should be given some form of recompense, even at the expense of white workers in the same plant, for the discrimination they have endured in the past, and further, that if unions continue to put seniority practices into agreements, the day of real equality on the job will never arrive.

Perhaps the most vicious aspect of the complex seniority issue for black workers has been the maintenance by plants, with union agrement, of separate lines of promotion and seniority as a result of which the black worker is virtually frozen into a dead-end polition. This issue has been discussed for years in scholarly journals. But early in 1973 it was brought to the attention of many Americans who knew little of the problems when newspapers throughout the country carried headlines reading "Bethlehem Steel Plant to Alter Seniority System to Aid Blacks." On January 15, 1973, Labor Secretary James D. Hodgson ordered Bethlehem Steel Operation to open job classifications formally restricted to whites only. The directive was issued under Executive Order 11246, which requires government contractors to follow nondiscriminattory employment practices and to take "affirmative action: to ensure that job applicants and employees are not discriminated against on the basis of race, color, religion, sex or national origin." The executive order, in turn, is based on the Civil Rights Act of 1964.

The order followed by slightly more than two years a finding by a federally appointed panel that Bethlehem practiced discrimination at Sparrows Point through its seniority system. It found that most blacks at the plant had been placed in inferior, dirty, low-paying jobs and that most whites had been placed in departments with more desirable, higher-paying jobs. For example, blacks were given refuse-disposal and coke-oven jobs, while whites worked as timekeepers and sheet-metal workers. The panel found that the company's seniority system "locked" blacks into their inferior positions and discouraged them from transferring to better units.

When black workers applied to the company for promotion to more skilled departments, their applications were refused. When they took their case to their trade union, United Steelworkers' Local 2610, requesting grievance papers to file a claim against the company, the union officials refused to give them the papers and told them to take their case to the Equal Employment Opportunity Commission. Meanwhile, white workers with less seniority were promoted to the positions the blacks had applied for.

Pressured by the EEOC, Local 2610 finally prevailed upon Bethlehem to accept the application of one black worker, George Mercer, for promotion to crane operator. The company agreed, and Mercer was promoted. But he continued to be paid a laborer's wage while operating one of the company's huge cranes. After five years, on May 27, 1971, Mercer and four other black steelworkers who had had similar experiences brought a suit, charging Bethlehem Steel with racial discrimination. The suit named the United Steelworkers as a co-defendant!

The suit prodded the Labor Department into action. In his order Secretary Hodgson called for the following measures to be taken: First, workers who have never transferred out of mostly black departments must be informed in writing of the opportunity to do so; second, transfers will be based on a plantwide seniority, which meant that a worker in a "white" department with only three years' service would no longer be able to move to a better job before a black worker with more seniority who applied for the job; and finally, workers who transfer to better jobs would be "redpencilled," whick meant that they would keep the wage they reached through seniority in the "Black" department even though the job in the "white" department paid less.[16]

A Labor Department lawyer described Hodgson's order as the "most far-reaching affirmative-action decision yet by the Federal Department."[17] He failed, however, to add that, although there had been several court rulings outlawing dual white and black seniority lines, the government had been slow to implement them. Indeed, one decision was in the case of Bethlehem's Lackawanna, New York, plants, where the company and steel union were defendants, charged with practicing the same type of discriminatory seniority and promotion lines that perpetually held blacks to low pay and undesirable jobs. Instead of penalizing Bethlehem by canceling government contracts, as the law requires, the government refused to act. Finally, after years of doing nothing, a federally appointed panel rule that no change be made in the seniority system in any of Bethlehem's plants because such a change would be "unduly disruptive" to the company's normal business.

Although Secretary Hodgson's order reversed that recommendation, insisting that the continued safe efficient operation of the Sparrows Point plant did not require the maintenance of the existing dual seniority system, many black steelworkers at the plant voiced skepticism that their job opportunities would improve as a result of the order. The order, they pointed out to a *New York Times* reporter, required the company and the union to end discrimination through normal bargaining channels, and they viewed this as being "like telling the fox to help the chickens." The account in the *Times* continued:

> "there is still discrimination at Sparrows Point," said William Jones, a black who was interviewed as he came off his shift as a cinder cleaner, atop one of the mills' big, hot coke ovens.
> Mr. Jones, wearing a hard hat and carrying the goggles and respirator he must wear all day to keep the red cinder particles from his eyes and lungs, has been working for 20 years in the same department, one consisting almost entirely of blacks."[18]

The skepticism of the black workers was based on experience. Not only had the company and the union fought the original ruling of the Office of Federal Contract Compliance, but their reaction to the Labor Department's order was not encouraging. Local 2610's head, Edward Binto, speaking for many white steelworkers at the Sparrows Point plant, called the order "discrimination in reverse."

White workers voiced fear that blacks would be "pushed ahead" of them, and one said bluntly: "You give a colored person a finger and they want the whole hand."[19] Evidently the best solution for the union and many of the white steelworkers was continuation of the discriminatory seniority system that had existed for years.

Sharing the skepticism of the black steelworkers, the National Association for the Advancement of Colored People's Legal Defense and Educational Fund announced plans to force a more basic corrective than provided for in Secretary Hodgson's order, including back pay for all minority workers who had suffered under the segregated seniority systems, and injunction eliminating the separate seniority lines against discriminatory testing procedures that blacks must undergo before they are permitted to qualify for previously white jobs, and a preferential quota for the immediate placement of blacks in supervisory positions and other job classifications from which they had been excluded. A number of these demands were achieved, over the bitter opposition of the United Steelworkers, and black workers have indeed received back pay for all of the years of suffering caused by the discriminatory seniority practices. The union, incidentally, wept over the enormous sums the company was required to pay to the black members of the organization, and pleaded with them to accept a "more reasonable" payment which was a good deal less than what they were entitled to.[20]

The Bethlehem-United Steelworkers' case pointed up sharply the fact that even though the barriers to union membership to black workers had been eliminated, they were basically second-class members not enjoying the same rights as white union members. Nor was this a problem confined to the United Steelworkers. In an article originally published in *Haper's Magazine* of May, 1971, and widely distributed as a reprint in the A. Philip Randolph Educational Fund and the AFL-CIO, Baynard Rustin, a black spokesman, took white liberals to task for creating the impression that "the unions are of and for white people." After praising the labor movement for its integrated character and its increasing black membership, Rustin conceded that "in some unions whites still possess a disproportionate number of the high-paying jobs and there is not yet adequate black representation at the staff level and in policy-making positions." But this situation, though it is to be lamented, could not properly be placed at the door of "racial discrimination in the unions."[21]

On whom then should it be placed? Rustin gave the answer in September, 1972 during a speech before the convention of the International Association of Machinists. He put the blame squarely on the shoulders of the black workers themselves. Addressing himself to the complaints of black unionists against union policies and practices, he said arrogantly:

> I want to say to our trade unionist Black brothers, nobody got anything because he was colored. That is a lot of bull. Not a man on the platform who got here merely because he was white.... Second of all, I want to say to my Black brothers, stop griping always that nobody has problems but you black people.[22]

This was delivered at the convention of a union that for sixty of its eighty years of history barred "non-Caucasians!"[23]

At the same convention, a resolution was introduced by Local 720B for advancement of black, Chicano, and women members to positions in the union from the local international level. It noted that while 26 to 30 percent of the membership of the IAM consisted of minorities, "direct representation entails a token 2 percent." The resolution did not call for specific quotas (the dreaded word in labor circles) or set any numeric guidelines for achieving its purpose; it merely asked that the top officers and executive board of the union's staff and leadership be more representative of the membership's composition.

The resolution's committee rejected the resolution and submitted a substitute proposal. The committee conceded that it "cannot disagree" with objectives of the resolution, but added: "We find ourselves on the horns of a dilemma, but we reject the notion that elected or appointed persons in the union's staff should meet certain standards based on sex, race, color, or creed." Its substitute resolution reaffirmed a nondiscriminatory policy and called on the union's officers to endeavor in good faith "to encourage use of the talents of women and minority group members in the paid positions and elected offices." The substitute resolution was adopted without discussion.[24]

It is impossible to believe that among the 30 percent of the members of the IAM who were blacks, Chicanos, and women, there were none sufficiently talented to serve in paid positions or as elected officers of the union. Equally incredible was the response of an International Ladies' Garment Workers' Union official to the charge that, while blacks and Puerto Ricans far outnumbered Jewish and Italian members, there were still no blacks on the twenty-three-member General Executive Board; the one Puerto Rican on it represented only the locals in Puerto Rico and not the overwhelming majority in the mainland industries. He stated "with some irony" that "General Motors could afford tokenism; the International could not and would not insult blacks by putting into leadership men who would be plain figureheads by virtue of their experience."[25]

We are expected, then, to believe that of the thousands of black ILGWU members there was not a single one who could be more than a "figurehead" if he or she were elevated into a leadership position. The contributions of blacks in leadership positions in unions like hospital; state, county, and municipal; distributive; meat-packing; fur; and West Coast longshore expose this as the insult it is to the black members of the ILGWU.

By the opening years of the 1970's many in the black community were convinced that, despite the burgeoning of rank-and-file groups of black workers, black caucuses and black power activists seeking, among other objectives, the end of institutionalized racism on the job and in the unions,[26] the incumbent union bureaucracies were so entrenched that their hopes of success were slim. But one group of black workers had more confidence. This movement, known as the "Coalition of Black Trade Unionists," began at a conference in Chicago, September, 1972, called by five black trade-union leaders: William Lucy, secretary-treasurer of the American Federation of State, County, and Municipal Employees; Charles Hayes, vice-president of the Amalgamated Meatcutters and Butcher Workmen of North America; Nelson Jack Edwards, vice-president of the United Auto Workers; Cleveland Robinson, president of the Distributive Workers of America, and also of the Afro-American Labor Congress; and William Simons, prsident, Local 6 of the American Federation of Teachers in Washington, DC. The call stressed the sponsors' distress over the "neutral" stand of the AFL-CIO Executive Council and some unions in the presidential election campaign, which they believed was contributing to the re-election of Richard Nixon.

About 1,200 black unionists, rank-and-filers and officials from thirty-seven unions, attended the conference. While major attention was paid to the Presidential campaign, the conference made it clear that it planned to go beyond it and deal with matters of particular concern to black workers. Among the issues stressed by many of the black workers and officials were the failure of the AFL-CIO to organize the unorganized and to bring substantial numbers of nonunion black workers into the labor movement; the necessity of greater black representation in union leadership; the necessity of the organization of the poor in black communities; the importance of supporting actions in opposition to the Vietnam war; and the need to back legislation favorable to federal revenue-sharing programs that would bolster social services in the black community. It was necessary for the "Coalition of Black Trade Unionists" to continue after the Presidential election regardless of who was elected and provide a forum for blacks concerning their special problems within the unions as well as to act as a bridge between organized labor and the black community. "We must have a change," declared Charles Hayes, "and there will be no change without organization."[27]

Before adjourning, the delegates from UAW locals, building trades and hospital workers' unions, the AFSCME, and dozens of other national unions decided to set up a continuing movement. A five-man steering committee was selected by the Chicago gathering to issue a statement of intent.

While the Chicago conference did not endorse George McGovern, the delegates voiced their determination to rally black voters in opposition to the re-election of Richard Nixon. The dismal showing McGovern made did not shatter the Coalition of Black Trade Unionists. The McGovern campaign, as William Lucy observed, had served merely as the "catalyst" for the new organization, and it would take concrete form at a constitutional convention to be held May 25-27, 1973, in the nations capital. Once formed, the coalition would conduct a membership drive to enlist black union members throughout the country and would embark on an intensive effort to organize poor blacks. The new coalition would not be "black separatist" or even a "civil rights" organization. It would work within the trade-union framework for black workers and the black community.[28]

The call, for the Second Annual Convention of the Coalition of Black Trade Unionists in Washington, D.C., May 25-27, 1973, read in part:

> In September of 1972, more than 1200 black workers, representing the single largest gathering of black unionists in labor history, convened in Chicago for two days of discussion on the 1972 elections and ways to enhance black influence and power in the American labor movement.
> In keeping with the mandate of that historic meeting, we invite you to participate in the Second Annual Convention of the Coalition of Black Trade Unionists.
> The primary focus of the meeting will be the adoption of a constitution and a viable permanent national organizational structure through which black trade unions can effectively project their views and maximize their influence in the labor movement.
> As black workers, it is imperative that we organize to gain a more substantial role in the development and implementation of local and national labor union policy....
> We call upon you to lend your support to the effort to achieve dignity, decency and a better standard of living for all people.

Some 1,414 delegates from 33 international and other unions attended. Most were from unions affiliated with the AFL-CIO, and 35 to 40 percent were black women. In general, the delegates represented basic industry, government, and service workers. A number of white delegates attended.

The new Coalition of Black Trade Unionists, formally established by the convention, was to meet at annual national conventions, and between conventions the Executive Council would be the governing body. The Coalition was also to be made up of state bodies and local chapters.

A separate statement on "The need for a Coalition of Black Trade Unionists," signed by William Lucy, Nelson Jack Edwards, Charles Hayes, Cleveland Robinson, and Bill Simons, made the point that the nearly three million black workers in organized labor constituted "The single largest organization of blacks in the nation." It then pointed out:

As black trade unionists, it is our challenge to make the labor movement more relevant to the needs and aspirations of black and poor workers. The CBTU will insist that black union officials become full partners in the leadership and decision making of the American labor movement.[29]

"The sleeping giant is awakening," is the way a black unionist described the Coalition of Black Trade Unionists at its founding convention.[30] The giant, however, faced many obstacles.

William Lucy, COBTU president put the matter bluntly: "The success of the Coalition of Black Trade Unionists will be measured by the degree to which unions open their leadership ranks to black workers."[31] By that sole measuring-rod, the COBTU has been a failure. To be sure, prodded by the Coalition and by a rank-and-file revolt of black and white steelworkers, the United Steelworkers, all-white at the top and in regional office, since its formation, finally added a black vice-president to its roster of union officials in 1976. In general, however, blacks in unions still have an infinitesmal percentage in top and middle-level union leadership. Most major unions, representing the overwhelming majority of union members, still do not have blacks in leadership beyond the local union level (and very inadequate even there). Charles Hayes, one of the black vice-presidents of the Amalgamated Meat Cutters and Butcher Workmen and a COBTU vice-president, observed at the 1973 AFL-CIO convention: "We got a situation here where the labor movement is made up roughly ten to 12 percent black representation, I would venture to say we have less than two percent represented as delegates."[32] The same exact statement could be made of the 1977 AFL-CIO convention.

In the last few years, most black organizations and the AFL-CIO took opposite positions on the issue of seniority in several landmark cases before the United States Supreme Court. Over the opposition of the AFL-CIO, black workers, supported by the NAACP, have challenged the traditional seniority provisions as discriminatory. At first they were eminently successful. On March 24, 1976, by a vote of 5 to 3, the Supreme Court ruled that blacks denied jobs in violation of Title 7 of the Civil Rights Act of 1964 (prohibiting discrimination in employment because of race, religion, sex, or national origin) must be awarded retroactive seniority once they succeeded in getting those jobs. The blacks must be given the same seniority they would have had if they had been hired initially, the Court said, with all the accompanying rights, including pension benefits and in the event of layoffs, better job security than that possessed by workers with less seniority. The ruling on the rights of blacks in jobs appeared to assure the same rights to women who were discriminated against on the basis of sex. But the ruling did not mean that every minority member or woman who is newly hired by a company that once discriminated could get retroactive seniority. The person must prove in Federal Court that he or she was denied the jobs because of unlawful discrimination after Title 7 went into effect. The decision also left unanswered the question whether retroactive seniority is to be awarded to a person who was denied a job on the basis of race or sex before the enactment of Title 7 or to a person who did not initially apply for a job because it was well known in the community that the employer did not hire blacks.

Despite weaknesses, the ruling considerably strengthened Title 7's provision for affirmative action as a remedy in discrimination cases. It established the principle that, in the Court's words "whites must share with blacks the burden of the past discrimination" in employment as they already must do in schools. Jack Greenberg, director of the NAACP Legal Defense and Educational Fund, Inc., which argued the winning side of the case, told a reporter that the ruling "assures the black victims of racial discrimination will be put in the rightful place."[33]

Greenberg was vastly over-optimistic. Despite the loss of newly-won jobs by blacks (and women) in the recession years under the last-hired — first-fired principle, the AFL-CIO leadership would brook not the slightest interference with the seniority principle. The organization mounted a vigorous campaign against the Supreme Court decision. On June 1, 1977, the campaign paid off. The Court retreated from its previous ruling, and declared 7 to 2 that the seniority systems which perpetuate the effects of past racial discrimination placing blacks at a disadvantage in the competition for better jobs and other benefits, are not necessarily illegal. The gist of the ruling was that unless a seniority plan *intentionally* discriminates against workers it covers it is not illegal. The burden of proof of proving intent — an almost impossible task — is on the workers who claim they were discriminated against.

The Court thus made it clear that seniority systems can legally perpetuate favored employment for white males if the systems were in operation before the Civil Rights Act took effect in July, 1965.

Further, the Court placed more stringent requirements for proof of individual discrimination against complaints in cases after 1964. It thus became clear that such changes in seniority systems in landmark settlements between black workers and steel companies (such as the one in Bethlehem Steel discussed above) which have given wider opportunity to blacks trapped in the least desirable, lower-paying jobs will be more difficult to achieve in the future. Indeed, the Court's dissenters, Justice Thurgood Marshall and William J. Brennan, Jr., declared that the Court's ruling would mean full equality for a full generation of minority workers would remain a "distant dream."

But William Pollard, civil rights director for the AFL-CIO, which had fought for the decision, hailed the ruling, and smugly told black workers that "the problem is economic downturn, and not seniority."[35] The argument that the real answer is full employment is raised whenever existing racist practices in the union are challenged, and is a frequent theme among black apologists for the trade union bureaucracy. But it has rarely been coupled since the recession hit hard in 1974 with meaningful trade union action on behalf of full employment. The AFL-CIO leadership, and especially George Meany, only reluctantly endorsed a mass rally in Washington, D.C., April 26, 1975 (sponsored by its Industrial Union Department) calling upon the government "to put America to work." The New York Coalition to Support the Rally took a full-page ad in the *New York Times* (April 3, 1975) urging,

> We've got to go to Washington. We've got to stage a peaceful rally where hundreds of thousands of Americans will tell President Ford and all our elected officers: We want action! We want jobs!

When the rally broke up into a series of bitter outbursts against the trade union leadership and establishment political leaders, the AFL-CIO leadership and establishment political leaders, the AFL-CIO leadership immediately let it be known that the era of mass demonstrations for jobs was over.[36] This was one pledge the AFL-CIO kept. Meanwhile, the prestige of the labor movement in the black community, already seriously damaged by the battle over seniority, sank to new lows, and this trend is also being reflected in other areas of American life. In May, 1977 the Roper organization found that public confidence in labor leaders had slipped from 50 percent in 1975 to 48 percent, and that among union members 51 percent had confidence in the "system of organized labor," down 13 percentage points from a poll in mid-1974![37] Undoubtedly, the failure of the trade union leadership to mount an effective campaign to alleviate the rising problems of unemployment helped explain the downward trend.

With continued inactivity on the issue of jobs, the Humphrey-Hawkins bill calling for government action to reduce unemployment remained simply a dream even though it had gone through several stages of toning down in an effort to broaden the sponsorship and support. It seemed unlikely in the summer of 1977, as black unemployment rose to new and unprecedented heights, that despite President Carter's campaign promise to support Humphrey-Hawkins that the bill would ever become law--or, if it did, would basically alter the picture.

This was the desperate situation facing black workers, and especially young black workers, when fifteen black leaders met on August 29, 1977 at the National Urban League's headquarters. Two general agreements were reached at the meeting. The first was that the participants would maintain a loose coalition to "counterattack" what they perceived to be an antiblack mood in the country. The second was that the top priority was to increase job opportunities for the nation's unemployed, and that the Carter Administration had failed to fulfill its promise to the black community, whose votes had elected him. What was significant about this meeting was that for the first time since the 1963 March on Washington, all sections of black leadership, including black trade unionists, had agreed on the key issue facing Black Americans. Another significant feature of the August, 1977 meeting, also reminiscent of 1963, was that the demand of the black spokesmen was endorsed by leading white trade unionists. George Meany had remained aloof, to be sure, from the 1963 March on Washington. But now he lost little time in identifying the AFL-CIO in his Labor Day message, with the black leaders' criticism of Carter and with the full employment demands. Other younger white labor leaders also were quick to associate themselves with demands of the black leaders' meeting.[38]

However, when asked what his view was on this issue very close to the black population of the United States, the suit of Allan Bakke against the right of the University of California to set aside a segment of each medical school class of blacks and other "approved minorities" as part of a proper plan of affirmative action,

Meany hedged. The AFL-CIO president replied: "I don't know what the Supreme Court's going to do. Some of our unions take a pro-Bakke position and some oppose." Blacks were hardly assured by this seemingly neutrality or that Meany did not instantly endorse the position of the American Federation of Teachers, whose president, Albert Shanker, bitterly opposes meaningful affirmative action, and which has filed an *amicus* brief on the side of Allan Bakke. The fact that the AFL-CIO itself is silent on Bakke, Ken Bode points out, "should not mask its underlying sentiment. Most of the unions of the federation hierarchy line up with Albert Shanker and Allan Bakke."[39]

To their credit, five unions have signed on a common *amicus curiae* brief defending the University of California. The five include the United Mine Workers, the United Electrical Workers, the American Federation of State, County and Municipal Employees, the Farmworkers and the United Auto Workers.

The theme of a labor-black alliance was mentioned once or twice at the AFL-CIO convention in Los Angeles, December, 1977. But basically the convention revealed that little had changed so far as black representation of black interests are concerned. Charles Hayes, vice-president of the Amalgamated Meat Cutters Union and a leading official of the Coalition of Black Trade Unionists, noted that there were probably less than 20 delegates at the convention. It is widely believed that there should have been at least 80, which would be closer to a fair representation of the black membership in the federation, estimated at 10-12 percent. Hayes voiced a widespread sentiment among black workers when he noted:

> We are really underrepresented here. That has been a problem of long standing and still is. We in the CBTU are seeking to get more blacks at the policy-making level. The CBTU has not been as effective as it should be, but we will be.

He added: "I would have liked to see more time at the convention devoted to domestic policies. Here we have the whole economic situation. What are we going to do about it? ... The Carter administration's program is inadequate. But just to talk about it is not enough. I don't think we have enough of a program to guarantee that the government is going to guarantee a decent way of life for people who are now out of work and are being written off as far as our economy in America is concerned."[40]

It is clear we still have to travel a long way before we can say that racism is no longer an important influence in organized labor. The solution is not to destroy but to transform the trade unions. Black workers, like other workers, have gained from the achievements of their unions in the form of higher wages, improved working conditions, and better fringe benefits. The evidence is overwhelming that the economic status of black workers is always higher in unionized than in nonunionized industries.[41] In a carefully documented study, Orley Ashenfeller concluded that "the average wage of black workers relative to the average wage of white workers is consistently higher in unionized than in nonunion labor markets." All this, he points out, however, does not mean that trade-union discrimination against black workers is a thing of the past. What it does indicate is that there is "apparently less discrimination against black workers in the average unionized labor market than in the average nonunion labor market."[42]

From a study of considerable evidence, Albert Syzmanski concludes that white workers often lose from economic discrimination against blacks since the entire trade unions struggle to achieve better conditions even for the white working class is seriously weakened. Racism, he argues, is a divisive force which undermines the economic and political strength of working people and acts to worsen the economic position of white workers as well as that of the black working class. The answer, he insists, is the total elimination of racism from the labor movement.[43]

Early in 1978 the Martin Luther King Jr. Center for Social Change granted its Social Responsibility Award to AFL-CIO President George Meany. In accepting the award — the justice of which I leave for future generations to assess — Meany emphasized that "full employment is absolutely essential if civil rights are ever to be fully enjoyed and exercised by every American." Later he observed: "Thanks to Arthur Burns and the Nixon-Ford Administration there is a new segregation in America. A segregation as bitter and brutal as the one outlawed by the Civil Rights Act. it is a segregation based on whether or not an individual has a job — those always working and those always jobless. Like segregation based on race, this new segregation must go." Still later, he noted that "black workers . . . are union members in greater percentage than their percentage in the work force generally. . . ."[44]

Not a word about the fact that these black workers are meagerly represented in the AFL-CIO conventions, on the AFL-CIO Executive Council, or in the leadership of the unions affiliated with the Federation. Not a word about the fact that for black workers there is no such thing as "a new segregation in America," since black workers have faced this so-called "new segregation" throughout the history of this country. Finally, we are supposed to believe that until "full employment" — certainly a worthy goal — is achieved the problems facing black workers must remain problems; that nothing need be done about the troublesome issues of seniority, the increasing trend of industry to move to suburbs where blacks cannot live, and the failure of so many unions to deal adequately with the legitimate grievances of their black members. This is a position which Marxists cannot and must not accept.

Notes

1. Bayard Rustin, "The Blacks and Unions," *Harper's Magazine* (May, 1971), p. 76.
2. *American Sociological Review* (June, 1970), p. 32.
3. Lester Thurow, "Not Making It in America: The Economic Progress of Minority Groups," *Social Policy* (March- April, 1976), pp. 5-8.
4. Among these studies the most interesting are the volumes published at the University of Pennsylvania Press under the direction of Herbert R. Northrup and Richard L. Rowan and carrying the general title *The Racial Policies of American Industry*. In all thirty-two volumes will be published "to determine why some industries are more hospitalbe to the employment of Negroes than are others and why some companies within the same industry have vastly different racial policies." Already more than twenty studies have appeared covering such industries as automobile, steel, hotel, petroleum, rubber tire chemical, paper, banking, meat, tobacco, bituminous coal, lumber, textile and drug.
5. Carl Bloice, "The Future of Black Workers Under American Capitalism," *Black Scholar* (May, 1972), pp 14-16.
6. *New York Times*, December 5, 1972.
7. *New York Times*, April 8, 1977.
8. *New York Times*, September 18, 1977.
9. *Wall Street Journal*, November 15, 1976.

10. AFL-CIO *American Federationist,* (May, 1977), p. 6.
11. *New York Times,* January 18, 1976.
12. *New York Times,* August 3, 1976.
13. Philadelphia *Sunday Bulletin,* February 23, 1975; *In These Times,* Sept. 14-20, 1977.
14. *New York Times,* July 12, 1976.
15. "Last Hired, First Fired — Layoffs and Civil Rights," A Report of the United States Commission on Civil Rights (February, 1977), p. 61.
16. *New York Times,* January 15-16, 1973.
17. *New York Times,* January 17, 1973.
18. *New York Times,* February 10, 1973.
19. *New York Times,* January 22, 1973.
20. *New York Times,* February 22, 1974.
21. Rustin, "The Blacks and Unions", p. 76.
22. *Los ANGELES Times,* September 8, 1972.
25. *Dissent,* (Winter, 1972), p. 48.
26. For a discussion of these various groups, see Foner,*Organized Labor and the Black Worker,* pp. 397-424.
27. *Labor Today,* September, 1972.
28. *Ibid.* See also: *Daily World,* December 12, 23, 26, 1972; *New York Times,* October 3, 1972; and Stanley Plastrik, "Coalition of Black Trade Unionists" (Chicago, Illinois, September 13-14, 1972), pamphlet.
29. *Daily World,* June 1-4, 1973.
30. *New York Times,* October 3, 1972.
31. William Lucy, "The Black Partners," *The Nation* (September 7, 1974), p. 180.
32. *Proceedings,* AFL-CIO Convention, 1973, p.242.
33. *New York Times*, March 25, 1976.
34. *New York Times*, June 2, 1977.
35. *Ibid.*
36. *New York Times,* March 25, 1976.
37. *Wall Street Journal,* May 3, 1977.
38. *New York Times,* August 30, 31; September 5, 1977.
39. Ken Bode, "Unions Divided," *New Republic* (October 15, 1977) p. 20.
40. *In These Times,* December 21-27, 1977.
41. *Alanta World,* December 28, 1972.
42. Orley Ashenfelter, "Racial Discrimination and Trade Unionism," *Journal of Politcal Economy* (May-June, 1972), pp. 403-13.
44. *AFL-CIO News,* January 28, 1978.

THE IMPACT OF MEXICAN IMMIGRATION: A PANEL DISCUSSION

John Womack, *Harvard University*
John Coatsworth, *University of Chicago*
Marc Zimmerman, *Minnesota Migrant Council*
Renato Barahona, *University of Illinois, Chicago Circle*

Chaired by John Coatsworth
Transcribed and edited by Marc Zimmerman

Dedicated to the memory of Joe Sommers, Writer and Teacher,
y su lucha por la causa de los indocumentados

WOMACK: As an introduction to further discussion, I will sketch out a brief history of the cycles of movement of Mexican workers into the U.S. I believe this panel will show how this matter, which may seem peripheral or secondary in the total configuration of U.S. capitalism, has great and growing significance for the future of this country and for the hemisphere.

It is important to distinguish the traditional migration of Mexican workers from the kind that has developed during the last fifteen to twenty years. The traditional migration has been going on since intensified capitalist expansion began in the Southwest at the turn of the century — as copper mines opened, as the railroads, large scale agriculture and the entire infrastructure of commercial capital began to develop. Once launched, the new enterprises required labor to build the railroads, to work the mines and fields. To some extent, this labor came from Europe and from European settlements in the east; it also came from China. But considerable numbers came from Mexico.

From the turn of the century up to the early 1960's, the migration of Mexican workers followed one basic pattern. It generally came from the same northwestern and central districts of Mexico (from Michoacan, Jalisco and Zacatecas) which were also the source of migration to new booming districts in Mexico itself. The same geographical sources of unskilled labor supplied workers for the Arizona mines and for the Tampico oil boom of 1910. Sixty to eighty percent of the annual Mexican migration to points in Mexico and the U.S. came from the zones which, in effect, specialized in the production of workers or the reproduction of labor power.

These migrant workers took traditional migrant jobs — they worked the mines and they became track workers on the railroad; they planted and harvested. The vast majority went to the traditional places — mainly to the belt that extends from Texas to New Mexico, Arizona, Colorado, to certain parts of Nevada and to California. These were the people that most of the literature on immigration is about, even today — people taking whatever jobs paid best, but mainly, over time, serving as the labor force for agri-business.

The most formal institutionalization of this migration on the part of the Mexican and U.S. governments took place with the so-called Bracero agreement of 1942, when there was an obvious demand for Mexican workers to replace the U.S. citizens who had gone into war and war-related industries. This formal and official agreement controlling Mexican migration to the U.S. lasted until 1964. Since that time, the migration pattern has been very different.

The push or expulsion of workers out of Mexico had changed by 1964. Beginning in the late 1950's and extending throughout the 60's, a new kind of industrialization took place in Mexico. Mexico was no longer striving to substitute imported consumer goods with the products of domestic industry. The country was now at a stage of industrialization involving the replacement of intermediate goods, which cost more to produce and required the importation of expensive machinery. Mexican industrialization became progressively more capital intensive. For their size, the new industries employed less labor; the need was for small numbers of highly skilled workers. Thus, although in crude terms Mexico's economy was growing, the kinds of employment possibilities it offered were proportionately diminishing. Unemployment became a considerable national problem throughout the sixties, and it intensified in the 1970's.

Mexico's unemployment problem may be measured from some very rough figures. The Mexican population is about sixty-

3: The Impact of Mexican Immigration

five million; the economically active population (the able-bodied, work-age people) number something like twenty million. Of this group, approximately fourteen million people are probably employed at any one time. Out of roughly twenty million who could work, something like six million are not working, or are working very sporadically; they are virtually unemployed.

Although the estimates vary from two to eight million people, I would suggest that the number of Mexican workers who are in this country illegally — that is, people without the proper immigration papers and without official permission to be here — totals roughly five million. This massive and still growing migration of undocumented workers stems from the enormous problem which Mexico has encountered as a developing capitalist country whose economy is tied to, and dependent on, the U.S. to such a degree that it provides a decreasing number of jobs for the survival of its own population. The victims of Mexico's distorted development need to eat like everybody else, so they come to the U.S. and spread out to work wherever they can find jobs.

Since the late 1950's, this migration has come not only from the traditional supply bases or recruiting grounds for migrant workers, but from all over the country — from Chiapas and Yucatan, from places where before there was very little immigration into the U.S. In addition, they are not just in the traditional jobs. The police for these people, the Immigration office, or "Migra" who track down, arrest and deport undocumented workers, have produced figures which show that these people are no longer just mine workers, railroad workers or agribusiness workers. They work in innumerable light industries (glove and shoe factories, garment district sweat shops and the like) or in service employment (car washes, restaurant kitchens, etc.), and they are not just in the old migrant centers of the Southwest. There has been a strong immigration into the Chicago area for a long time now, starting as early as World War I but it has increased in recent years. There are immigrants in urban and rural centers scattered through the entire country now. They are in light industries and small businesses — places where it is somewhat easier to hide, places where there are no union contracts, and where the inspectors can be evaded. This means that the question of undocumented workers poses an altogether different set of problems for analysis than it did twenty to thirty years ago.

So far as I can tell, there are no coherent policies for managing this problem; and given the structures and relative power of the U.S. and Mexican economies as well as the contradictory interests favoring and opposing this immigration from different perspectives, the problem may well continue to be unresolved, or may lead to a series of psuedo-solutions with rather explosive consequences.

By the year 2,000, there will be roughly 120 million Mexicans; there will be 40 million ready and able to work. If things continue at the present rate (which is in fact likely to accelerate), there will probably be more than twelve million unemployed Mexicans attempting to cross the border. By that time, the migration into this country will already have made the Mexicans by far the largest minority in this country — distinctly larger than the Black population. This creates obvious social strains on top of the structural and class problems that already exist. We will have a vast population of unskilled, poorly educated Spanish-speaking workers inserted into a society based on advanced technology and capital-intensive labor. We will have a population needing housing, social services, education and jobs in a nation whose own capitalist logic will probably leave it ill prepared to deal with the contradictions it has engendered.

In this sense, the question of undocumented workers may be very important for the future of the U.S., and for Mexico as well. Here, to shift perspectives, undocumented and immigrant workers have been a fundamental resource in U.S. development. For Marxists, their potential importance for future progressive labor organization should not be underestimated. This is true not only for the U.S. Many of these people are often cycling back to Mexico, and the organizations they develop here may well have an impact south of the border.

COATSWORTH: I am going to start by adding two comments to what John Womack has said. The first has to do with the push and pull of migration from Mexico. Mexican immigration to the United States was first stimulated by imperialism, by large scale foreign capital investment (mainly from the U.S.) in the late nineteenth century. The impact of imperialism on Mexican society has continued to be the fundamental cause of migration to the U.S. ever since. It is nonsense, therefore, to assert, as many politicians and media now do, that the problem of Mexican immigration is a problem Mexico has created for us. It is a "pro-

3: The Impact of Mexican Immigration

blem" that imperialism has imposed on both our peoples.
The first large scale foreign investments in Mexico went into railroad construction, beginning in the 1880's. The railroads caused profound changes in Mexican society. First, they helped to revive the large haciendas (the agri-businesses of their time) whose owners expanded their holdings by expropriating the lands belonging to the Indian villages. Second, they made Mexico's mineral resources, especially those in the sparsely populated northern states along the U.S. border, more accessible than ever before. More foreign capital followed to exploit these resources and to set up light industries around Mexico City where the new rich preferred to live and spend their money. The landless villagers who fled the predations of land companies and *hacendados* were later joined by fugitives from the poverty created in the rest of Mexico through the enormous concentration of foreign capital in the northern states and the Mexico City region.

The problem of structurally unbalanced economic growth was created largely by the uncontrolled search for profits by American investors. In recent years, the depression in vast areas of Mexico, due to the continuation of this investment pattern, has led to the still greater regional diversification of migration that John Womack has already discussed.

For the past few decades, Mexico has been trying to cope with the problems of industrialization which emerged after post World War II governments reopened Mexico's borders to foreign investment. These decades have been a time when foreign investment in the strategic sectors of the economy has not increased employment rates. A good part of the problem faced by Mexican government officials in their negotiations with the U.S. stems from a situation which our own corporations have created because of the manner in which they have exploited Mexico's resources.

The effect of immigration from Mexico to the U.S. on conditions in Mexico is a complex and serious matter. It is quite clear that the Mexican government views emigration to the United States as a positive factor, for two important reasons. First, emigration is a safety valve that takes some of the pressure off the unemployment situation in Mexico. When workers migrate across the border, whether legally or not, and find employment outside the country, they are no longer a problem to the Mexican government. Second, the Mexican economy benefits from emigration to the U.S. because Mexicans who work in the United States send money back to their families. Incredible as it may seem, these exploited and underpaid workers spend more to alleviate poverty in Mexico than the Mexican government. The small sums they painfully set aside from their meager earnings each week add up to tens of millions of dollars. These dollars not only mitigate the desperate poverty of many families, they also help reduce the balance of payments deficit which foreign capital has inflicted on Mexico in recent years — a problem so serious that it forced the Mexican government to devalue the peso in 1976.

The effects of immigration on the U.S. pose another set of issues that have been discussed widely in the last few years. The most important issue affecting our rulers as well as people in the trade union movement is the matter of substitution or competition, especially in a period of recession. When Mexican workers arrive in the U.S., do they take jobs that American workers would have or could have taken? Do they keep wages below levels American workers can accept? Is there a substitution effect? The answer depends partly on the sector one examines: services, agriculture, industry. But even in those sectors where there may be actual displacement, the effect is relatively slight. There is considerable evidence that workers coming across the border are not taking jobs away from American workers.

There is also the issue to which the growers in the U.S. border states give high priority. They argue that Mexican immigration is necessary, because if U.S. workers have to be recruited to work the fields under existing conditions, they will demand higher wages and thus push up the price of fruit and vegetables to consumers throughout the country. The growers have used this argument to persuade the public of the need for importing cheap labor. In fact, from California to Oklahoma and on into Wisconsin and Minnesota, the wage bill of U.S. agri-business could double without increasing produce prices by more than five percent. A decent union contract calling for wage hikes of even one hundred percent would have only marginal effect on prices if the agri-business drive for super-profits could be held in check.

In general, prevalent policy positions on undocumented workers reflect the conflicting interests and the incoherent and misleading information that has not accidentally underlied the public debate of the issue. In spite of the frequent outcries against un-

3: The Impact of Mexican Immigration

documented workers, a number of particular important interests besides the growers welcome their presence. Industries drawing on a large pool of low-wage "illegals" can keep their labor costs down. Undocumented workers have no access to any public services that taxpayers might provide; they have only limited and precarious access to those possibilities for organizing open to citizens fully protected by the law. Clearly the present situation is optimal for employers in those low wage industries where the difference between success and failure may lie in their ability to hire very cheap, non-union labor. Cutting off immigration would mean paying higher wages to people who are already working here. Legalizing immigration could mean serious problems resulting from the organization of trade unions. For many employers of immigrant labor, the present situation is quite satisfactory. Even those who might prefer legalizing mass immigration have recognized the advantages of employing unprotected workers.

North Americans must, in the end, face the question whether to restrict immigration drastically (and enforce that restriction), or allow open and legal immigration. This is a question that has engaged the discussion of Marxists and trade unionists for half a century. One of the most important debates in the old American Socialist Party before World War I was precisely over the question of the policy that party should adopt toward foreign immigration: whether they should follow the tradition of craft unions and the AFL in calling for restrictions on the flow of immigrants into the U.S. or resist nativist and racist appeals for exclusion. The Socialist Party never worked out a consistent position on the issue.

There are short-term reasons from the point of view of some trade unions for expecting that unrestricted immigration — that is, a large increase in the labor supply — will cause a decline in wages. With that rather simple-minded analysis, many trade unionists, and particularily those whose experience suggests that restricted entry to a given occupation boosts wages, have a tradition of arguing against unrestricted immigration. It is not possible, however, to predict the effects of unlimited immigration by using supply and demand curves alone. The argument has been made that if there were unrestricted legal immigration, hordes would pour across the border in larger numbers than ever before. That proposition has never been tested, and it is impossible to test it without some kind of experiment. Would unrestricted and legal immigration increase or decrease the flow of immigrants? There are costs involved for people who wish to cross the border, and there are historical and cultural motives that prevent many from coming. Since illegal immigration is largely unrestricted and impossible to control already, the prospect for a substantial increase in the number crossing the border is quite open to question. One recent argument made about the effect of immigration restrictions on Mexico centers on the view that immigration is so important to Mexican economic and political stability that a really strict policy of limiting immigration would produce serious economic effects and lead to a political crisis of major proportions, with turmoil south of the border, and with the added prospect of this turmoil spilling over from Mexico into urban and rural communities in the U.S. It is clear that any change in U.S. policy could have quite serious consequences for Mexico. An economic or political upheaval in Mexico could trigger a potential crisis in the United States.

The possible negative effects on Mexico, of severe restrictions on Mexican immigration are related to the broader issue of equity between two countries. Until now, most discussion has focussed on the questionable premise that we need to cut off immigration so that U.S. workers will get more and better paying jobs. But the issue must also be discussed in relation to the problem of runaway shops established under the aegis of the Border Industrialization Program during the past few years. U.S. firms now have the right to enter border states of Mexico to set up assembly plants, where cheap Mexican labor puts together U.S.-made components that are shipped back across the border. There may well be a negative correlation between illegal immigration and border industrialization, so that the impact of runaway shops on the U.S. economy, and especially on U.S. workers, may turn out to be far more severe than any influx of Mexican workers. More jobs could be lost in the long run to workers who never leave Mexico than to migrants who spend wages here. In fact, the simultaneous promotion of these shops and of restricted immigration policies could signal a strategic trend very much conducive to certain sectors of U.S. capital, at the expense of the U.S. economy as a whole. Those interested in the fate of U.S. workers cannot limit themselves to any narrow economic specifications based on labor supply and demand.

In the face of such realities, it is rather difficult to give serious credence to the package proposed by the Carter government. The Carter proposal would, in theory, legalize undocumented

3: The Impact of Mexican Immigration

workers who were here in 1970, expell the remaining undocumented immigrants, and simultaneously impose far greater obstacles against future border-crossers. This supposedly humane and realistic mid-way compromise between restricted and unrestricted immigration is both inhuman and unrealistic. As Marxists, we should be able to find a more viable and humanly meaningful solution. But it is no simple matter.

A Marxist solution is easiest to find for the long run. The experience of socialist countries suggests ways of dealing with inequities that arise because of different wage levels and migration flows between full-employment socialist economies. Our context is obviously more intractable. In the long run, we could solve the problem if on both sides of the border, there were economies that could plan to provide decent wage levels and full employment for their populations, while reducing inequities over time.

The short term issues are much harder to deal with. Moreover, the problem cannot be solved without close and continuous consultation between Marxists on both sides of the border. The first step Marxists here should take, therefore, is to explore the possibilities for developing a dialogue with those elements of Mexican society who are concerned about this problem and have a tradition of organization and struggle for socialism. I believe that most Mexican political parties on the serious left would welcome this kind of initiative from North American Marxists, and would be happy to engage in a constructive discussion of the issues. Since this is a matter involving workers in both our societies, it seems to me that we must consult workers and representatives of workers from Mexico. This is not an easy undertaking, but I believe it can be accomplished.

Of course, Marxists don't run Mexico and they don't run the U.S. But in both countries, Marxists influence trade unions and popular organizations, and even some agencies of government. One of our initial tasks should be to reach a reasoned consensus with Mexican Marxists on a programatic solution and a set of short term objectives.

My own preference would be for a policy of unrestricted immigration from Mexico. But this policy must be linked to efforts to provide state and federal enforcement of existing legislation that would give immigrants as well as U.S. citizens access to social security, to welfare, legal services, education, housing and health services — legislation that establishes minimum wage and hours, and legislation (which should be strengthened) that protects the rights of workers to organize.

In the short run, and in a programatic sense, an analysis of current problems would suggest that Marxists should be working to support unionization of farmworkers and workers in those other service and industrial sectors where there are large numbers of Mexican immigrants. We should be working for legislation that protects workers who are still illegal immigrants from the union-busting tactics of the Immigration Department. At the present time factory owners and corporations facing union elections in plants that deliberately employ undocumented workers can simply call the Migra, and *they* win the election for him. That kind of thing must be stopped.

Even without changing the immigration laws, the right of legal as well as illegal immigrants to unionize should be protected by special legislation and of course by pressure. Efforts to extend to those sectors of industry and agriculture the services which are not covered effectively by present social legislation should also be high on the list of priorities.

ZIMMERMAN: Perhaps more than the other speakers here, I have experience in a day to day sense with the plight facing Mexican workers in the U.S. This is because I work as a counselor in an agency administering a Department of Labor program of emergency aid and urban resettlement for roughly twenty thousand farmworkers, almost all of Mexican origin, who come to Minnesota seeking work every year.

On the intake form of every person who enters our office needing help, we have to answer the question, "legal resident alien or U.S. citizen?" Of course, by law we are not supposed to provide services or funds for people who fit neither category. And while we are not imployees of INS, we are responsible for making a "reasonable determination" of the applicant's legal status. Therefore when we find ourselves dealing with an undocumented worker (which happens even in Minnesota), we meet face to face with all the difficulties these people have in finding food and shelter and merely surviving, while they seek jobs which they are not legally allowed to have, and which, if they find them, may well pay the minimum wage or lower and are likely to rank with the worst labor situations available in the U.S.

The fact that I and others have come so far north to improve our Spanish may provide some sense of the total sweep of the new phase of migration from Mexico, and the international web of relations implicated in the migration flow. For the bulk of this new migration to Minnesota comes to work in the sugar beet industry that grew up after the blockade of Cuba. The vast majority of the people I serve are legal resident aliens or U.S. citizens coming from the south of Texas, but they too are part of the total push process that starts much further south and that spreads northward and outward to all parts of the U.S.

One of the effects of this process is that some of the "legal" clients say that "it's because of those *mojados* that I had to come north," or (if they do not qualify for funding), "Oh, you only help *mojados*." And I have even heard *mojados* say it. So that the issue of undocumented workers has created tension among U.S. Latinos and Chicanos, as well as among the majority population.

My conviction is that much of this tension is an effect of manipulation. There are tremendous employment problems in the border areas; some undocumented workers do take jobs for lower wages than legals can afford; and this is a factor in some of the push up into the north. But many of these people would come in any event, because the economic blight in the southwest is such that, barring vacuum-sealed borders and a concerted collective will to struggle over years, the wage scales and employment possibilities for their skills would not be enough to detain them. It is not that there is so much more opportunity northward, but there is a sense and a hope that for some, at least, there might be more. And so each spring, thousands leave.

It is true that when we talk about the problem of undocumented Mexican workers, we have to keep in mind the problem of documented ones as well. The overall economic situation of the U.S., especially in the last few years, has created a virtual crisis for a growing population who, documented or not, have in large number, still not gotten off the lowest rung of the economic ladder — people with little education and with a constellation of problems stemming from Spanish language dominance as well as racial and cultural discrimination.

I should be more precise in my use of the word, *problem*. For my point is that the problem to which I allude is an economic one *for* Mexican workers — and especially for the undocumented among them. While undocumented workers may create residual difficulties for some Chicanos and other impoverished sectors of labor, they pose no serious problem at this time to the broader working masses of the U.S. The problem of capitalism casts its shadow on all workers, and the problem of undocumented workers exists mainly as one for the undocumented workers themselves. That problem begins in central Mexico where they find sporadic, menial employment, and it continues and deepens as they move first to northern Mexico and then into Texas. Some go towards Florida, where they join other undocumented persons from Jamaica and Haiti, and then work their way up to Maine, where they meet French-speaking workers coming from Canada. Others move toward California, Washington, Vancouver and even Alaska. Still others work their way in a broad and often zigzag sweep through the middle and upper midwest and up into Winnipeg and beyond. And then there are those "free wheelers" who wander in varying directions and patterns throughout the entire vast migrant labor area of institutionalized racism, hardship and exploitation.

And of course this situation is not peculiar to the dynamics of the U.S. and Mexico. Southern Mediterranean workers fill the workingclass slums of Northern Europe; impoverished and ragged Columbian *indocumentados* pour into oil-rich Venezuela. And so it is in many parts of the world.

But in the midst of these situations created by the unevenness of capitalist development and by the capacity of certain countries to feed on others, there is also a very crushing dose of political manipulation that escalates difficulties to the point of crisis. One thing is the predictable tension created between those poor workers with and without papers. But when this country undergoes economic recession or depression — that's when it gets toughest for the undocumented workers. *All* workers are alerted that their low wages and high taxes (their expiring life possibilities and dreams) are the result not of the capitalist system, but of a foreign dirty and immoral swarm of undocumented *mojados* and *alambristas*. And, as if to confirm the propaganda, such times are when large numbers of undocumenteds are indeed most likely to arrive, because if the situation has grown bad here, it's bound to have worsened to the breaking point in the miserable Mexican towns they are coming from. Then we may witness the spectacle of government spokesmen and business officials blaming the economic strife and unemployment on the pool of illegal labor which has mainly taken the low-paying jobs that few legal workers in any advanced capitalist country would ever care to hold.

3: The Impact of Mexican Immigration

In the 1930's, one of the ways to deal with the depression was to generate an atmosphere of hostility and fear on the part of workers and other sectors of the population, to the point that thousands and thousands of people, including many with papers, could be rounded up and routed post-haste out of the country. In the 1950's, Operation Wetback, an even grimmer, more colossal dose of mass manipulation, so galvanized public opinion that no viable opposition could succeed in stemming the deportation of over a million Mexican workers. And now we have a new onslaught which feeds upon inner fears, feeds upon racism, feeds upon every worst instinct which the capitalist system can engender, to displace large-scale structural and socio-economic problems and point to a plague of illegals as the real *something* that is rotten in the state.

This new campaign was unleashed in the early 70's, by attorney General Saxbe, in a series of calculated statements before the media; it has developed since then in the more genteel and demogogic forms of the Carter Administration. Saxbe was troubled by the high unemployment rate. The official charged with protecting civil rights sought to defend the rights of workers by blaming their problems on the most unprotected, defenseless and disenfranchized group of workers in the nation.

Following Saxbe's lead, INS was quick to register alarm over the spiralling numbers of illegals now in the country. Blurring the distinction between total apprehensions and the number of specific individuals apprehended, INS officials based their hyped-up tally of illegals on a crude correlation between raw deportation figures and the number of employees on the INS payroll. These officials have a vested interest in their own bureaucracy, and like the Attorney General, the INS director owes his job and allegiance to the administration in power. And so it is not surprising that a few months before Gerry Ford was to run for office, INS launched its campaign to create hysteria about illegal aliens. The goals should be clear: to bolster Ford's image as well as INS funding and job prospects by displacing the blame for economic woes away from the Republican administration; to prepare the ground for new immigration policies favorable to the particular political and business interests that the administration (including INS) was committed to serving.

Early in the game, INS sponsored the Gallup "Study of Attitudes toward Illegal Aliens," based on a rapid fire survey conducted in April, 1976. It is no accident that the poll sample was heavily middle class: Ford's people had commissioned Gallup to test the mood of middle America. According to the study, Americans felt that undocumented workers were growing in number, taking away jobs and generally draining the economy by flooding the welfare rolls, receiving social security and other benefits, and committing crimes at a rate that exceeded the national average. Many people felt that undocumented workers should be deported and that companies should be penalized for employing them. But paradoxically, some of the same people felt that a certain percentage of the undocumenteds should be granted citizenship.

As a matter of fact, the survey was rather inconclusive; the deep and widespread sense of alarm about what the survey consistently called the "problem" of undocumented workers was itself undocumented. But of course the survey becomes not a means of determining public opinion, but a means of molding it. As elections drew near, INS Director Chapman, an ex-Marine general, toured the country dishing out costly copies of the Gallup study and discussing the "enormous illegal alien problem" that sapped the national life and infirmed the body politic.

It is clear that INS used the Gallup study first to promote and record negative impressions, then to intensify these impressions and substitute them in the public mind for the facts. Indeed more objective sources give a picture that differs qualitatively from the one INS sought to project. The facts seem well established that undocumented workers produce a value of thousands and thousands of dollars and that, even subtracting what they may return to their families, they pour large sums into the U.S. economy. Directly or indirectly, most undocumented workers pay income and social security taxes, unemployment and disability insurance, but rarely receive any benefits. Many of them who would in every other way be entitled to Food Stamp, medical and welfare assistance rarely seek them. Overall, undocumented workers have only limited legal rights and are afraid to utilize the small recourse they have, for fear that the effort to do so would subject them to deportation. The crime rate among undocumenteds *is* higher than average, for the simple reason that post-deportation re-entry is itself a felony. The illegal's chief crime is being illegal.

In spite of these facts, INS persisted in its attempts to amplify the atmosphere of hostility and alarm over undocumenteds even in the months following Chapman's tour and the elections. This atmosphere has carried over into the Carter administration. Chapman is out, and now we have a Chicano director, Leonel Castillo, who is to somehow legitimize INS policies and actions. The government now has a rhetoric that oozes with humane concern, but there has been no fundamental shift in approach. The aura of crisis surrounding this issue is basic to the strategy behind the promotion of new policies. And we may be sure that to the degree the Administration wants to increase its hold over Mexico, and wants to find scapegoats for nagging internal problems, the crisis atmosphere will continue into the future.

Given this situation, I am not sure that we shouldn't look at what Carter has in mind, because if in substance, his "amnesty proposal" is a feeble compromise, it may have powerful consequences, either in itself or as an item on an international bargaining table. And we should look at the efforts of Carter's Administration to promote legislation on the model of the Rodino Bill. Such legislation would make it illegal for employers to hire undocumented workers. Latinos would have to carry counterfeitproof identification cards, and they could be surer than ever of employment problems, since employers could claim "reasonable doubt" over legality to justify discrimination. Racist patterns would be enforced, and employers would in effect become agents of INS.

The Rodino approach is not the only repressive aspect of the Carter package. The "amnesty" itself only implies relief for a small percentage of those undocumenteds presently in the U.S. But most undocumented workers will be afraid to submit to the tests necessary for amnesty. Most of them will be unable to prove five years' residence. How would they do so without incriminating themselves and others in the process of coming forward? Amnesty for some will mean the basis for deporting many others here, and for persecuting the great numbers of undocumenteds who will cross over from Mexico in the years to come. And so long as the Mexican economy fails to provide sufficient jobs (and Mexico has still not felt the full brunt of the peso decline), workers without papers will come. Even if a new *bracero* act were passed, others passed over by the legalized program would still find other ways to enter. If INS builds a wall in El Paso, pole-vaulting schools will open in Juarez. For the gnawing facts of poverty inspire a collective ingenuity that surpasses government plans and restrictions.

Now the Carter Administration is juggling competing demands from different sectors of capital. The multi-nationals are saying, we need capital-intensive enterprises, and we don't need competition from petty industries using labor-intensive means. The growers and middle level industries insist on a continuing need for the influx of cheap labor. Farmworker organizers are caught in the middle, wary of undocumented strikebreakers, but wary too of discrimination and persecution that will affect all workers. These and other interests coming from different social sectors are among the cross-influences shaping the package Carter has proposed. But it seems likely that no compromise package will long satisfy any of the parties involved.

In Mexico, the most touted solution is the one proposed by Jorge Bustamante, if only because it represents a significant wing of Mexico's ruling Partido Revolucionario Institucional (PRI). Bustamante believes that Mexico should establish new productive centers able to employ potential undocumenteds and improve the national economy by turning out export goods that would not compete with U.S. products here, but would be shipped to markets elsewhere. Now who is to fund these production centers? Not the U.S., because that would be imperialism. So Bustamante turns to international lending agencies. But whatever the source, the reality would be financing through U.S. or internaitonal capital, which would increase Mexican dependency and provide money for a small national bourgeoisie, but would still not solve the problems for thousands of workers who would still seek to cross the border.

I agree with John Coatsworth that solutions to this very contradictory problem created for workers by imperialist relations have to be sought from both sides of the border — but here I do not mean representatives of the two capitalist-controlled governments coming up with self-serving programs that improve the situation of a few and increase the oppression of the many. In the short run it would be valuable if not only Marxists, but progressive community groups and trade unionists from both sides would join together and attempt to work out certain local pilot solutions. But in the long run, I fully agree that the best answer is a campaign for an open border. It seems to me that whatever problems are created by fighting for and winning an open border will lead to solutions that are much more in keeping with some kind of progressive historical development than the proposals posed by U.S. government and PRI spokesmen. The influx of immigrants might well generate a new stage of labor organization

3: *The Impact of Mexican Immigration* 87

in the U.S. In the last analysis, the problem for undocumented workers may be a problem *of* these workers *for* capitalism itself. And that problem engendered by capitalism may find its own solution by contributing to the dissolution of the system which creates it.

BARAHONA: I would like simply to add some comments to the previous presentations by putting recent studies and news items into the overall framework thus far established. I believe Marc Zimmerman was referring to the Litton study regarding how Mexican undocumented workers use the social services. The Litton study came out in late 1976. It showed that less than two percent of the Mexican undocumented workers actually used the welfare or unemployment rolls. Seventy-seven percent of them paid taxes, and the level of unionization of undocumented workers is almost on a par with that of American workers. Seventeen percent of undocumented workers from Mexico join labor unions. Yet one of the tried and true trite statements of the AFL-CIO oligarchy is that you will never be able to unionize Mexican undocumented workers. In fact, their propensity to unionize is very great and very high, and it would probably be higher if they were not without civil rights and not under constant threat of deportation.

In late December, Senator Cranston of California made one of those marvelous statements that we see in the press from time to time. He said, "The solution to the alien problem is prosperity." The question is, prosperity for whom? And what kind of prosperity? A group of Mexican economists has estimated that in the first nine months of 1977, the United States transnational corporations received 7.46 dollars for every dollar they invested in Mexico (see "Immigration: Facts and Fallacies," in *NACLA*, 1977). These are staggering profits, and they are some measure of prosperity — the prosperity of the transnational corporations, and of the different international lending agencies, which advance monies to Mexico. So my question remains: Prosperity for whom?

It has often been said that migration creates unemployment. In fact, it's quite the opposite, as far as the Mexicans are concerned. It's unemployment in Mexico that breeds migration. The penetration of U.S. capital into Mexico since 1940 has multiplied by ten — and that's a conservative estimate. Even in spite of the recession in the U.S., this penetration has accelerated in the last six or seven years. And this has led to a further disequilibration of Mexico's economy, and a greater migration, not only from Mexico to the U.S., as we know, but also internally from the depressed areas into so-called agricultural boom areas of Sinaloa and Sonora in the north.

Between September, 1976 and September, 1977, over a million Mexican nationals were deported through the Rio Grande, so that when people talk about the problem of undocumented workers, they're talking primarily about Mexican workers, who are more than ninety percent of the million plus people that have been deported. However, we should not lose sight of the fact that in some areas, there are substantial numbers of undocumented workers of other nationalities. For example, the *New York Times* recently reported that there are over a quarter of a million Haitians and Dominicans in New York alone — undocumented workers with exactly the same problems as the Mexican population, and many of them with the additonal problems of being political exiles and refugees from their own areas. We should keep this perspective in mind at all times.

Some people believe that the Carter proposal (namely H.R. 9531 and S. 2252) will be the basis for dealing with Mexican immigration in the next few years, whether any form of the proposal passes or not. However we should be very careful about this. Many states have already enacted laws barring employers from hiring undocumented workers. Florida, Kansas, Massachusetts, New Jersey, Vermont and Virginia have already passed such legislation, and it is pending in six other states. It passed in California, but a judicial hearing will decide whether the measure is constitutional or not. It is currently pending in the legislatures of Indiana, Nebraska, Michigan, Ohio, Rhode Island, Wisconsin and the District of Columbia. It did not pass in three states — Colorado, Texas and Illinois. But even before the Carter proposal comes to a vote in Congress, we know that in varying ways, it is already on the books or on the agenda in several states. The constitutionality of these state laws is being tested, but some of them will probably be upheld. It is much to the credit of grassroots community groups (including the local branch of CASA) that a Carter-style bill was defeated in Illinois.

One of the most stunning things about Carter's proposal is the very limited number of people that it would actually cover. Leonel Castillo himself has estimated that perhaps only sixty to a hundred thousand people at most would actually benefit from the post-1970 amnesty. But what troubles many people even more than the limited numbers who would benefit from a so-called amnesty is one of the other proposals that would create a five-year temporary worker status for Mexican undocumented workers, with no social or civil rights — no rights to unionize, no rights to use social services — and with a proviso which in some cases even prevents them by law from bringing their families from Mexico to the U.S. This is clearly untenable.

One of the other aspects of the Carter proposal that troubles people greatly is the provision for an increased militarization of the Border Patrol, which would grow from two thousand to four thousand agents. This is part of the carrot and the stick policy. The carrot is a very restricted amnesty for a few, but then Leonel Castillo says that we need more INS officials because his agency is so understaffed. And on some of the patrols and outings that he himself has accompanied, he has pointed out time after time the need for increasing border patrol staff and equipment.

Not only that, but recently, Castillo, speaking at the Legal Conference on the Representation of Aliens in Washington (February, 1978), said that the U.S. must deal with the alien problem or build fences such as this country has never seen. He called on Hispanics and other minority groups to "help create a legislative package that will be be sensible and equitable." And, Castillo continued, "I would urge all of you who have the capacity to begin to develop a rational, detailed analysis of solutions to the problems." (*Chicago Sun Times*, March 3, 1978).

In other words, what Castillo wishes (and he has said this quite vocally in the recent past) is for Hispanics to help the Migra resolve the immigration problem. Every now and then he summons psuedo-community representatives to Washington to help him cook up new solutions.

Now, the reference to the fence is not a new one. The INS has entertained it many times, particularly during Chapman's tenure at INS: the building of a militarized electrified zone, exactly comparable to the dividers the U.S. built between the two Vietnams before that country tore away the false borders. This is an idea which periodically comes up in INS proposals, and we should be on the alert for it.

Just a few more words on the question of exports. Drs. Jorge A Bustamante of the Colegio de Mexico and Wayne Cornelius of M.I.T. have pointed out the necessity of creating more jobs in Mexico, to help that country stem the so-called "illegal tide." This job-creation would be financed by American capital, by American companies and lending agencies, and it would involve international organizations such as the Inter-American Development Bank. In one of the recent issues of NACLA ("Immigration: Facts and Fallacies," 1977), there is very convincing criticism of these proposals, confirming points already raised by this panel, and showing the extent to which further penetration of American capital in the area leads to greater dependency in Mexico.

NACLA corroborates John Coatsworth's view that the most recent incursion of U.S. money into Mexico, the helping hand of the Border Industrialization Program, has led to the creation of very few jobs in Mexico, because many of these runaway shops are capital-intensive and employ very little Mexican labor power — mainly that of underpaid women workers. So people who believe with Alan Cranston that Mexico needs more prosperity, should know that U.S. investments create greater dependency and economic instability in Mexico. In fact the solution to the problem is to have greater taxation and greater control of American profits and the nationalization of many of the basic industries.

NACLA also shows that much of the capital in Mexico has gone into the buying of businesses that were already in existence previously, so that businesses are not being created from nothing, they're being created, expanded and co-opted on the basis of enterprises that already exist.

Now Jorge Bustamante believes that one of the things Mexico should do is to export goods to the U.S., and he suggests that this be done in small manufacturing centers across the border under Mexican control. It is interesting to point out that the people who would be employed in the given components of his industrialization project are those who have not been caught by INS. In other words, the people who would be employed in those sectors would be those that have a blemish-free record — therby already creating an interior discriminatory process within the Mexican nation itself. Secondly, it is very clear that Mexican exports are only going to be competitive if Mexican labor power is further exploited at home. I have followed with great interest on radio and TV the demonstrations of American farmers in Texas, near Hidalgo, protesting against what they call cheap Mexican imports of meat and tomatoes. In fact, the people the farmers should be protesting against are not those of the Mexican nation, but those of agri-business, a sector which takes a wide share of profits on the Mexican-grown produce. But these demonstrations do show

3: The Impact of Mexican Immigration 91

on the other hand the extent to which U.S. farmers as well as Mexican *campesinos* are being "cleaned out" by American agribusiness in northern Mexico.

I should point out that Bustamante is one of the major Mexican researchers to have studied the question of undocumented workers. At the national meeting of the Latin American Studies Association, held last November in Houston, Bustamante outlined a political scenario of what he thinks could happen as a result of the problem of the undocumented workers. Bustamante's thesis is that the inability to solve the problem is going to lead to fascism in Mexico. He reaches this conclusion by a step by step rehearsal of the situation: border problems, increasing tensions, unruliness, social unrest, disruption, the sending of the Mexican army to the border, corresponding to the show of force of the U.S. on the American side, and so forth.

Bustamante's scenario is an interesting one, but the gist of this scenario is to justify a no-policy situation on the part of the Mexican government, by thrusting the whole blame on the U.S. government. On the pretext of the threat of fascism, Bustamante justifies continued inaction, continued non-policy on the Mexican side, and therefore what are at best reformist patchup measures. Bustamante criticizes the no-policy situation in Mexico, but clearly he believes that the Mexican government can really do very little about the immigration flow. Now we may readily assume that there is not much we can expect from the Mexican ruling classes and their PRI representatives. And we can confirm this appraisal by the way that the Carter proposals seem to have been received in Mexico. Bustamante claims they were attacked. But I have yet to see any very strong and articulated attack on the part of the Mexican government and the ruling classes against the Carter proposals. And this implies to me a certain amount of acquiessence or bowing down to them. And yet, it may be significant, that at least in the mind of a key establishment expert like Bustamante, a failure to solve the undocumented worker problem poses the threat of fascism for Mexico.

I think that perhaps the Carter proposals and the responses they have garnered bear further discussion — what they mean and what a proper response should be — as the proposals evolve in the months to come. I am generally in accord with the other members of the panel, in that I too favor an unrestricted immigration, an open border, and full democratic rights for Mexican undocumented workers in this country.

SPEAKER FROM THE FLOOR: I agree that the issue of the undocumented worker has become subject to a very concerted policy of scapegoating, and I also agree that, open border or not, the immigration will continue. Among the contradictions of capitalism in the U.S. is the fact that, in spite of moves toward mechanization, agri-business in the southwest continues to be very dependent on the exploitation of Mexican labor. And that's one of the main reasons why border restrictions have not been effective. In fact, undocumented workers remain extremely exploitable; they can be used for cheap seasonal labor, and their social needs do not have to be dealt with, because after the season is over, they can be deported. So there are contradictions preventing real enforcement of the exclusion of Mexican labor, and that situation is going to continue as a polemical issue.

Finally, contrary to what Marc Zimmerman said about the attitudes of Mexican communities inside the U.S. being hostile to *mojados* or undocumented workers, I think that in fact one of the things that has been surprising in the last couple of years is that increasingly Mexicans in the U.S. seem to be recognizing that attacks against undocumented workers are not only on the recent arrivals and the labor that is coming in, but in fact on the entire Mexican community. There is more recognition than there has been in the past, and communities have formed coalitions to prevent attacks on the undocumented.

ZIMMERMAN: The scapegoating issue is very strong and very clear. Again, the problem of undocumented workers is really a problem *for* undocumented workers to a very great extent in this country. And the manipulation is obvious. The effort to say these people are taking our jobs, spending our tax monies, the effort to divide workers — all this is very clear. It is part of the INS policy carried over from administration to administration, and it is basic to local, national and international dimensions of our political economy.

There is a conflict among the ruling sectors of capital, and the oppositions constituting this conflict are, I think, shaping the contradictions within the Carter proposal itself. In this respect, we should add that there is a sector that wants to trade off immigration policies against the opportunities of deeper, more massive penetration of the Mexican economy — and here we should not forget Mexico's oil holdings. While the government generally

3: The Impact of Mexican Immigration

favors the interests of the multinationals, local officials of INS and the Department of Labor, at least, have a history of collaborating with companies and growers requiring cheap labor, especially in those areas in the Southwest where these enterprises are very crucial local economic factors and where undocumented workers can be manipulated in the manner you describe. Many people have observed that the oscillations between strictness and laxness in INS's enforcement of immigration laws corresponds not with staff size but with the specific needs of the labor market.

As for the attitudes among Chicanos, my own sense is that there has been a great effort to manipulate the Chicano communities on the issue of illegal aliens, and I agree that the resistance to that manipulation has grown. Community attitudes have always been contradictory, because on the one hand Chicanos can be fearful of losing their jobs and of being labeled *mojados* themselves, but on the other hand, there is a sense of comaraderie, of shared experiences of culture and exploitation, to the extent that the harboring of undocumented workers from seizure has always been a consistent pattern, even to the point of being organized. I think that the very fact that some Chicano sectors at a certain point moved toward support of the Rodino Bill (for instance, the UFW, when they saw the use of undocumented scabs as a threat to union organization) has led now to a reverse reaction. The consequences of that kind of *ad hoc* solution have made people realize all the more that the persecution of undocumenteds harms every Latino in the country.

I believe we must give credit to grassroots Chicano organizations throughout the U.S. for helping to evolve a more progressive community stance on the issue of undocumented workers and their rights. Organizations like CASA, the legal assistance programs and many others have made Chicanos aware that an attack on undocumenteds is a political attack affecting them all. Further, several of these organizations have helped undocumenteds to become aware of at least certain means to fight back against their oppression. Chicano communities have come out increasingly against the Carter proposal. And perhaps most optimistically, we should note that recently documented workers joined with self-declared undocumenteds in a strike victory in the southwest.

These are the trends which lead me to believe that we must seek alternatives in immigration policy tactics not from the PRI or our own Democratic Party, and really not only from the Marxists, but from the grass roots and trade union groups themselves.

I see much hope for further developments in this direction. But all of this optimism should not cloud the seriousness and force of government and big business manipulations on undocumented workers. Nor should we lead ourselves into the complacent belief that there is now, nor in the immediate future, any complete Chicano community consensus about this issue. Believe me, this is a reality I have encountered every day in my job, and one that is likely to continue for some time into the future. It is clearly a reality which all of us must attempt to counteract.

SPEAKER FROM THE FLOOR: Mr. Coatsworth raised one point which was passed over very lightly, but which I think has some significance in the evaluation of the question of undocumenteds. He referred to the position of the Socialist Party before World War I. Mexican immigration was not the great question in those days; there were other important groups, from Europe, Japan and so on. I can't say that the Marxists of today can get too much inspiration from the Party's approach, and certainly not from people like Victor Berger and others who were social racists when it came to the question of immigration. But some socialists made an important contribution to the struggle for a coherent Marxist class position on immigration that certainly has importance today, especially since the same issues that we raise had to be confronted at that time.

To be sure, there weren't many undocumented workers, but the great influx of immigrants from Europe during the early twentieth century raised the issue of whether they represented a threat to the American standard of living and organizations of labor, or a potential element for the building of the labor movement. There was considerable debate on this issue, and it is worth noting that whereas AFL officials, like AFL-CIO officials today, took the position that these workers were unorganizable, others, progressive Socialists among them, sought to prove that they were. If the approach that these workers couldn't be organized had prevailed, we would never have had a successful United Mine Workers, because it was only when the UMW organized the unorganizable Slavic workers that they succeeded. The IWW is another example. So I don't think we can deal with this issue unless we can find the roots of the question and demonstrate the errors of those who believe that Mexican workers are not organizable and that their continued influx would therefore ruin the labor movement. It's an old argument, it's been dealt with in the past, and we ought to learn from it.

WOMACK: I couldn't agree more with your statement. It is striking the extent to which the issues we are facing now with respect to undocumented workers are similar to those that were raised by the turn of the century up to the First World War and beyond it within the American Socialist Party. It is true that the official position of the old Socialist Party is not a good model, and I think we can do better.

Since I talked very generally earlier, there are some specific points I would like to make, in agreement with what my comrades here have said. In the first place, I think it's very important that Marxists take a straight class, but reasoned, position in favor of legalizing the immigration. The reason is that you can't stop it. It's not going to stop in the immediate future, and as it proceeds now, it is organized already, but essentially by labor smugglers. That is, there is a black market; in the same way that there is a dope trade, there is a labor power trade. The movement of Mexican unemployed from various points to the border, across the border and from the border to places of employment in the U.S. is already organized by gangsters. Legalizing immigration would do something toward removing the criminal features from the movement of labor, and it would allow some room for continued pressure toward legalizing the right to organize unions and other struggle organizations.

In the second place, I think it's important to organize the Mexican workers who come here — it is important for them to organize themselves and for them to get whatever help they can from their own Mexican organizers and from friendly people in this country. It happens that historically, and for good reasons, migrant workers in industry and agri-business have been particularily militant. Immigrant workers early in this century (the undocumented workers of their time mentioned by the previous speaker) provided some of the most militant, reasonable, conscious, determined, brave leaders of the working class in those years. And I think that both Mexicans and Americans are missing a great fund of union organizing energies in not helping to free these workers who are going to be moving in and out of the U.S.

Finally, with reference to specific matters John Coatsworth in particular alluded to about the Carter proposal: It is important to keep in mind that there are eight or nine outstanding issues between the U.S. and Mexico. To cite a recent State Department document, these issues are: financial problems (that is, investments and credits), oil (Mexico has discovered vast reserves), natural gas (the Pipeline), trade (protectionism — the border runaway shops), the border lands, drugs and narcotics, and of course the migration. All these matters seem very separate, and the State Department does not seem to argue publically that they should be linked. However, as Marxists, we have to anticipate the linkages and find solutions that keep all dimensions in perspective. In so doing, I am sure we will discover that the question of undocumented workers is one of the key places in the puzzle of capitalist reality and the struggle to overcome it.

ZIMMERMAN: After having voiced some negative views, I would like now to expand on John Womack's revolutionary optimism and take it to its logical consequences. My own perspective also stems from a concern with linkages — between undocumented and documented migrant workers of the fields and factories, among Mexican, Chicano and Latino workers, and, of course, ultimately among all oppressed minorities and all oppressed workers.

The fact is that as an extremely oppressed and beleagured group coming from one exploitative subsystem into the heart of the "beast," undocumented workers, by their experience, their persistent role and their likely future, are among the most potentially progressive and radical sectors of the labor force.

Certainly they are subject to the unevenness of cultural and economic development, and to some of the negative qualities peculiar to every oppressed group. Nevertheless, these qualities are far from universal or eternal; nor are they completely negative in the overall dialectics of human development, if only because they may breed a powerful counterforce over the years. And I do believe that the potential of undocumenteds to rise in concert with, and to in fact galvanize other sectors is very important, especially given the vision of the year 2,000 which John Womack has offered us.

The total population of Mexican immigrants, Chicanos and Latinos is growing at astronomical rates — no other sector in the U.S. is growing as rapidly. And this is not just due to immigration, but also to the fact that this is an extremely young population with a very low median age and (here an aspect of the positive dialectic even of seemingly negative factors) still with a propensity toward large families. The potential of this vast population is severely limited if large numbers do not overcome the extremes of capitalist oppression to become progressive fighters and workers united against the forces of exploitation. But to the degree that all of us are successful in helping this happen, this population has the potential for re-vitalizing the struggle for workers and for socialism in the U.S.

We have already witnessed the potential in certain limited ways with the great UFW drive in California. Compromised on the issue of undocumenteds, overwary of leftward ties and trends, the UFW, though still a vital and positive force, is only a foreshadowing of the future possibilities for organized Chicano workers in America.

The struggle, then, for Chicano workers and the struggle for undocumented workers are not diametrically opposed, but dialectically linked as part of the effort to maintain a future basis of a socialist-oriented labor movement in the U.S. The struggle to open the border, the efforts to keep undocumenteds here, to wage war on the Migra, to fight for their social and political rights, is a struggle to build the potential base, in the U.S. and in Mexico, for the future assault on capitalism. Indeed, as the long-standing U.S. exploitation of Mexican and Latin American peoples becomes more and more a situation internal to the U.S., as the U.S. becomes part of Latin America just as Latin America is now part of the U.S., we may find the basis for the complex historical development that will one day liberate the hemisphere.

That is the real problem *of* undocumented workers *for* capitalist society — it is the fact that the very population which sectors of capital need to maintain their profits is a potential source of their overthrow. That is why even capitalists who today thrive on the exploited labor of illegal aliens in another more profound and long range way, fear the effects of the influx. That is why they sometimes encourage the cry against the very sources of their profits; that is why they seek to have the American masses pay partial compensation for the complete exploitation they seek to maintain. That is why they try to modulate and control the influx, so that it only serves their interests in their times of need. That is why they broadcast the threat of fascist repression — for the sake not of solving the problem, but of preventing it from reverberating against them.

These are ultimately the reasons why the problems for undocumenteds are the problems of the capitalists, and part of the solution for Marxists and progressives in the U.S. And it is for these reasons that, as part of our overall struggle against oppression, all of us must find means to fight on this front.

Among the means, I would suggest that we have to make use of every mechanism which capitalist contradictions have placed at our disposal — the migrant programs, the legal services, the trade unions, the community groups.

We must work with lawyers to inform undocumenteds of their rights. We must challange INS for their incessant violations of rights and procedures — for their searches and sweeps, for their collusion with big business and their political agents, for their deportations without due process. We must challange the violation of confidentiality rights by which government agencies like Social Security, Food Stamps and the police turn over suspected undocumenteds to the INS. Above all, as a short range goal, we must attempt to build the support groups that give undocumented workers the confidence to challange INS — to come out in numbers, to strike, to protest, to resist deportation and to fill the court dockets with so many complex and contradictory immigration cases that we can bring INS to its collective corporate knees. In the long run, we must fight for an open border and a *total amnesty* for all undocumented workers already here.

As one who has had the fortune to spend the past few years of his life actually earning a living by working for migrants and migrant rights, I would urge more of you to involve yourselves with the issues and the people. You may do so with the firm conviction that whatever you accomplish at least stands a chance to contribute in an important way to the struggle against capitalism and for the emergence, however far off still, of a socialist world.

II.
CLASS, RACE AND EDUCATION

DEVELOPMENTAL EDUCATION
A BELEAGURED SPECIES

Michael H. Washington Sr.
University of Cincinnati

The struggle for access to higher education in the sixties and early seventies led to a tremendous influx of working class, poor and minority students, otherwise considered "non-traditional" clientele. Because many of these students had spent all previous years of educational training in a public school system designed as a control mechanism to maintain custody of its clients until society could absorb them into the lowest rungs of the labor force, they were illprepared to do college level work. As a consequence, through a process known as selective retention, i.e., retaining only those students who were properly prepared, these students were carefully weeded out. It was this process that gave rise to developmental education programs, whose function was to overcome the academic deficiencies and provide the necessary support services to strengthen the success possibilities of newly admitted "nontraditional" students.[1]

As adjuncts to an historically established institution designed to service the upper class, these programs have experienced extreme difficulty in their efforts to survive. Their inability to fit into the traditional organizational framework of four-year institutions of higher education has a definite class basis. The insidious effects of their systemic marginality and exclusion not only results in the perpetuation of class oppression among minority and working class students but it has a repressive effect on the staff members, who are often considered as adjunct faculty.

An article in the student newspaper at the University of Cincinnati vividly describes the situation of adjunct faculty members:

> Negative as the non-tenured situation is, . . . adjuncts are even worse off. Not only is job security even more tenuous, but pay is much

lower and basic job benefits such as health insurance are non-existent. More significantly, essential outside-the-classroom tasks in providing quality service to students (personal contact and curriculum development), are not considered important enough by administrators to include in adjunct pay. Adjuncts are also barred from participation in faculty governance of the University, the only way faculty can stem the increasing administrative control of the educational process.[2]

Soft-money-funding overtly dispalys the depth and breadth of the lack of commitment to adjunct programs on university and governmental levels. The year-by-year funding cycle of these programs has an effect which is analogous to the "last hired first fired" phenomenon so prevalent in the hiring practices of industry. For in times of economic crisis, some of the first programs to be "cut back" or even "cut out" are the very programs which service minority and working class students.

The psychological effect on the staff of such tenuous financial arrangements hinder the effectiveness of these programs. The fact that faculty members do not know if they will be hired from one year to the next creates a serious impediment to their level of commitment to developmental education, or to the specific organization for which they work.

The lack of adequate funding necessarily creates an administrative phenomenon that Frederick Taylor referred to as scientific management, which has the effect of maintaining class and caste relationships between developmental education staff members and the rest of the university faculty. Because developmental education teachers are not covered under faculty union bargaining units, it is not unusual for them to have greater teaching loads than traditional faculty and to have advising loads commensurate with those of social workers, while receiving less pay than even the lowest paid instructor who is a member of the union. And if the developmental education staff member is only part-time, which is more often the case than not, the intensification of labor becomes even more blatant. Remuneration for doing the equivalency of a full-time job is often less than what would be received for public assistance. The dismal condition of having absolutely no control over one's career is exacerbated by the fact that there is little hope of ever being promoted. And when the questions of promotion are raised, committees and subcommittees are formed in order to formally reject their acceptance into the professional world of academe.

The actual commitment to developmental education by most academic and political officials can be further demonstrated by examining the quantity as well as the quality of support services designed to make the transition from community to academic life a less traumatic experience. Rarely if ever will we find a real institutional commitment to cultural, psychological, or day-care services to assist non-traditional students in their struggle for higher learning. When such programs do exist, they are primarily the result of individuals whose personal interest alone is the chief reason for their survival from year to year.

As a microcosm of society, the university has often constructed certain discrete units in specific campus locations to house, educate and service non-traditonal students. Such units are viewed by traditional faculty and students alike as being the ghetto section of the campus. Being blamed for the inability of public school bureaucracies to properly equip them with the necessary academic skills, these students are viewed as culprits to be held responsible for the "deflated degree" phenomenon. This victim-blaming syndrome has the effect of describing the segregated social and academic life patterns of these students rather than revealing the true causality of their oppression.

In conclusion, institutions of education in any society, whether elementary, secondary or higher education necessarily reflect the interest of the ruling class. In a capitalist society where sharp class distinctions must exist in order to provide the basis for the economic structure, it is the function of educational institutions to help perpetuate the differences in class. Also, because educational institutions are reflections of the society for which they exist, the social conditions of society will manifest themselves in the schools as well. With these points in mind it is easy to understand the lack of commitment on the part of the university and government officials. For if the perpetuation of class distinctions is a necessary function of schools under capitalism, then in relation to developmental education programs, the universities should be commended for a superlative performance.

Notes

1. For a detailed account of these programs, see John and Suzanne Roueche, *Developmental Education: A Primer for Program Development and Evaluation* (Southern Regional Education Board, 1977).
2. *News Record*, Tuesday, April 11, 1978, p. 4.

THE STRUGGLE FOR DESEGREGATED QUALITY EDUCATION: THE CASE OF APPALACHIA

Marvin Berlowitz
University of Cincinnati

1. Class Struggle and Schooling
The analysis of the role, the stakes and the prospects of white urban Appalachians in the struggle for desegregated quality education is another in the countless reaffirmations of Marx's maxim that "all history is the history of class struggle."

The unprecedented number of school closings and general fiscal bankruptcy of our nation's school systems indicate that educational disfranchisement is no longer limited to minority students contained in segregated ghettoized schools. There is now a spectre of doom haunting the rights of the entire working class to free public education. The struggle for desegregated quality education is at the same time the first foothold in the necessary counter-offensive to retain these rights and the critical pre-requisite for the unit indispensible to its success.

A brief reflection upon the recent bourgeois counter-offensive against victories in the areas of desegregation and affirmative action makes it clear that the U. S. ruling class has a far clearer conception of the critical importance of class struggle and its dialectical relationship to the centrality of the struggle against racism than do many educators. The opposition to desegregation includes the most reactionary, chauvinist, racist, anti-working class representatives of finance capital — for example, the Ku Klux Klan and the Nazi Party. In the governmental arena, we find Richard Nixon and his Supreme Court appointees, Louise Day Hickes in Boston, and more recently Patrick Moynihan and Howard Jarvis.

2. Socio-Historical Perspectives

Despite the sophistical proliferation of "victim blaming" rationalizations for the failure of schooling in the U. S., it is Harrington's portrayal of poverty as "the other America" and the Kerner Commission's famous prediction, or perhaps more accurately, postdiction, that racial isolation in the U. S. would give rise to "two Americas — one black and the other white," which lay the foundation for a scientific explanation of the "crisis of urban education."[1] Briefly, the dynamic basic to the school's role in the reproduction of the capitalist social division of labor is the segregation of students by race and socio-economic status into subsystems, each having their own separate books, curriculum, teachers, physical facilities, expectations, norms of teacher and administrative conduct, pedagogy and, of course, separate outcomes including lower achievement and higher dropout rates for poor, minority and working class students.[2]

Although many progressives including the historical revisionists might agree with this thesis, they put forth a caricature of Marxism which not only explicitly rejects the central role of the working class in the struggle for free, compulsory and quality public education (i.e., the labor education thesis), but they also fail to see the integral dialectical relationship between quality education and desegregation.[3] In reality, a significant body of evidence exists to support the relationship.

3. The Labor Education Thesis

First, let us turn to the labor education thesis. Historically, the struggle for free, compulsory public education has been an integral part of the struggle for democratic rights in our nation. Such concerns were even reflected in the zeal of the American Revolution as Thomas Paine called upon America, " . . . to make men as wise as possible, so that their knowledge being complete, they may be rationally governed." Thomas Jefferson even went so far as to call upon the Virginia legislature to make "provisions for talented though poor students to be educated, without cost to themselves, all the way through college."[4] In the 19th century, incipient working class organizational forums such as Workingman's Associations and Mechanics Guilds put educational demands on a par with concerns as central as the establishment of mechanics liens and the abolition of imprisonment for debt. The Chicago Federation of Labor launched a specific struggle for comprehensive high schools expressing the fear that separate vocational high schools would result in a segregated tracking system injurious to the interests of working class children.[5] During the period of Reconstruction, abolitionists, women's groups and missionaries concerned with the specific plight of Blacks made demands for the provision of education for the disfranchised. The writings of Black leaders, including Frederick Douglas and W. E. B. Du Bois, reflect similar demands.[6] Spokeswomen for the women's movement including Blackstone, Stanton, Anthony, etc., also placed a high priority on educatoin for their constituencies.[7]

At the 1976 AFL-CIO convention, members stressed the importance they gave desegregated quality education, and made clear their desire to isolate those who would slander the democratic essence of labor. The Ohio AFL-CIO drafted their own resolution affirming those positions.[8]

4. Desegregation and Quality Education

The relationship between desegregation and quality education can first be developed by a general explication of the stake of whites in the struggle against racism.

In a discussion of racism and the labor movement, W. E. B. Du Bois observed:

> The object of white labor was not to uplift all labor; it was to join capital in sharing the loot from the exploited colored labor . . . And white labor loved the white exploiter of black folk far more than it loved its fellow black proletarian.[9]

As unemployment rises in the throes of the present economic crisis, it is quite clear that "the loot" is to be shared by increasingly fewer whites. It is the exploitation of labor which is to be shared more widely as we witness economic crisis leading not only to the depression of wages but to an intensification of labor, to unprecedented "speed up" and the increasing abandonment of concern for safety on the job and in the very environment the worker drinks and breathes.

However, despite the rejections by the labor movement DuBois further admonished that "the labor movement was the most promising movement of modern days and we [Blacks] who

are primarily laborers must eventually join it."[10] Had the invitation been extended earlier, workers of Ohio would not be finding it necessary to organize a lobby for legislation to deal with the problem of "runaway shops" for there would not be sanctuaries of cheap, vulnerable, unorganized labor throughout the South.
Reich's study of the relationship between racism and labor in the South is instructive.[11] He not only found that the wages and benefits of unionized workers were far superior to those of unorganized workers, but that those unions with desegregated locals fared far better than those with segregated locals and other more racist practices.

Looking at the situation in more analytical terms: If "white skin privileges" were anything more than a short-lived delusion, then white workers in the South would not only enjoy greater employee benefits than their Northern counterparts but would also enjoy far superior social services. Bureau of Labor statistics provide quite the opposite picture, with social services including education ranking lowest in the Southern states on all indices.

The history of the labor movement is, in itself, instructive.[12] Even the incipient industrial unionism of the I.W.W. found desegregation and the general struggle against racism critical for its successes. The crisis of the 30's along with advancing technology and the increased division of labor gave rise to the need for a decisive break with the racist practices of the A. F. of L. as essential to the formation of the C. I. O. Similarly, in the field of education the National Education Association (N. E. A.) found that its capitulation to the practice of segregated Southern locals cost it dearly in its competition with the American Federation of Teachers (A. F. T.) for the membership of urban school teachers. When the N. E. A. abandoned the segregation of Southern locals in order to survive the competition of the A. F. T., it not only found that it was able to survive in the South, but gained in strength generally.[13]

5. *Desegregation-Cost Effectiveness Terms*

Reacting to the role of state laws in maintaining separate institutions for Blacks, DuBois remarked:

> there is no doubt that this is unfortunate and even idiotic. It is *needlessly costly* and it is a direct contradiction to that democratic equality toward which all education in the end must strive.[14]

5: The Struggle for Desegregated Education

In a recent Federal Court decision prohibiting the Cleveland Board of Education from closing the city's schools, Judge Batiste cited cost analyses by experts as unconcerned with social issues as accountants, to demonstrate that the extra financial burdens imposed by the historic maintenance of *de facto* segregation were the major factor in bringing the schools to financial ruin. In Cincinnati, we also find the maintenance of under-enrolled segregated schools in order to maintain racial isolation. Thus Boards of Education which like those in Cleveland and Cincinnati make the maintenance of racial isolation a priority infinitely higher than the provision of educational services, are in contempt of the people. What else can we make of a situation, in which officials make extravagant expenditures in order to defend criminal violations of federal laws at the same time when they answer demands for the improvement or even the maintenance of services with pleas for austerity.

Counter arguments harping on the costs of busing rest on foundations of sand. Anti-segregation busing costs constitute less than 1% of general school transportation expenditures, but do not include costs of busing for the maintenance of racially gerrymandered school districts.[15]

Furthermore, the indirect costs of school segregation and racial isolation must not be overlooked. Real estate prices are audaciously inflated for the dubious privilege of attending segregated white schools which are themselves of questionable quality.[16] The ghettoization and racial isolation of Black youth in schools with low achievement and high dropout rates . . . help to maintain a 40-60% unemployment rate among urban minority youth, which constitutes an "industrial reserve army" constantly threatening the entire working class. In this regard, the Kerner Commission reports the following:

> Our survey of riot cities found that the typical participant was a school dropout. As Superintendant Briggs of Cleveland testified before the Commission: Many of those whose recent acts threaten the domestic safety and tear at the roots of the American democracy are the products of yesterday's inadequate and neglected inner city schools.[17]

Even in times of relative domestic tranquility, abandonment of youth to a life of despair and anomie gives rise to the proliferation of unnecessary and costly demands on social service agencies of all kinds.

On the question of unity so integral to the struggle of the working class, the struggle for desegregation can only serve to forge our strongest link. Racism is a cancer which has historically infected our body politic. Those who suggest that the struggle for desegregation itself poses a threat to working class unity are not unlike a medical charlatan who advocates cancer treatment by means of benign neglect or goodwill rather than radical extrication; they display a despicable temerity and a racist historical blindspot. The pursuit of their logic would have led to the abandonment of the Abolitionist movement for fear of a civil war, and a similar abandonment of the struggle against Jim Crow. The triumph of Little Rock would never have come to pass, for the summoning of the 101st Airborne and the challenge of Governer Faubus would have been insurmountable obstacles. It is precisely because such illogic did not prevail that we have had the victories which prepare us for the struggle we not face for desegregated, quality public education.

6. Court Ordered Desegregation: Success or Failure?

The next point of analysis is to look more specifically at the success of court ordered desegregation.

A recent national survey of the Civil Rights Commission reveals that the overwhelming majority of court-ordered desegregation plans have resulted in "dramatically improved achievement scores, reduced dropout rates, and increased . . . percentage of students seeking higher education after desegregation when changes were made in ever area affecting the curriculum." The survey cites a typical court ordered situation of desegregation:

> The school system introduced an ungraded individualized, sequential plan for the development of basic skills; added courses in Black history and literature; maintained the number of minority teachers at a level proportionate to minority student enrollment; provided staff training in human relations; and took steps to ensure that disciplinary treatment is administered equitably.[18]

Socio-psychological studies of desegregation completed by academic institutions reveal similar results.[19]

It is interesting to note the type of negativism, cowardice and lack of objectivity which characterizes coverage by the media. Community groups in Boston, including the Freedom House Institute on Schools and Education, express outrage at the fact that the sensationalism of South Boston appears to take priority over the peaceful transition in almost eighty other districts.[20] Recent television coverage of the successful aftermath of Little Rock is a pleasant exception — a particularly significant one when we recall the rabid Governor Faubus in the doorway of the school building and the necessity for the intervention by the 101st Airborne. The successes must be qualified. Certainly the analyses and reports of school desegregation might be more favorable if they were based on longer periods of time. Certainly the use of more sophisticated statistical techniques such as trend analysis would be useful to overcome certain negative appearances during the initial stages of school desegregation campaigns.

7. *The Appalachian Bourgeoisie and New Left Ideology*

In some circles, the decade of the 60s witnessed a romantic approach to national liberation struggles which gave rise to a New Left proliferation of "internal colony" theories that were applied in analyses of the situation of Blacks as well as Appalachians.[21] On a theoretical level the validity of the notion was dismissed by Winston and Jackson in the case of the Blacks and by Walls in the case of the Appalachians.[22] They demonstrate that neither group constitutes a separate or stable geographic, economic, cultural, linguistic or political entity. With respect to Appalachians, Walls attacks the "internal colony" theory, noting that "A loose analogy is no substitute, in the long run, for a precise theory that can lead to more detailed investigations."[23] A mechanical application of the theory would lead to utopian schemes such as secession, the formation of Appalachia as an autonomous republic and the like. Walls points out that the only hint of concrete strategy proposed has been, "a weaker version — a state of Appalachia has been mentioned."[24]

The petty bourgeois class orientation of the New Left has given rise to a preoccupation with marginal groups, utopian schemes and right opportunism. Walls adds credence to such notions in his speculation on the popularity of "internal colony" theories saying, "One explanation may be that the vocabulary of colonization is more comfortable than that of class conflict, and regional and ethnic chauvinism is more acceptable than talk of socialism."[24] Walls speculates that such forces may see an

Appalachian state as providing the basis for a new class of "hillbilly millionaires"[25] or perhaps they have more modest ambitions to model themselves after what Perlo terms "the illusion of Black capitalism."[26] Finally, the lucid socio-historical work by Linda and Paul Nyden on "the struggle in the coalfields" reveals that the Appalachian region is not only plagued by the general fallacies of New Left ideology but also with its malignant outgrowths of Maoism.[27]

8. Appalachian intelligentsia

Don West points out that the proliferation of Appalachian Studies programs and projects such as Foxfire are largely entrepreneural undertakings "in pursuit of grants," limiting themselves to a focus on "the quaint, picturesque and romantic" to the exclusion of the "rich history of struggle which is central to the Appalachian culture and heritage."[28] Thus, we are reminded of Marx's comment that, "Those who control the material forces of society control the intellectual forces." John Gaventa drives home the relevance of Marx's words on the following observations:

> The point has often been made that higher education came to Appalachia first and foremost to satisfy, not the region's needs and interests but those of a new industrial order . . . Appalachian colleges and universities have failed to produce critical studies of Appalachian issues or to be a source of resistance against the region's exploitation or to be the architects of an alternative Appalachian future . . . By focussing with an alien method upon the 'unique', folksy culture, the kind of sociology and history which Appalachian studies produces is more often the scrutiny of the victims, not the victimizers.[29]

The most blatant right opportunism of the Appalachian petty bourgeoisie is succinctly embodied in the work of Harry Caudill, whose recent book, *A Darkness at Dawn*, generalizes the victim-blaming theories consistently utilized against Blacks and even white immigrants in the 1920's, to Appalachians. And Caudill goes so far as to carry the banner of eugenics against his own people:

5: The Struggle for Desegregated Education 117

The ceaseless hemorrhaging of the best blood has already had a discernable effect. The deteriorating situation moved one wag to note that, "the best thing the federal government could do for the mountains is to move a big army camp in. The soldiers would get the local girls pregnant and the fresh genes would do more good than all the free grub they're giving away." The observation evoked laughter seasoned with the realization that it contained more truth than wit.[30]

However, conceptions more suitable to the liberal palate abound. The National Institute of Education, representing that sector of finance capital which the historical revisionists have aptly labeled "the corporate liberal ideology", is feverishly bankrolling a proliferation of projects based upon the concept of "ethnicity", a brainchild of Nathan Glazer and this right opportunist ilk.[31] Paul Laska addresses this phenomenon which he terms the "ethnico-populist attitude.":

> ... The "people" are seen separately from the working class as an ethnic identity either real or imagined ... In Appalachia, for example, a new Narodnik movement is shaping up as an awakened and aroused "intelligentsia" rushes to embrace the "true folk" of the region, in whom are said to reside all the decent values quashed in the "outside" world of mass capitalism.[32]

The formulation is also gaining ground among opinion leaders in the area of urban Appalachian education.[33] The obfuscation of class struggle and the centrality of the struggle against racism inherent in the ethnicity construct portend an epoch of divisiveness between urban Blacks and white Appalachians. The lack of initiative among petty bourgeois urban Appalachian leaders on the issue of desegregation reinforces that possibility. Furthermore, at the very moment when Jonathan Kozol, the veritable guru of the "free school movement," has abandoned the movement and its theoretical underpinnings have been devastated by numerous critics of Ivan Illich,[34] the strategy is now being put forth as a solution to the problems of urban Appalachian school children in areas such as Cincinnati. The fact that racist Boards of Education such as those in Cincinnati, Chicago and elsewhere are hastily creating "alternative education programs" and "magnet schools" as a last ditch smokescreen in their efforts to circumvent court ordered desegregation adds an additional cause for concern. Increasing Maoist influence among urban Appalachians also poses a danger in view of the anti-desegregation position taken up by the so-called "Revolutionary Communist Party."[35]

Many progressive Appalachians have pointed out that they would do well to follow the leads of the Black liberation struggle in the formulation of their strategies and tactics. When this statement is made without further specification, it smacks of white chauvinism, for Blacks are objectively being viewed as a monolith. Unfortunately, the analysis thus far reveals that the most appropriate analogues with the Black liberation struggle appear to be Frazier's insights on *The Black Bourgeoisie*, DuBois' indictments of "negro Colleges" on the issue of "accommodationism" and Winston's charges concerning the "opportunism of cultural nationalism."[36]

9. The Taproot of Racism or Tomorrow's People?

The present paper has paid a good deal of attention to petty bourgeois influences among Appalachians. However, as Marxists we understand not only that we must proceed from a class analysis, but that the vanguard role of the proletariat must be central to our discussion of strategies. An examination of the heritage of workers' struggle, so neglected by most writers on Appalachia, will also indicate the tremendous promise of the area's contributions to the campaign for desegregated quality education.

The demarcation of the Appalachian region itself is a reification of class struggle. Those immigrants who settled in Appalachia brought with them a history of struggle against religious and political persecution in the Old World. When they arrived in the established coastal colonies, continued persecution and intense economic rivalry forced them to move westward and soutward into the mountain areas. As we look further at the settlement of the southern part of the U. S., the distinction between "colonists vs. immigrants" is particularly instructive. The "privileged sons of the aristocracy . . . along with upper class adventurers" not only carried with them charters gained by virtue of their privileged position in the Old World; they also brought their accumulated capital and their propensities for indolence and exploitation, which laid an excellent basis for the development of "a tidewater slavocracy."³⁶ The lower status immigrants who landed in the tidewater region soon left because they were repulsed by the tidewater aristocracy or their status as indentured servants and redemptioners came to an end.³⁸ The Appalachina people demonstrated their propensity for democratic struggle by forging a model constitution before the drafting of the Declaration of Independence and by serving an exemplary role in the Revolutionary War: The Regulators were the first to raise the cry against "taxation without representation"; the legendary Swamp Fox was a son of Appalachia.³⁹

In the struggle against slavery, the first abolitionist newspaper was founded in Appalachia when William Lloyd Garrison was only ten years old. Don West captures the class nature of the Appalachian involvement in the abolitionist movement in his biography of Robert Tharin:

> Tharin understood too well (for his own personal safety) how the slaveholding aristocrats despised and misused both the slave and the white non-slaveholder. He understood how they used the brave non-slaveholders, whom they had helped madden with false statements, to fight and die in order that they might lounge around, in comparative safety on their cotton plantation.⁴⁰

The Appalachian region continued as a major conduit in the underground railroad. As the tidewater aristocrats sought ratification for the move to secede, they found stiff opposition in the Appalachian region. Civil disobedience continued throughout the war in areas such as Lookout Mountain, Tennessee, which suffered savage assaults because they continued to fly the union flag throughout the war. Union volunteers from Appalachian counties within Confederate boundaries exceeded the draft quotas they would have been assigned had they been in the union; and these volunteers often "bushwhacked" Confederate recruits before they could enter combat.⁴¹

Similarly, the United Mine Workers has carried on the tradition of militancy by their struggle against racism in their ranks. Most schools within the region were desegregated as a matter of course until forced to segregate as a function of the imposition of Jim Crow laws; they immediately conformed to the

1964 Brown decision without the necessity of coercion by specific desegregation orders.[42] The multi-national character of the student body of the Appalachian South Folk Life Center and the harmony and discipline among the extremely impoverished student body would be the envy of any urban school administrator.[43] Careful study of the much maligned Kanawa County textbook dispute also reveals that the racist content of the struggle was largely the responsibility of petty bourgeois leadership elements emanating from the Ku Klux Klan and similar ultra-right forces. However, it must be kept in mind that the KKK has never gained a foothold in the Appalachian south.[44]

Serious Marxist study of the region will move from New Left theories of the "internal colony" to concrete studies of the contradictions of "new versus country," the impact of industrial capital, the unique features of extractive industry, the advent of monopoly capitalism and the recent combination of steel and energy multinationals whose vicious onslaught was recently defeated by the heroic efforts of the United Mine Workers and their supporters. The Appalachian people have often played a pioneer role in the struggle against those multinational corporations who constitute the frontrunners of U. S. imperialism as a uniquely Appalachian rather than a worldwide phenomenon, it is important to stress how the Appalachian proletariat has contributed to the finest traditions of proletarian internationalism, the force which will ring imperialism to its knees. We have merely to measure Appalachia against some of the unique features which characterize this epoch, including the existence of a Socialist bloc, the proliferation of national liberation struggles and a resurgence of a rank and file movement in U. S. labor. The United Mine Workers have been pacesetters in the development of rank and file unionism; they have also set a precedent in their struggles against South African coal. Numerous delegations of trade unionists and other progressives to the Soviet Union have also had their origins in Appalachia.

Jack Weller labels Appalachians as "yesterday's people"; Harry Caudill sees the region through an imagery of darkness and despair. The nihilistic, cynical symbolism of these petty bourgeois elements is symptomatic of their failism in relation to the Appalachian proletariat.[45] In viewing the prospects of regional and urban Appalachians in the struggle for desegregated quality education, dedicated Marxists will find that the appropriate way to describe them would be as "tomorrow's people."

Notes

1. William Ryan provides a superb refutation of such theories in *Blaming the Victim* (New York: Vintage, 1971). For Specific refutations of the theories as applied to appalacians, see Paul Nyden, "Appalachian Syndrome Theory," in *Goldenseal* (Charleston, West Virginia: State Capitol, 1978); Stephen Fisher, "Victim Blaming in Appalachia" and "Cultural Theories and the Southern Mountaineer," in Bruce Ergood and Bruce Kuhre, *Appalachia: Social Context, Past and Present* (Iowa: Kendall Hunt, 1976), pp. 153-162.
2. For empirical support of this thesis, see James Coleman et al., *Equality of Educational Opportunity*, (Washtington: U. S. Department of H. E. W., Office of Education, 1966). See also Patricia C. Sexton, *Education and Income* (new York: Viking, 1961); Mark Borinsky, *Comparison of Schools with High and Low Proportions of Poverty Pupils* (Washington: U. S. Department of H. E. W., National Center for Education Statistics, 1975); and *Racial Isolation in the Public Schools: Conclusions and Findings of a Report of the U. S. Commission on Civil Rights* (Washington: Government Printing Office, 1967). The Children's Defense Fund provides an excellent national survey of the institutional mechanisms which push children out of school, along with a statistical treatment which overcomes the artifacts which tend to obfuscate the extent of the problem in *Children Out of School* (Washington: Children's Defense Fund, 1974). On the inequities of teacher assignment see my article, "Institutional Racism and School Staffing in an Urban Area," *Journal of Negro Education*, 43 (1974), pp. 25-30. Finally, see my paper with Henry Durand, *School Dropouts or Student Pushouts?*, Working Paper No. 8 (Cincinnati:

Urban Appalachian Council, 1978).
3. On the "historical revisionists," see Samuel Bowles and Herbert Gintis, *Schooling in Capitalist America*, (New York: Basic Books, 1976), pp. 230-231. Bowles and Gintis include the following scholars as advocates of the position in question: Michael Katz, Clarence Karier, Marvin Lazarson, Carl Kaestle, Joel Spring, David Tyack, and Colin Greer. These thinkers believe that "Schools were promoted first and foremost as agents for social control of an increasingly culturally heterogeneous and poverty stricken urban population in an increasingly unstable and threatening economic and political system."
4. See Herbert Aptheker, *The American Revolution*, (New York: International Publishers, 1974), p. 247.
5. William Russell, "The Contributions of Labor to Education in the 19th Century." Presented at the 1976 American Educational Research Association Meeting.
6. See Philip Foner, *The Life and Writings of Frederick Douglas* (New York: International Publishers, 1950), Vol. II, pp. 38-43; Vol. IV, pp. 288-95 and 414-417; Vol. V, pp. 370-75. See also W. E. B. DuBois, *The Education of Black People* (New York: Monthly Review Press, 1973).
7. Cf. June Sochen, *Herstory* (New York: Alfred Publishing Company, 1974), pp. 111, 189.
8. Ohio AFL-CIO-resolutions-Reports of the Constitutional Committee on Resolutions Presented to the 10th Constitutional Convention, 1976.
9. W. E. B. DuBois, *op. cit.*, pp. 123-124.
10. *Ibid.*
11. Michael Reich, "Economic Theories of Racism," in Martin Carnoy, *Schooling in Corporate America*, (New York: David McKay, 1972), pp. 67-80.
12. Gil Green provides an excellent summary of the problems of labor in *What's Happening to Labor?* (New York: International Publishers, 1976). A few classic works include Richard O. Boyer, *Labor's Untold Story* (New York: United Electrical, Radio and Machine Workers of America, 1955); William Z. Foster, *American Trade Unionism* (New York: International Publishers, 1947); and, of course, Philip Foner's exhaustive four-volume work, *History of the Labor Movement in the U.S.* (New York: International Publishers, 1965).

13. See Celia Zitron, *The New York City Teachers Union, 1916-1964* (New York: Humanities Press, 1968). For a more specific treatment of this issue, see Patrick J. Gross, "Teacher Organizations and School Desegregation," *School and Society* (December, 1962), pp. 441-52; Rolland Dowing, "The American Federation of Teachers and Desegregation," *The Journal of Negro Education* 42 (1973) pp. 79-92.
14. W. E. B. DuBois, *op. cit.*, 133.
15. Many of the myths concerning busing are exploded in "Your Child and Busing" (Washington, D. C.: U. S. Commission on Civil Rights, 1973). A very useful pamphlet entitled, "Busing, Myth and Reality," is available from the Cleveland Branch of the Women's International League for Peace and Freedom.
16. Victor Perlo, *Economics of Racism* (New York: International Publishers, 1975), Chapter X.
17. Otto Kerner, *Report of the National Advisory Commission on Civil Disorders* (New York: Bantam, 1968), p. 425.
18. Arthur S. Fleming, *Fulfilling the Letter and the Law: Desegregation of the Nation's Public Schools* (Washington, D. C.: U. S. Commission on Civil Rights, August, 1976), p. 113. The Presidential condemnation of this report marked a turning point in which the executive branch of our government has moved in closer alignment with the more racist, reactionary sectors of finance capital. The executive role in the Bakke case is a clear indication that the trend continues.
19. See Nancy St. John, *School Desegregation Outcomes for Children* (New York: Wiley and Sons, 1975); also, Martha Carithers, "School Desegregation and Racial Cleavage, 1954-70: A Review of the Literature," *Journal of Social Issues*, 26, 4 (1970), pp. 25-47.
20. Caroline Durrum and Toye Lewis, *Boston Desegregation: Questions and Answers* (Boston: Freedom House Institute on Schools and Education, 1975). See also Rayleen Craig's paper, which follows in this volume.
21. For perspectives on New Left romanticism, see Ileana Rodriguez and William L. Rowe, ed., *Marxism and New Left Ideology* (Minneapolis: Marxist Educational Press, 1977).
22. Cf. Henry Winston, *Strategy for a Black Agenda* (New York: International Publishers, 1973), Chapters I-V; James Jackson, *Revolutionary Tracings* (New York: Inter-

national Publishers, 1974), Chapter XXIV; and David Walls, "Internal Colony or Internal Periphery? A Critique of Current Models and an Alternative Formulation," in Helen Lewis, *et al.*, ed., *Colonialism in Modern America: The Appalachian Case* (Boone, North Carolina: Appalachian Consortium Press, 1978).
23. Walls, "Internal Colony," p. 340.
24. *Ibid.*, p. 324.
25. *Ibid.*, p. 340.
26. Victor Perlo, *Economics of Racism*, Chapter XI.
27. Linda and Paul Nyden, "Showdown in Coal: The Struggle for Rank and File Unionism" (Pittsburgh: Miner's Report, 1978), p. 13.
28. Donald West, "Miseducation of Appalachians," speech at university of Cincinnati (May 5, 1978).
29. John Gaventa, "Inequality and the Appalachian Studies Industry," *Appalachian Journal*, Spring (1978), 328.
30. Harry Caudill, *A Darkness at Dawn*, (Lexington, Kentucky: University of Kentucky Press, 1976), p. 36.
31. See survey of the literature on ethnicity in Phillip Obermiller, *Ethnicity and Education: The Intercultural Dimension, Working Paper No. 5* (Cincinnati: Urban Appalachian Council, 1974).
32. Paul. J. Laska, "Political Poetry and the Politicalization of Art," in *The Unrealist*, (Prince, West Virginia: Unrealist Press, 1978), p. 19.
33. Obermiller, *op. cit.*
34. See Jonathan Kozol's critique in his *Free Schools* (New York: Houghton Mifflin, 1972); Herbert Gintis, "Towards a Political Economy of Education: A Radical Critique of Ivan Illich's *Deschooling Society*," in Ian Lister, ed., *Deschooling* (Cambridge: Cambridge University Press, 1971), pp. 24-34.
35. See "People Must Unite to Smash Boston Busing Plan," in *Revolution, National Newspaper of the Revolutionary Union*, 2, No. 9 (October, 1974), p. 1. The Revolutionary Union is now known under the name Revolutionary Communist Party.
36. For E. Franklin Frazier, see his classic, *The Black Bourgeoisie* (Glencoe, Illinois: Free Press, 1957); for Du Bois and Winston, see notes 6 and 22.
37. Charles Hanna, *The Scotch Irish* (New York: Knickerbocker Press, 1902), Volume I.

5: The Struggle for Desegregated Education

38. Henry Pratt Fairchild, *Immigration* (New York: Macmillan, 1925), Chapters I-III.
39. On these matters, see Donald West, *Freedom on the Mountains* (Huntington, West Virginia: Appalachian Press, 1976), and Suzanne Crowell, *Appalachian People's History Book* (Louisville, Kentucky: Mountain Education Associates, Southern Conference Education Fund, 1971).
40. Donald West, *Biography of Robert Tharin* (Huntington: Appalachian Movement Press, 1976), p. 24.
41. Robert Kimmel does an excellent job of putting to rest the myth of class solidarity between the tidewater slavocracy and the southern mountaineer in a succinct seminar paper entitled, "Disloyalty in the Confederacy," mimeographed by the Department of History, Miami University, Ohio.
42. The information gathered from Don West in an interview in August, 1978, is of particular significance when one takes into account his long history as a teacher and school superintendent in the Appalachian region.
43. This perspective emerged with clarity in my travels throughout Appalachia. I not only visited the educational facilities at the Appalachian South Folklife Center in Pipestem, West Virginia, but also went deep into the back hills to interview some of the students; I observed poverty and deprivation far worse than most of that known to us in urban areas.
44. Linda and Paul Nyden, "The Kanawa County Book Boycott: The Politics of Reaction," mimeographed (1975). See also Linda and Paul Nyden, "Showdown in Coal," p. 13.
45. Waller's book, *Yesterday's People* (Lexington: University of Kentucky Press, 1965), is a widely used (and criticized) subjective slander of the Appalachian people based upon the author's sour grapes rationalization over his failure to enlist the free labor of the indigenous opoulation in the pursuit of his church projects. (See note 30) Caudill's *Night Comes to the Cumberlands* (Boston: Little, Brown, 1962) sets the stage for his recent commitment to eugenics theory in *A Darkness at Dawn* (see note 30). For even Caudill's earlier work alleges limitations in the American Indian gene pool, describes American Indian behavior as "savage, childlike and superstitious," and provides a pejorative, stereotyped, paternalistic caricature of Black slaves and white Appalachian workers.

THE DEVELOPING PARENT MOVEMENT IN BOSTON: DYNAMICS OF CHANGE

Rayleen M. Craig

1. Introduction

Since 1974, Boston has achieved international prominence because of the racist reaction that surfaced in response to Court-ordered school desegregation. This paper examines the role of parents through Court-ordered citizen participation structures which grew up out of efforts to stem the racist tide and establish popular mechanisms that would facilitate improved, equitable education for children throughout the Boston area.

More generally the paper focuses on the inherent and persistent aspects of institutionalized racism and the obstacle this presents to parent unity. The paper offers suggestions for positive action on the part of parents that have implications for both educational change and broader social change as well. The lessons and strategies of Boston can well be applied to other urban areas in the U. S.

2. Structure and Purpose of Parent Councils

In the U. S. District Court order of October 4, 1974, Judge W. Arthur Garrity mandated the creation of Racial-Ethnic Parents' Councils (REPC's) at all schools affected by Phase I of desegregation and the formation of a City-wide Parents Advisory Council (CPAC) to represent parents interests on a citywide level. As spelled out in that first Court order, the Councils purposes were:

1. to insure adequate and impartial investigation and responsible recommendations on racially and ethnically oriented problems arising at the school,

2. to create a means of communication between parents, students, teachers and administrators regarding the solution of such problems; and
3. to promote an environment of understanding and common purpose among the various elements of the community so that the best available education may be afforded to all children.

The following year, Phase II of desegregation was implemented, affecting all schools in Boston. REPC's were mandated for each school and expanded in composition to include equal numbers of black and white parents as during the previous year, plus proportional representation of Asian and Hispanic parents. Since there were now nine school districts, CPAC was expanded to include one black and one white parent from each of the districts, and two Asian and two Hispanic parents to be elected from city-wide caucuses. Additionally, the Phase II order of June 5,1975 mandated the creation of nine Community District Advisory Councils (CDAC's) to advise Community District Superintendents on district concerns, priorities, relationships with university and business collaboratives, etc. The CDAC's were comprised of one half parents and one half "community" representatives, from business, the universities and schools, the police, labor and community agencies, etc. The CDAC's were to communicate their concerns to the newly created City-wide Coordinating Council (CCC), a monitoring body that Judge Garrity described as the "eyes and ears" of the Court.

All parents of schoolchildren were eligible to participate in REPC elections, both as voters and as candidates. CPAC and CDAC representatives were elected by REPC members. At all three levels, white parents elected whites, black parents blacks, etc.

The August 24, 1976 Court order only mandated minor changes in the Councils, based on the previous year's experience. No parent could serve on more than one Council. Parents elected to CDAC's and CPAC were required to vacate the seat of the REPC from which they were elected. The separation of responsibilities between CDAC's and CPAC was further spelled out. CPAC was to represent parent interests at a city-wide level. Each CDAC was to deal with the programs, buildings, transportation and security of schools within its district and to watch over the progress of desegregation in these schools. To accomplish these ends, the CDAC's were to recruit volunteer monitors, with the stipulation that no parents could monitor a school which a child of theirs attended.

Massive confusion resulted from the inability of parents or others to discern where parent and programmatic concerns were separate. Relations between the CPAC and the CDAC's became strained and tense, primarily because of the lack of structural clarity. Based upon the experience of the past two years, CPAC and CDAC representatives developed a plan to present to the Court calling for modifications in the Council structures. The September 1, 1977 Court order on citizen participation reflected many of the substantial changes recommended in the council jointly by the CPAC and CDAC.

At the REPC level, participation was broadened to include what the Court order termed "linguistic minorities," wherever there was a bilingual program in effect. the CDAC's were expanded to include parent representation from each school. CDAC's primary function would now shift to providing assistance to the REPC's and to strengthening parent involvement within the districts. REPC's were to become involved in monitoring within their schools, a total about face from the previous year. REPC's were to hold quarterly meetings for all parents in the school, and CDAC's were to hold quarterly meetings for all REPC's in a district. These meetings were to serve the purpose of both sharing information and insuring that the Councils represented their constituencies. Another complete turnabout from the previous year was that dual membership on Councils instead of being prohibited, was mandated. A CDAC member would sit on both the CDAC and REPC. CPAC members, likewise, would sit on both CPAC and the CDAC of the district from which they were elected. However, in the case of CPAC membership, the representative would vacate his/her REPC seat and the REPC would select another member to sit on the CDAC.

CPAC's role was more explicitly delineated: to represent parent concerns on a citywide level, to co-ordinate monitoring of all desegregation programs in conjunction with the CDAC's and to initiate city-wide forums around issues of particular concern to parents, such as, bilingual or special education. CPAC, as written in the Court order, was also to work closely with the City-wide Coordinating Council as it prepared to assume its full powers, once the Court withdrew its jurisdiction.

Ironically, the one group which still has no direct representation in the parent structures is the American Indians. They must run for a seat on a Council and vote in another group's caucus. Because the School Department has refused to admit that many Mic Mac children need bilingual services, the American Indians cannot even take advantage of the most recent expansion of parent participation. Efforts will continue to try to include Native Americans in the parent structure through CPAC and/ or Court action.

3. Class Relations of Black, White and Other minority Parents

A disturbing phenomenon has occurred since the inception of desegregation and the creation of the Court-ordered Councils: the participation of black parents has declined steadily each school year between September and June. In September 1977, the numbers of black and white parents initially elected to REPC's were almost equal (584 whites, 508 blacks and 105 other minorities) whereas in the previous years whites had outnumbered blacks by three to two. In some schools, only black parents were active and in some only white. By January of each year, however, the overall black parent participation began to decline; and by June, relatively few schools had any black parent participation at all. A similar situation prevailed in CDAC's and CPAC. Although there was a concurrent decline of white parent participation, the decline was not nearly as severe as among the blacks. Indeed, it is safe to say that in previous school years, where there were Councils at all, the Councils were, with few exceptions, dominated and controlled by whites.

The overall decline in parent participation will be considered in the following section. However, the nonparticipation of other minorities and the high attrition rate of black parents from participation in the parent councils must be examined from a race and class perspective in order to gain a clear understanding.

According to the Marxist definition, "a worker is one who is compelled to sell his or her laboring power . . . to an employer in order to live."[1] But this definition also includes persons not now employed because there are no jobs: the underducated who have never worked, employable welfare parents, youths requiring a special lift into employment — all those condemmed to take "job leftovers," and even white collared professionals who sell their brain power for wages, are members of the working class.

In the Boston public schools, children from petty bourgeois homes (of small independent business people, physicians, lawyers,

6: The Developing Parent Movement in Boston 131

governmental bureaucrats) constitute 3 to 5 percent of the student population; children of the capitalists (those who make their profits on the work of others) constitute a miniscule proportion. Even to the casual observer, then, it is obvious that the vast majority of children attending Boston public schools came, as in most U. S. urban school systems, from working class homes.

The racial composition of the Boston Public Schools is 41 percent white, 44 percent black and 15 percent other minority. There are relatively few Boston blacks and other minorities who are petty bourgeois and less than a handful who are capitalists; almost all the children of black workers are in the public schools; inversely, since non-working class children (minority or not) generally go to private or special examination schools, almost all black and other minority children who attend the public schools come from working class families.

On this basis, we can make the following generalizations about the parents of Boston public school children:

1. The vast majority belong to the working class, with a small number belonging to the petty bourgeois class.
2. There are almost equal numbers of black and white parents.
3. Other minorities constitute 15 percent with Hispanics being the largest group.
4. The majority of parents with children in the school system is composed of non-white workers (both employed and non-employed).

The working class as defined above is far from monolithic, and it is characterized by little unified working class consciousness. This is especially the case in Boston, largely because of the absence of basic industry and its accompanying trade union movements. In basic industry cities, workers (men and women, black and white) have had more opportunities through their trade union associations for popular types of expression. From experience, they have learned the need to join together in struggle for whatever changes or benefits they wanted. To varying degrees, they have also learned to identify the enemy and the fundamental problems that confront them. Also from experience, they have learned to be wary of leaders who speak out but do not act.

In Boston, contrary to cities having large industrial unions, the labor organizations that dominate are craft unions. As the history of trade unionism indicates, the craft unions fought against the right of industrial workers to organize. To date, they still represent the most racist and reactionary element of the trade union movement. They have consistently fought against union membership for minorities, and the Massachusetts State Labor Council publicly stated its opposition to Boston's desegregation order.

Racism is the major tool that the ruling capitalist class uses to keep workers divided. As Gil Green puts it:

> American capitalism has been racist from its inception . . . To the extent that white workers have accepted the holding down of other races in the belief that it benefits them, they have been trapped in a dilemma. They dilute and distort class awareness by finding common racial ground with the very class that is their antagonist.
>
> This has been, and remains, the chief obstacle to greater class consciousness and a wider workers "and peoples" unity. It is the meaning of Marx's trenchant observation that labor in the white skin can neverbe free as long as labor in the black skin is branded.
>
> Black workers have always been ready to unite with white workers on a basis of equality. They have shown this on numerous occasions. Yet time and time again their hopes have been dashed. So all-encompassing is the effect of racism on their lives that some find it difficult to identify with white workers as members of a common class fighting a common foe for common ends.[3]

And in his recent critique of the views of Daniel Moynihan and Robert Allen, Henry Winston states:

> According to both . . . [men] each "ethnic" or "interest group" has a stake only in its "own" particular interest which can pre-

sumably be advanced only in opposition to the needs of other "ethnic groups" and "interest groups." Such theories encourage Black and white to regard each other as the enemy: in particular, they influence white workers to accept racism — and in effect to maintain it.

What has happened in South Boston symbolizes the logic of these concepts: an "ethnic" group is made to feel deprived by the anti-racist struggle and thus white workers are misled into helping to forge the chains of their own enslavement.

The "ethnicity" and "group interest" theories reverse reality for both Black and white, portraying the anti-racist struggle, not racism, as contradicting the interests of the white masses.[4]

The propagation of racist and ethnocentristic ideologies and institutional practices in Boston has been manifested in the most virulent and overt forms. Neighborhoods as well as schools have been intentionally segregated through red-lining practices of banks. Churches and civic organizations, political leaders and intellectuals have all contributed to the foment of racist hysteria either through inflammatory rhetoric or through silence. Voices of reason on the part of the so-called responsible and liberal white leadership of Boston could not be heard until after the vicious attack on Attorney Theodore Landsmark in Government Center. Only then did the ROAR signs disappear from the windows of City Hall and did the Mayor call for a march for peace.

Unemployed white workers seeking government-funded jobs were often told that that could not be hired because the jobs, though unfilled, were waiting for blacks and minorities. Given the high unemployment rate among blacks (almost double that of the white community), such a hiring policy, if actually carried out, could have contributed to the overall economic growth of minority neighborhoods. However, the rumor and not the policy was in effect. Blacks did not know that they were being scapegoated, while whites did not know that their civil servants were lying to them.

This is the back drop against which white and black parents came together in the Court-ordered Councils. Fear and mistrust of each other abounded. Given what was happening in the city as a whole, it is a wonder that during the first two years, there was any interaction of black and white parents at all. When Councils did function with black and white participation, whites came slowly to the realization that blacks were not the cause of their problems. No, blacks did not want to take over their neighborhoods and schools. No, blacks did not have as a primary goal that their sons marry the daughters of the whites. No, they were not all on welfare.

Through the interaction with blacks, working class whites in economically depressed areas such as Charleston, South Boston and the North End came to realize that their schools were no better than and sometimes inferior to schools that black children had attended in Roxbury. Those white parents whose children were bussed into predominantly black neighborhoods began to find out that black neighborhoods were not the dens of vice, iniquity and filth that they had been led to believe. And black parents learned that in some white neighborhoods, housing and school conditions were as bad or worse than in their own.

Nevertheless, attitudes built up over generations are not easily swept aside even when the objective conditions change. Therefore, white parents continued to treat black parents as something other than equal. This unequal treatment manifested itself in a variety of ways:

1. The locations of meetings were often inconvenient for black parents.
2. If blacks occupied a leadership position (most Councils had co-chairs — one white and one black), the black parent leadership was usually by-passed or ignored.
3. In some cases, blacks were treated in a condescending manner by their white peers.
4. References continued to abound about the "decline in the quality of education," "disadvantaged children who are holding others back," etc.
5. White parents identified more readily with school administrators and personnel than they do with black parents.

It is interesting to note that both black and white parents have been quick to exonerate themselves for any responsibility to reach out to Hispanic, Asian, Native American or other minority parents. Both groups are quick to point out that "their culture is different," "they don't go out at night," "they're not interested in their children's education," etc. One gets no sense of a bond of commonality between English and non-English-speaking parents. Thus, as parents of bilingual students begin to organize, they are quick to blame both the black community and white community for their problems.

Traditionally, the more progressive parents have been elected to the CDAC's and CPAC. However, once elected they usually fail to maintain contact with the REPC's from which they come. Thus, these parents grow as individuals and the "higher" Councils grow, but the REPC's are left much on their own, with no help from anyone. White chauvinism is also manifested at the CDAC and CPAC levels, but is counteracted more effectively, since the most militant, aware and vocal black parents aspire to these seats.

Since the summer of 1977, a group calling itself the "Concerned Black Parents" has been meeting with regularity. This group, primarily composed of CPAC and CDAC members, is attempting to develop a city-wide strategy to involve black parents in their children's education. They are committed to integrated education and housing, but they understand that black parents and children need greater support than they have received so far. Their understanding is that integration implies that all parties come together from equal positions of strength, and that black parents must develop their own strength and their own agenda.

It is safe to say that parents, both black and white, are becoming increasingly aware that their interests are more similar than dissimilar. They acknowledge more readily that all of their children are being short-changed in the educational process. Although there still exists fear and suspicion, by and large, parents have stopped blaming each other for the failure of the city's schools.

4. Relations of Parents with School System

The Boston Public School system views the parent Councils with a mixture of trepidation and scorn and more recently awe. In the 1974-75 school year, the school system did not take the Councils very seriously. Interpreting the Court order in the narrowest possible fashion, they saw the Councils as dealing with racially-oriented problems only. In fact, since most parents on the Councils looked to the School Department for direction, they were told that they had no business dealing with anything but racial incidents and conducted themselves accordingly. Despite the adverse publicity about incidents at South Boston and Hyde Park High schools, very few other schools had racial problems per se. The School Department, whenever possible, dealt only with the Home and School Association, Boston's peculiar version of a Parent Teacher Association. By charter, the Association is to provide support to the school administration. It is an overwhelmingly white, politically conservative, even reactionary, organization.

With each Court-order giving more clearly defined and broader powers to the parent Councils, and with the Councils becoming increasingly aware of the powers they had, the School Department began to realize that it would have to deal with the Councils in some way.

As stated in the Citywide Coordinating Council's March, 1977 report to the U.S. District Court:

> The School Committee and school administrators are no longer perceived as having the final say as to whether the educational system is doing its job. Institutions of higher education, businesses and cultural institutions of have long affected the interests of public schools — perhaps most decisively in decisions to admit, employ, and serve their graduates. Now they have taken on new roles and responsibilities for direct participation in the education process. Most importantly, parents who have been given a new legitimacy and organized access to information and decision-making are more and more insisting that they be treated as respected peers.
>
> A previously closed, hierarchial structure is being shaken by the prospect of a more open, democratic model that demands effective participation by all those who have a stake in the public schools. Public schools in Boston are shifting gears — moving forward to meet the needs of a socially and

6: The Developing Parent Movement in Boston

technically complex present and away from behavior that preserves modes of living no longer practical for today or tomorrow.[5]

By September, 1977, the School Department and Committee had reluctantly accepted the inevitability of the presence of the Councils. Through the Council structures, parents have, in some cases initiated, in others supported, and in still others opposed, changes in the schools.

During the first two years of desegregation, something just short of a miracle occurred. Every school with a functioning REPC had a hot lunch program. On the face of it this may seem insignificant. However, in most of these schools, all of the equipment for hot lunches was present, except for a $40 adapter plug. In fact, the equipment, in most instances, had been installed in these schools more than five years before the Court order. But the Department of Planning and Engineering had been able to evade principals for five years, saying they could not get the plugs. When parents arrived on the scene, they were not willing to accept such a ludicrous explanation from the principals, in response to inquiries about hot lunches. So school by school, parents went to pay visits to the Chief Plant Engineer. In some schools, the REPC's organized to get other parents' signatures on petitions. Other REPC's went directly to the School Committee to complain about the situation.

This example is but one minor indication of what has happened when the inefficient bureaucracy of the school system was confronted by what it perceived to be an organized force. The School Department's initial fear of retaliation by the parents, and even the Court, if it did not respond positively to parents demands and requests, allowed the Council structures to gain many victories. It also gave the nascent Councils much needed time to develop and become informed.

Many management studies have been done on the Boston Public Schools. While they had variations and disagreements, in detail, all of them agreed that the structure of the School Department itself was creating many of its problems. In effect, there is no central administration of the school system, although the Superintendent of Schools has overall responsibility for all educational programs and personnel in the hierarchy that directly or indirectly relate to students. The Chief Plant Engineer is responsible for all public school buildings and grounds and has control over all noninstructional contracts, all ordering of equipment and all custodian, engineering and crafts personnel. The Secretary to the School Committee manages all the hiring of all clerical help and all school lunch personnel. The Business Manager is responsible for all financial matters, the ordering of supplies and the approval of bills for payment. Each of these four people are hired by and are directly responsible to the School Committee. They each act independently of each other, and they often act in contradictory fashion. The Superintendent of Schools has no authority over the other three officials.

To further exacerbate the situation, the School Committee itself acts on each personnel matter and all contracts above $500. The School Committee approves all hirings, all name changes due to marriage, all requests for maternity leaves of absence, all bids for overtime and promotion, all terminations and retirements. Therefore, at each meeting, much time is spent on personnel matters that are purely administrative in nature. This four-headed monster managed by a five member unpaid elected board thus becomes fertile ground for graft, patronage and corruption.

The school system had its problems of internal communication and external credibility before the advent of the Court-ordered Councils. But the onslaught of parents through the Councils exposed as never before just how bad things were. A closed, corrupt, highly inefficient system was suddenly stripped bare — much to its embarrassment.

As a result, alliances began to develop both within the School Department and between some school employees and parents. Personnel within the school department, who had previously had antagonistic relationships, found it necessary to band together against their new common enemy. This was especially true of the corrupt and incompetent. Banding together on the basis of status became less important than doing so to create a self-serving unified front. The highly stratified hierarchical arrangement of positions began to melt away, as teachers, principals, secretaries and janitors began to support each other against parents.

Simultaneously, personnel, expecially teachers and lower level administrators, who had attempted throughout the years, to effect reformist changes, sought out parents involved in the Councils. These frustrated reformers felt that they, at last, had an ally whose interests paralleled their own, but whose power exceeded theirs. (Also, as mentioned frequently by reformer types, parents faced less risk in confronting issues — they could not be fired). The reformers provided parents with much needed information about what was happening in the schools, and also about who was responsible for what. Working mainly undercover, the reformers, particularly teachers, became the "eyes and ears" for parents, much as the CCC functioned for the Court.

The Court, the State Department of Education and even the Superintendent of Schools mandated parent involvement in several areas — screening, interviewing and later evaluation of principals, assistant principals and guidance counselors; approval of proposals; consultation in development of individual school plans; participation in the development of each school's annual report. Depending on the school, parents on REPC's found themselves either deluged with paper work or fighting for their right to be involved. Rarely were they given encouragement or support. As I stated in an earlier study of the subject:

> At the local school level, some parents found themselves being given only that information which the principal saw fit to give them. In other schools and on the District and City-wide Councils, parents found themselves deluged with an avalanche of information that they had no way to process or sort out. Minority parents find themselves confronting not only the institutionalized racism of the school department and the racial prejudices of many of their white counterparts, but also, a sometimes subtle, sometimes overt class discrimination. The School Department and the U.S. District Court both operate on a 9-5 day. Meetings at which information gets shared, and decisions get made are held during those hours. Only those parents who are affluent enough to be able to spend their days attending meetings and visiting schools, or those whose jobs allow them to be professional parents, can participate in a meaningful manner. With few exceptions, these parents are white and because they come to meetings with so much more information than others, their mere presence inhibits the involvement of minority and

working parents. The "non-professional" parents are made to feel inferior.[6]

The frustrations and obstacles parents face far exceeded the rewards. On a purely economic level, many parents found themselves incurring expenses that they could ill afford — for child care, transportation and time off from work to attend school related meetings — especially since school personnel often refused to meet after the regular working day. Given the enormity of the task, and the cost in human and economic terms, many parents, after the initial encounters, simply walked away and never returned.

But some parents did chose to stick it out and fight — to become the vanguard of the parent movement against the school system. Largely as a result of their persistence, two racist, reactionary incompetent principals were removed from schools in 1977; class sizes have remained close to the demanded 26:1 ratio of students to teacher; bilingual and special needs programs have been introduced into schools, and many schools got much needed repairs. In the case of one particular school, the REPC prevented nine teachers (the entire Faculty Senate) from either being dismissed or transferred because of their co-operation with the REPC in having a principal transferred. The charge against the teachers was insubordination.

5. The Uniqueness of the Boston Parent Councils and their Politicization

Studies on citizen participation in education have examined both the functioning of advisory groups and the movement of community control, particularly in the 1960's and the early 1970's. While a comprehensive review of the literature has not been done for this paper, the author has found nothing, in theory or descriptive analysis, that approximates the Boston situation.

Where advisory councils have been established these have usually been formed with the tacit or implicit approval of the local school system. They have either been all parent bodies, or a combination of parents and non-parents. They are also normally formed in areas where there is a relatively good school system. The major concern of advisory councils, then, is improvement of education that is already considered adequate or more than adequate. Exceptions to this hypothesis are those advisory councils mandated by federal or state legislation, but generalizations of these models are not being made, because each is tied to a particular program within a system or school and not to a total system or school.

The Boston councils mandated by the Federal Court were designed to be advisory and investigative bodies, reporting back their findings and recommendations to either School administrative personnel and/or the U.S. District Court. Underlying the design of the Council structure was a belief by the Court that, once in place, they would receive the co-operation of the School Department. They were also, by design, to be integrated bodies. Even with its history of racism and reaction, the U.S. District Court never envisioned the problems that were to confront parents or the councils. No one outside the School system thought that parents would ever pose such a perceived threat — not even the parents themselves. The Councils were designed to open previously closed doors to parents who would then be able to co-operate and collaborate in improving public education generally.

The community control movement was born from the frustrations of black and other minority parents who had typically, been involved in attempts to integrate urban public schools. In the case of American Indians, the thrust for community control emerged from strong dissatisfaction with the Bureau of Indian Affairs Schools, often located hundreds or even thousands of miles away from children's homes. These schools operated on a philosophy that stressed assimilation and denial of Indian culture, values and norms, and were controlled and run primarily by whites. Thus the community control movement was a nationally separatist movement attempting to wrest power away from school systems that were contributing to racial oppression and exploitation. Some community controlled schools operated within public school systems as model or demonstration centers; others were set up out side the parameters of the local education agency, and were financed through federal, state or private sources.

Because of their experiences with the Boston school system, parents, through the Councils, are demanding more and more of a voice in decision-making. As these demands focus on programmatic, personnel and budgetary decisions, parents are exercising or can exercise more control. In May, 1977, a Conference of Councils was held for parents involved in the Court-ordered bodies. one of the resolutions passed was to work on forming a parent union; another to have parents involved in collective bargaining. Should parents be able to achieve these goals, they will indeed be in a powerful position. A lot will depend on whether they can become involved in collective bargaining and what their role in that process will be. Parents clearly recognize that their relationship with the school system is one of a shift in power. The more the school system resists, subverts or bungles, the more power parents want. Parents feel that unless they are there, unless they have control, the school system will not do its job of educating their children. Parents have developed a new political sophistication as a result of their involvement in the Councils. In 1976, virtually every parent reached out to others to inform them and to defeat the Mayor's 1976 charter reform plan. Many of these parents had not previously even bothered to vote. However, the plan, as presented by the Mayor, would have stripped the parents of what little control they now exercise. Similarly in 1977, CPAC mobilized parents to support the candidacy of John O'Bryant for School Committee. A strong anti-racist campaign was waged by parents, black, white and Hispanic, to elect the first black School Committee person in Boston in this century.

Parents United, the monthly newspaper of CPAC, mailed to the home of every parent with a child in Boston Public Schools, is becoming more and more of a political publication. Recent issues have focused on the Council and School Committee elections, the need to organize, the fight against racism, class size and conditions within the schools themselves. Through *Parents United*, an anti-racist ideology is being propogated to almost 40,000 homes. What is becoming increasingly apparent and more and more accepted is that without parents' active particpation and without a struggle, things will not change for the better.

6. Symptomatic Problems of the Parent Councils in the Struggle for Change.

The greatest impediment to parent unity, as to the unification of working people as a whole, continues to be racism. To go back to Karl Marx, labor in the white skin will not be free as long as labor in the black skin is in chains. This axiom holds true for Boston parents as well: White parents will not realize any significant gains in education for their children if they expect to make these gains at the expense of black parents and youth. Although the Fascist element, typified by ROAR, has largely disappeared from the scene, the attitudes and behavior of white parents still reflect the racist nature of the social system.

Ideologically, CPAC is developing a strong anti-racist position. The training CPAC provides for CDAC's and REPC's and the materials for CPAC prepares for them address the issue of racism. In practice, however, the deeds fall far behind the words. There is little support for black parent leadership. Black parents are under-represented if represented at all, at planning and strategy meetings. The reasons for the decline of black parent participation are purposely not discussed. Under CPAC's leadership, concrete steps must be taken to combat the institutional manifestations of racism within the Council structure itself.

At the same time, black and white parents must be ready to lend support to Hispanic and Asian parents. The current Court order has not adequately addressed the needs of these and other racial-linguistic minorities. As a result, a separate bilingual shift is being prepared. Such a suit will seek redress for legitimate grievances by these groups. However, there is a very dangerous current emerging among those responsible for organizing Hispanic parents to blame black parents, the black community and the U.S. District Court for their present problems. If this current trend is not reversed, it will cause a wide rift between the Black and Hispanic communities generally, and parents particularly, that will be difficult to heal in future years.

Another problem facing parent councils is that generated by the divisive anti-communist red-baiting tactics of persons within the School Department, and those inside and outside the parent councils. This nation has not yet fully recovered from the McCarthy years, and apparently communist or socialist sympathies and tendencies are little understood by most people in the U.S. Red-baiting as a tactic has been and continues to be used to isolate progressive and even moderate parent leadership. As this weapon was used to divide workers in the early years of the labor union movement and during the McCarthy era, so it is being used now, to split the ranks of the parent movement. This tendency, like others, needs to be confronted and combatted.

Because the parent movement represents a progressive struggle that is disturbing the current balance of power, it is a threat to the local ruling class. As Paul Sweezy notes, "The local ruling class wants to keep the ghetto, so to speak, a profitable asset. And since the present educational system is one of the principal means of preserving the existing pattern of neighborhood and racial relations (in the words of Eleanor Leacock, 'the educational system functions to train the children of the poor to accept their station in society as poor'), the local ruling class and its supporters naturally reject or sabotage all efforts at educational reform."[7]

These are the major dangers within the parent movement that must be faced and struggled against at the same time that parents confront the school system. Racism, sectarianism and anticommunism are the major methods that can be used to keep the parents divided and fighting among themselves, diffusing and dissipating their energy and willingness to fight the school system itself.

As the bourgeoisie and petty bourgeois have usually opted to send their children to schools outside of Boston or to private schools within, so there is a tendency within the Boston system for parents with petty bourgeois leanings, to send their children to schools with a known track record of success and to become involved in these so-called "magnet" districts. In Boston, the prestige schools are largely located in District 9, the magnet school district par excellance. The competition for entry into the prestige schools has always been keen. Now, each year, more and more parents are "by hook or crook" trying to get their children admitted. Parent involvement in the magnet school districts far exceeds involvement in the remainder of the city's schools.

The U.S. District Court paired the magnet schools with businesses, universities and cultural institutions to a greater degree than any other schools. It was hoped that the magnets would serve as a model, and would thus contribute to the uplifting of all Boston schools. The magnet school district is by and large successful when viewed in and of itself. However, there is a dominant petty bourgeois tendency among school department personnel and parents within the magnet district to create a separate, elitist system. No district 9 group has exercised any responsibility or demonstrated any concern about schools in the remainder of the city. Rather, even though schools within this district have a disproportionately high share of financial and human resources, the concern is always with more for these schools, which ultimately means less for the rest. Unless reckoned with, parents, both black and white from within the magnet school district, will be soon fighting their parent peers throughout the city, as the class distinctions and loyalties become more apparent, and as parents in the other districts become more involved.

Parents must face up to some very important decisions. A

6: The Developing Parent Movement in Boston 145

dilemma faces all parents who must decide what they think is best for their children. When one has options to exercise, one tends to chose the option with the greatest gains attached. When one's own child's educational (and ultimately economic) future is at stake, it is often easiest and seemingly most logical to choose whatever is perceived to be best. Only with the development of a class consciousness, do parents realize that their children's future is inextricably intertwined with the future and fate of children in general. The parent movement can become a vehicle for the development of this class consciousness.

The immediate task before parent leadership is to strengthen the Councils particularly the REPC's at the local school level and to reach out and involve more new parents. It is important that the intended racial composition of the Councils be maintained, and that the parents elected to Council seats represent the interests of the larger parent community. Discussions are currently underway concerning the development of a Parent Learning Center, which will serve the needs of parents of children in Boston Public Schools, those on Councils as well as those not now involved.

Some parents have the tendency to view the Councils as ends in themselves. Once these bodies function as they should and a constituency base for them is soundly built, then these Councils should and can become the vehicles through which to create a movement of educational and broader social change. The overall economic condition of Boston adversely impacts on its schools. The Councils can become the vehicles through which to educate and mobilize parents around such issues as full employment, federal aid to cities, youth jobs and so on.

Finally, all encouragement and support must be given to black and Hispanic parents as they try to develop their own agendas and stragegies. This support and encouragement must be forthcoming from their white parent peers.

Most likely, the Councils will continue to fight for the expansion of bilingual programs, a curriculum without racial, sex and class stereotypes, an education that equips youth for life beyond high school. They will continue to lead the fight against incompetent, reactionary and corrupt administrators and teachers, behavior control in special education and tracking on the basis of race.

As the parent movement grows and becomes solidified and as it reaches out to form alliances with other progressive anti-racist forces, it can well become the catalyst for other types of social changes. A lot depends on the present and emerging leadership and the commitment of this leadership to end the exploitation of the masses by the few.

Such developments are fraught with dangers of cooptation, subversion and destruction, but they remain potentially viable in Boston. While parent Councils are clearly the unique outgrowth of problems and structures specific to Boston, they could, with modifications in tune with local differences, serve as a model for anti-racist, anti-elitist programs aiming at positive social change elsewhere throughout the U.S.

Notes

1. Gil Green, *What's Happening to Labor* (New York: International Publishers, 1976), p. 78.
2. *Ibid.*, p. 216.
3. Henry Winston, *Class, Race and Black Liberation* (New York: International Publishers, 1977).
4. Citywide Co-ordinating Council, "Quality Education: Changing Definitions and Heightened Expectations," Report to U.S. District Court Judge W. Arthur Garrity (March, 1977), p. 3.
5. Rayleen M. Craig, "Parent Involvement in Boston: A Perpetuation of Institutionalized Racism," paper presented at the Massachusetts Sociological Association Conference on Racism (Cambridge, March, 1976.), p. 3.
6. Paul M. Sweezy, "Afterword: The Implications of Community Control," in *Schools against Children* (New York, Monthly Review Press, 1970), p. 290.

III.
THE CRISIS AND CONSCIOUSNESS: A DEBATE

LATE CAPITALISM AND MENTAL ILLNESS:
Toward a Critical Theory Of Psychic Crisis

Robert B. Sipe
Sangamon State University

1

Our burgeoning psychic crisis is intimately connected with the social, economic and political crisis of late capitalism. This psychic crisis reflects a larger social crisis. It also plays a crucial psycho-functional role in perpetuating the existing social order.

The enormity of the problem of mental pathology in America has recently been attested to by President Carter's Commission on Mental Health, which found that "psychiatric and psychological disorders among Americans were worse than previously believed and that one quarter of the population suffered severe emotional stress."[1] This conclusion enlarged the earlier National Institute of Mental Health (NIMH) estimate that sixty million schizophrenics walked the streets of America.[2] A famous study of the late 1950's, the Midtown Manhattan Study, had maintained that approximately 23% of the population sampled needed psychiatric assistance. Yet another index of the crisis is the NIMH estimate that one out of every three American hospital beds is a psychiatric bed.[3] One out of every ten Americans will be hospitalized for mental illness in the seventies. Psychoactive drugs continue to be the most heavily prescribed drugs in the United States.

The number of psychiatrists in the American Psychiatric Association has risen from 11,083 in 1960 to 17,298 in 1970. Within the last twenty years the cost of caring for the mentally ill has increased tenfold to $17 billion. The soaring costs of mental health services, coupled with the increasing number of people in need of such services, suggest a growing crisis arena within American capitalism.

The general public, interested professionals and academics all muddy the issue of defining and treating mental pathology. The dominant medical model, with its emphasis on symptomatology and nosography, has engendered a method of treatment which supports the class nature of both the medical establishment and the larger social order. This model defines mental pathology as an illness within the individual rather than as a dysfunction of the larger society. The resultant method of treatment not only leaves the social roots of neurosis untouched, but actually fosters the individual's conformity and adjustment to a repressive social order. The failure of this approach is increasingly apparent to radicals and nonradicals alike.

Unfortunately, Marxists to date have not developed an analysis sufficiently comprehensive or sophisticated to deal with mental pathology in late capitalism. The variety of alternative explanations has failed to touch the core of the problem. In this paper I have developed some preliminary theoretical considerations which link the contradictions of the larger macro-social world of late capitalism to mental pathology. Such an analysis is important both for the development of new types of therapy and for the establishment of another critique of capitalism. I ultimately suggest that the demise of capitalism is the precondition to mental health.

Classical Marxism stresses the dynamic unity of theory and practice. When these poles no longer mutually determine one another, theory ossifies into an ideology which distorts our understanding of the world and its potentials for change. In order to avoid this ossification, Marxism must be recreated by each generation in response to the changing social relations of capitalism.

This effort demands new eyes for the relation between society and psyche. "The separation of society and psyche is false consciousness: it perpetuates conceptually the split between the living subject and the objectivity that governs the subjects and yet derives from them," says T. W. Adorno.[4] How do we understand this interrelationship between objective and subjective dimensions? Neither dimension can be explained totally in terms of the other nor can either be adequately understood in isolation. What is now needed is a distinct Marxist psychology which relates mental pathology, particularly depression and schizophrenia, to the entire social field. What is needed is the engagement of the individual in struggle with the social forces which shape his or her environment. What is needed, at the very least, is a psychological approach which does not validate the reified social relations of "trapped subjects" in an era of synchronized capitalism. In the following pages I will attempt to delineate such an approach, stressing the dialectical connectedness between psyche and society, and unmasking the "well-adjusted personality" as the chimera of a one-dimensional society.

2

Mental pathology in contemporary society is grounded in the social hierarchy of the capitalist production process. Thus, the interrelation of one's work activities, social class, and personality formation suggests that we examine the capitalist production process for its effects upon psychic well-being.

Such questions become particularly meaningful if we understand human nature as better described as *homo faber* than *animal laborens*. Karl Marx, who understood that part of our basic "species-being" is a need to engage in creative and purposeful activity, preferred *homo faber*. Work is the "everlasting nature imposed condition of human existence,"[5] whereby men and women, in shaping the world and themselves as a social totality, emerge as beings of praxis.

By praxis, Marx means something radically different from the common meaning of "practice." Praxis is "conscious life activity" by which social life stands as an object of both will and consciousness. In praxis, men and women use their human faculties of reason, imagination, and communication to develop critical consciousness. In this mode of cognitive awareness men and women are "able to discover the structure of natural and social processes in which [they take] part . . . [and] make extrapolations for the future, project goals, and look for the most adequate means to satisfy them."[6] Praxis is the creative activity of constructing and reconstructing a social totality in accordance with real, historically created, human possibilities.

Homo faber suggests the unique interiority of every individual in instinctual basic needs, capacities, talents, etc. This interiority is not ahistoric; it is realized within given historical contexts. Every individual enters the world with a set of potentialities. But in isolation or abstraction, these potentialities cannot be realized. The development of this inner nature is dependent upon the nature of one's social relations, and upon the society of which one is a part.

The socio-economic conditions of a society thus become the crucial structures by which an individual develops his or her species being.

This view of the human as a being of praxis who is engaged in the world through specific social and economic structures suggests the human growth process as a continuous series of "free choice" situations confronting the individual throughout his or her life. Every individual is situated in a particular social matrix in which the benefits of growth and development are dialectically contrasted with the safety and security of remaining at the present level of awareness. Forward growth is always threatening because it involves movement into unexplored, unfamiliar areas. The insecurity of growth implies an individual's longing for the safety and security of familiarity. "We grow forward when the delights of growth and anxieties of safety are greater than the anxieties of growth and the delights of safety."[7]

The relative dominance of "growth" and "safety" within an individual is a function of the objective, socio-economic structures of society. Synergetic (i.e., growth fostering) societies embody a socio-economic structure which enhances the delights of growth and maximizes the anxieties of safety. Nonsynergetic (i.e., growth inhibiting) societies maximize the anxieties of growth and the delights of safety. Normative considerations for mental health and mental pathology stem from this relationship. Hence, an immanent critique of capitalism must consider the type of societal arrangements which would facilitate or hinder the expression and development of our essential "species-being." The following attempts to pursue this aim by explicating some of the crucial mediations between the objective relations of capitalist society and individual self-development.

3

The primary function of the structural relations of capitalism (production structures plus social structures) is to provide the objective conditions for the capitalist class to secure an ever-expanding process of capital accumulation. Central to these conditions is a relationship which insures the hegemony of the capitalist class over the working class in all areas of social and economic life. Mental pathology among workers is the structural powerlessness they experience in the capitalist social hierarchy. My analysis differs from most other Marxist analyses in its emphasis on the effect of the prevailing objective conditions upon the realization of workers' "species-being" as delineated by Marx. Thus, the central importance of the objective conditions for the psychic apparatus necessitates that we further develop their impact and rationale.

Let us consider how class domination directed the evolution of the capitalist social hierarchy from guild to factory system. Steven Marglin and others have argued that the origin and early functioning of the capitalist division of labor and its ensuing social hierarchy had little to do with economic efficiency or technological superiority.[8] On the contrary, its real significance was the power it gave the emerging capitalist class to intensify its control over the activities of the artisan class and independent producers. Breaking the autonomy and independence of this group was an essential precondition for the development of the capitalist mode of production.

Thus, Marglin argues that the basic reason for this hierarchical control of the production process was to ensure the capitalist class an essential role and provide a requisite social structure which would ensure the central imperative of capitalism, the accumulation of capital. Only through the domination of the work force and the production process could a sufficient level of savings (capital accumulation) be obtained to guarantee the successful functioning of the capitalist system. The factory — and its descendant, the modern corporation — thus became the *modus operandi* by which the capitalist class was able to ensure its control over the production process.

The early factory system was not technologically superior to either the "putting out" system or other modes of domestic manufacture. Its advantage lay rather in the fact that it permitted entrepreneurs not only to control the basic resources of production but also to organize the work process in a manner which maintained the centrality of their control. Separation of tasks in the production process further restricted the workers' control over their product, ensuring their dependence upon the interests of the capitalist. The factory system also guaranteed the capitalist the power to introduce new technologies which would enhance the minute specialization of tasks and thereby restrict even further the autonomy of skilled artisans.

While the factory stands as the most important mediation in legitimizing the capitalist's dominant position within the hierarchy of production, aspects destructive to the physical and mental well-being of the workers occur throughout its organizational dynamics. This becomes even more important during late capitalism, when the organization of office and white collar work in general reflects the processes and modes of organization employed in the factory.

The extensive degree of mental pathology in contemporary society is grounded in the social hierarchy of capitalist production, as reflected in particularly destructive and psychologically debilitating modes of work organization. These are, in turn, essential for maintaining and perpetuating the pyramidal social hierarchy of the capitalist and working classes.

The turn of the twentieth century witnessed the growth of an extensive body of literature concerned with the application of new and improved organizational techniques and principles of the social hierarchy of capitalist production. The simple social division of labor of earlier times (assigning different tasks to different individuals in the production process) gave way to a sophisticated mode of organization theory called "scientific management." This approach attempted "to apply the methods of science to the increasingly complex problems of the control of labor in rapidly growing capitalist enterprises, from the point of view of the management of a refractory work force in a setting of antagonistic social relations."[9]

The effects of the principles of scientific management on the work-place were pronounced. Scientific management stimulated a proliferation of time-motion studies, reductive technologies, and various schools of industrial psychology and human relations, which attempted to adapt and integrate the worker into a production process organized along such principles.

The introduction of scientific management enabled the capitalist to introduce a high level of precision, calculability, stability and predictability into the production process. In addition, the capitalist's power and legitimacy within the social hierarchy (vis-a-vis the working class) was further enhanced. Most of these advances occurred at the expense of the basic class interests of the workers, reducing them to the commodity level of labor power, and making survival increasingly dependent upon the will of the capitalist class. This destruction of worker subjectivity is central to mental pathology.

By controlling the basic means of production and the organization of the workplace, the capitalist class was able to assume and subsequently ensure itself a dominant position within the social hierarchy of production. Not only was it able to control the products of labor, but increasingly the laboring class itself. This control was achieved at the expense of the workers' autonomy and well-being. Domination grew as the social hierarchy of the capitalist production process was transmitted to other, interlocking social institutions. In particular, with the bureaucratization and hierarchical control of social services, family, church, armed forces, all levels of government, and educational institutions, a social structure emerged which would continue to perpetuate the "legitimate domination" of the social hierarchy first established by the hierarchical relations of capitalist production. The extension of this control to all facets of life becomes a functional imperative for the survival of this social hierarchy as it attempts to contain the ever-increasing contradictions engendered by the dynamics of capitalist production.

4

From these socio-economic relationships, certain social processes emanate, which bear directly on the behavior, as well as the physical and mental well-being, of workers. The most vital of these social processes for our concern with mental pathology is alienation. All forms of alienation are forms of mental pathology and all forms of mental pathology are forms of alienation. This is not to deny that an extremely small percentage of cases involve organic mental pathology, but to suggest that the investigation of alienation — of being alien to one's products, activities, and social world — is a more constructive approach for understanding mental pathology.

Marx's theory of alienation, particularly as delineated in his important essay, "Estranged Labor," should be familiar to all of us. It stems from the central feature of capitalism, social production and private appropriation. Alienation is the de-realization of the subject when control over production is separated from the producer. In such a process, human beings become disconnected from the world they have created.

Reification is at the core of capitalist alienation. Reification can be defined as that "moment in the process of alienation in which the characteristic of thinghood becomes the standard of objective reality."[10] In more technical terms, reification is "that form of immediacy wherein the object is experienced as an in-itself over and against a subject."[11] Reification is the individual's loss of subjectivity and consequent loss of human activity, or praxis. The social world, a product of human activity, loses its distinctly human dimension and becomes a world of things. For Georg Lukas, a brilliant twentieth century Hegelian Marxist, reification expresses both an objective relationship in which "a world of objects and relations between things springs into being," and a corresponding subjective dimension in which "a man's activity becomes estranged from himself, . . . [and] turns into a commodity which, subject to the non-human objectivity of the natural laws of society, must go its own way independently of man just like any consumer article."[12] Thus the process of reification has a profound effect upon the needs, talents, capacities, and consciousness of men and women. According to Lukas, "his qualities and abilities are no longer an organic part of his personality, they are things which he can 'own' or 'dispose of' like the various objects of the external world. And, there is no natural form in which man can bring his physical and psychic 'qualities' into play without their being subjected increasingly to this reifying process."[13]

The important issue for this paper is how reification shapes and influences the particular needs, capacities, and mental health of the working class. Various forms of mental pathology, particularly depression and schizophrenia, can be more thoroughly explained by reification than by such standard explanations as biochemical imbalances, unresolved Oedipal struggles or communication breakdowns.

Psychiatrists generally identify the following traits as typical, with different emphases for each individual, of people diagnosed as schizophrenic:

1. Fragmentation of experience into bizarreness. Human objects, as well as relationships, and even space and time, are fragmented. Bizarreness results. Feeling is split off from idea, act from thought, one thought from another.
2. Fusion or confusion of the imaginary with the real. Reality and fantasy merge. Word becomes thing. Reality testing is hampered. A private personal world is created.
3. Loss of boundary around ego or self. The subject is alienated from his or her

productions in action, thought, and feeling. Thoughts may seem to be stolen from, or inserted into, one's own head by others. An illusory fusion or merging of self with other may occur.
4. Perception of self as object or thing. The sense of being the subject of one's experience is lost, except for regressions to infantlike states of total subjectness. Complaints of feeling 'dead' or 'empty,' or of being controlled by others for their purposes, often predominate. Dread of an encroaching numbness develops.
5. Terror, fragility, and isolation. Impermanence and insecurity threaten, while trusting relationships with others are precluded.[14]

The subjective experience of these traits is a normal response to the reified nature of social relations in capitalist society. They are emotions and awareness which most of us experience to some degree in our "everyday life" in capitalist society.

The increasing reification of social relationships under capitalism produces "ego disturbances," which Freud mistakenly analyzed as the socialization crisis of the bourgeois family. In reality, the capitalist organization of the work processes and social structures manipulate the behavior patterns required of workers. I do not mean to imply that subjective factors are thereby reduced and determined by objective factors. Human behavior not only reflects the socio-economic environment, but also has the capacity to change it. The foundation for this dialectical principle resides in the theory of human nature as structured by praxis and interiority.

5

The crucial question for us concerns the effect of capitalist social structures, and the processes which emanate from them, on the mental apparatus of the individual. Above, I noted that in a synergetic society, socio-economic structures were external instrumentalities developed by human beings to facilitate their social and self-development. However, the socio-economic structures of capitalism — premised upon profit maximization, class exploitation, and a hierarchy of power — have the opposite effect. They mold individuals into prescribed roles and behavior patterns which induce system-legitimizing behavior responses. Mental pathology develops in response to the loss of conscious praxis in the social world.

Schizophrenia, depression and other forms of mental pathology are reflected within the individual in terms of the contradiction between the need for self-realization and the capitalist socialization process. In a capitalist society, a necessary double bind exists for each individual, since the needs for self-realization cannot express and reinforce the given socio-economic relations. This double bind situation produces mental pathologies to various degrees among all individuals in capitalist society, because the systemic needs of late capitalism are inherently contradictory to those of individual self-realization. Acute psychotic episodes occur when this tension becomes unbearable within an individual's psyche.

Perhaps more important for our concerns are those individuals who do not immediately and consciously experience the severity of this tension. Such individuals achieve their orientation and self-realization in the world in terms of a capitalist *Weltanschauung*. This, of course, produces an identity between the needs of the individual and those of society. In any event, mental pathology still ensues, as a pathology which involves the proliferation of false needs and a false consciousness among the vast majority of the people.

The capitalist social hierarchy, by permeating all aspects of life, not only fosters extensive mental pathology, but also thwarts the ability of the working class to develop a critical class consciousness of its relationship to capitalism as a social totality. By class consciousness, I do not mean that each worker must manifest a general knowledge of the socio-historical laws of capitalist development and the totality of capitalist social relations. However, working class consciousness must reflect some awareness of the connections between the dynamics of everyday life experiences and the larger social order. Class consciousness demands a conscious knowledge among workers of the nature of their unmediated needs, the nature of their interactions with significant others, and the function of the various institutions of the capitalist social system. Most importantly, this understanding of class consciousness suggests the centrality of man's psychic structure to the

7: Late Capitalism and Mental Illness

determination of his social being. It takes cognizance of the fact that the conditions of social being are reflected, anchored and reproduced within the psychic structure. The capitalist socialization process, reflecting the functional needs of the capitalist mode of production, attempts to integrate the conditions of hierarchy and domination into the self-systems of individuals. This results in "psychic reifications" and other forms of mental pathology which minimize the possibility of an emerging alternative consciousness or structure of social action. It is this relationship between psychic reification and the structural dynamics of capitalist production that constitutes the key obstacle to the development of a class consciousness capable of relieving the alienation and exploitation of the capitalist social totality.

Lukacs has offered some fruitful insights into the problem of psychic reification and the phenomenon of "commodity fetishism." Following Marx, he posits "the fetishism of commodities" as the central problem of modern capitalism. Its universality, according to Lukacs, "influences the *total* outer and inner life of society" in a manner which reduces man's consciousness to a reified "second nature," unable to grasp the real dynamics of capitalist production.[15] Commodity fetishism produces reified social relations which directly shape and condition the functioning of human subjectivity in terms of object relations. With the capitalist reduction and redefinition of the human social world to the movements of commodities, human beings become mechanical parts in a mechanical system. The subject finds his or her locus in the dynamics of the capitalist production process and circulation of commodities. One's intrinsic value is determined by the prevailing rate of exchange. Human needs are satisfied in terms of commodity exchange.

For Lukacs, the destruction of craft labor, the reduction of work to a set of repititious, mechanical motions, the repressive organization of the factory system, and the extension of these processes into the larger social institutions of society "extends right into the worker's 'soul.'"[16] The fragmentation of the personality system produces a mental pathos reflected in passive subjectivity among workers, which is necessary to the functioning of late capitalism. Lukacs observes that "the personality can do no more than look on helplessly while its own existence is reduced to an isolated particle and fed into an alien system."[17] Thus, a reified consciousness is also a passive consciousness, devoid of the subjectivity which is the essential prelude to meaningful praxis.

6

It is within this extended realm of commodity fetishism that worker alienation and mental pathology must be ultimately understood. The power and domination of the capitalist system are generated at the expense of the worker, who is transformed into a thing, a reified consciousness — a commodity. In the final analysis, then, the reason for the failure of the American working class to develop a critical class consciousness lies in the ability of the capitalist system to penetrate the psychic apparatus of the working class, and reconstruct it as a reified consciousness.

By reshaping the needs, personality and consciousness of workers to the needs of advanced technological production, a pathological identity is forged between the worker and established society. "Substitute mechanisms" are introduced into the psychic structure for tension reduction within an antagonistic social reality. These substitute mechanisms repress and manipulate working class sexuality, destroy the worker's autonomous ego, and impose a capitalist "social character." Profound alienation emerges from this process. Workers' needs become identified with their position in the occupational hierarchy. Their identity and place in the world become functions of their activities in the production process. The traditional antithesis between proletariat and capitalist is transformed into a one-dimensional "unity of opposites," which reinforces the domination and alienation associated with the established social hierarchy of production.

The domination and redirection of the id, ego, and ego ideal of the worker's psychic apparatus into the "performance principle" of late capitalism have resulted in the development of a "social character" among workers, which channels their energy and behavior into system-supporting outlets. The increasing proletarization of the work force has intensified and extended this social character to ever greater numbers of workers. The main function of the channeling of this social character has been to prevent, among workers, any possibility of, or need for, self-realization which would threaten the social dynamics of the established order. It further serves as an important mechanism for adapting workers to the increasingly dull, mechanical work relations of capitalist society. As such, social character plays a definite social role in the functioning of the institutions of late capitalism. The effect of social character is to integrate and assimilate the individual to the dictates of the established society. In neutralizing the psychic apparatus of the worker, this social character has minimized the worker's freedom to develop a meaningful opposition to the established social order. Workers are increasingly unable to develop a critical consciousness and praxis as a revolutionary class; rather they have become, through the incorporation of this social character into their psychic structure, objects of administration. Thus, the development of a pervasive social character completes the transformation of the workers in late capitalism from conscious subjects to reified beings reflecting the commodity fetishism of the era.

This analysis suggests that worker alienation and mental pathology must ultimately be understood in terms of the interactions of the objective and subjective dimensions of the capitalist production process. The maintenance and perpetuation of the social relations of the capitalist mode of production depend on containing the subjectivity of the workers within the parameters of established social reality. The more dialectical mode of subjectivity, essential to man as a being of praxis, is truncated by the one-dimensional socialization process of late capitalism. The highly mechanized and automated work processes of late capitalism are bound to the dynamics of domination within the social hierarchy of the capitalist production process. A regressive dimension in which the social contradictions of capitalism are interiorized in the psychic apparatus of the workers has appeared more exact. This interiorization produces ever increasing levels of neurosis, alienation and mental pathology among workers. This interiorization stands in the way of socialist revolution and must be broken.

Notes

1. *The New York Times*, September 15, 1977.
2. Stanley Diamond, "Lecture on Cross Cultural Views of Mental Illness" (unpublished lecture, Columbia University, New York, 1975).
3. Phyllis Chessler, *Women and Madness* (New York: Doubleday, 1972), p. 311.
4. T. W. Adorno, "Sociology and Psychology," *New Left Review*, 46 (1967), n.p.
5. Karl Marx, *Capital*, I (Moscow: Progress Publishers, 1965), p. 183.
6. Stephen A. Marglin, "What the Bosses Do; The Origin and Function of Hierarchy in Capitalist Production, Part I," *Review of Radical Political Economics* (Summer, 1974), p. 66.
7. Abraham Maslow, *Toward a Psychology of Being* (Princeton: D. Van Nostrand, 1962), p. 60.
8. Marglin, pp. 60-112. See also Stanley Aronowitz, *False Promises: The Shaping of American Working Class Consciousness* (New York: McGraw-Hill, 1973); Loren Baritz, *The Servants of Power: A History of the Use of Social Science in American Industry* (New York: Wiley, 1965); Harry Braverman, *Labor and Monopoly Capital: The Degradation of Work in the Twentiety Century* (New York: Monthly Review Press, 1974) and E. P. Thompson, *The Making of the English Working Class* (New York: Random House, 1963).
9. Braverman, p. 86.
10. P. Berger and S. Pullberg, "The Concept of Reification," *New Left Review*, 35 (1966), p. 61.
11. *Ibid.*, p. 59.
12. Georg Lukacs, *History and Class Consciousness: Studies in Marxist Dialectics* (Cambridge: M.I.T. Press, 1971), p. 87.
13. *Ibid.*, p. 100.
14. Terry Kupers, "Schizophrenia and Reification," *Socialist Revolution*, 6 (1976), pp. 116-117.
15. Lukacs, p. 84.
16. *Ibid.*, p. 88.
17. *Ibid.*, p. 90.

ALIENATION AND HUMANIZATION: SUBJECTIVE AND OBJECTIVE FACTORS

Irving J. Crain M.D.
Benjamin Rush Society

In his paper, "Late Capitalism and Mental Illness: Toward a Critical Theory of Psychic Crisis," Dr. Sipe raises the complex question of the interrelationship between the "enormity of the problem of mental pathology" and the existing socio-economic order. After briefly outlining the increasing incidence of mental illness and the sharp increase in the use of psychoactive drugs, he states that "the general public, interested professionals and academics all muddy the issues of defining and treating mental pathology," while Marxists to date have "not developed an analysis sufficiently comprehensive or sophisticated to deal with mental pathology in late capitalism." He proposes to elaborate such an analysis in his paper, feeling that doing so "is important both for the development of new types of therapy and for the establishment of another critique of capitalism." This is indeed a bold venture!

To begin with, in an effort not to "muddy the issue" of definitions, I am not sure if Sipe agrees with the conclusion of Diamond, who states that 60 million schizophrenics walk the streets of America. Either this is a typographical error, or he is saying that 25% of our population is schizophrenic. That, obviously, is not true; most observers believe that 3-5% is a more accurate figure. Twenty-five percent of our population may be in need of psychiatric care, but they certainly are not all schizophrenic.

Another point of clarification: it seems to me that "late capitalism" might be more accurately called imperialism. This again may be a less "muddy" way of understanding present day capitalist economics.

And now to the more theoretical and philosophical issues. Sipe criticizes the dominant medical model's approach to mental illness for defining mental pathology "as an illness within the individual rather than as a dysfunction of the larger society." How can Sipe then speak of *mental* pathology or the development of our "inner nature" or our "unique interiority" as being dependent on one's social relations? He quotes Adorno: "The separation of society and psyche is false consciousness: it perpetuates conceptually the split between the living subject and the objectivity that governs the subjects and yet derives from them." This is a basic Marxist dialectical concept of the interconnection and interpenetration of opposites; like buying and selling, living and dying — one cannot exist without the other. Though society and psyche are certainly interconnected, they are not identical and can be studied separately, like the pneumonococcus and the human lung, neither of which is the disease called pneumonia. Mental pathology has both objective and subjective elements, but each form of pathology is qualitatively different. The man who loses his job can become depressed and suffer the associated mental anguish; but the boss is not depressed, even though he is the source of the economic pathology. Black lung disease is *in* the lungs of the miners and not in the polluted mines. People become mentally ill and suffer. The illness is within them and their brain and their central nervous system and their whole body. To place mental illness into "the larger society" is to be insensitive to the suffering the individual goes through when plagued with psychic torment. One does not have to be a doctor or follow a medical model to understand this.

Sipe states, "The resultant method of treatment not only leaves the social roots of neurosis untouched, but actually fosters the individual's conformity and adjustment to a repressive social order." Assuming it is capitalism that breeds mental illness, shall the patient have to wait until the "social roots" of his neurosis are overcome, and shall the malnourished wait for an equitable social order to be fed? As for adjusting and conforming, that assumes that there is no active struggle on the part of the patient, the therapist, and the people in general against a passive acceptance of the external pathology in the larger social order. Even a one-cell amoeba reacts to a prick of a pin.

What does Sipe mean when he asks for "new types" of therapy and for "another critique of capitalism?" He suggests that the "demise of capitalism is the precondition to mental health." This presents a simplistic view of mental illness. There is mental

8: Alienation and Humanization 169

illness under socialist conditions also, and the socialist world is making its contribution toward more effective prevention and treatment of these problems.

He states, "Marxism must be recreated," but Marxism and its literature are replete with analyses of the relation between society and psyche. The works of Vygotsky, Pribram, Luria, and others are current outstanding contributions in the field of communication patterns, the psychic apparatus, cognitive development, and related fields of pathology. Marx, Engels, and Lenin have written extensively on literature, love, beauty, culture, ideology, consciousness, the family, and the conditions of everyday life. There is, of course, much to be done in applying Marxist principles and analyses to modern American life. A proper application, and not a recreation, of the Marxist approach is necessary.

Sipe says, "What is needed is the engagement of the individual in struggle with the social forces" and a psychological approach which does not validate the reified social relations of "trapped subjects." What about the countless thousands who have been and still are involved in labor strikes, the peace movement, civil rights struggles, the women's movement, Black liberation struggles, and those of other oppressed minorities? Are they not in "struggle with the social forces?"

When it comes to schizophrenia, Sipe is on more shaky ground. I shall not go into a polemic about the role of social forces and this illness, but investigators from East and West tend to agree that the incidence of schizophrenia is about the same, regardless of social structure. This points to the problem of genetic and biological factors in this particular illness. How different societies treat the schizophrenic is a different matter. Though many studies indicate that schizophrenia is more prevalent in the lower socioeconomic groups, these figures are based primarily on the records of state hospitals, where the poor are relegated. Upper and middle class schizophrenics are more likely to be found in private hospitals, clinics, and psychiatrists' offices.

I agree with Sipe on the creative role of conscious action, or praxis in history. Marx has consistently emphasized that consciousness is always conscious existence and is an ever deepening process. But Sipe tends to contradict himself when he states that growth is "always threatening," because of movement into unexplored areas. Two sentences later he quotes Maslow, who refers to the "delights of growth as against the anxieties of growth."

When Sipe refers to "nonsynergistic (i.e., growth inhibiting) societies," he does not hesitate to identify them with capitalism. When referring to "synergistic (i.e., growth fostering) societies," I think it would not be inappropriate at a Marxist scholars' conference to identify such societies with socialism. It, too, exists.

After a detailed evaluation of the capitalist mode of production, distribution, and accumulation, he concludes that, "Mental pathology among workers is the structural powerlessness experienced by workers in the capitalist social hierarchy." Does he believe, therefore, that all workers have mental pathology? Incidentally, there is no reference at all to mental pathology among capitalists. One must not confuse mental pathology with ideology. The former is properly called an illness, the latter is a reflection of class relations. Though there can be an interconnection between mental illness and ideology, they are qualitatively different aspects of mental functioning.

In dealing with the development of capitalism from guild to factory system, Sipe refers to various colleagues who feel that this movement "had little to do with economic efficiency or technical superiority." But that its real significance was "power . . . and control" over the independent producers and artisan class. Why such a need? Power and control for their own sake? Sipe later states it was for accumulation of capital. What about private profits? Furthermore, this transition was an historic necessity in the wake of the objective development of the engine, machinery, and advances in physics and chemistry which contradicted the individual artisan approach to production. In other words, I believe that the capitalist mode of production was a necessary historical stage over feudalism, and not primarily due to a subjective desire for power. Even capitalists-to-be are affected psychologically by outside social and historical factors. Once influenced, their subjective feelings of power and greed are intensified as the objective process continues. To understand these subjective factors in the capitalist class, one has to follow capitalism as it has advanced to imperialism, with its drive for maximum profits.

Sipe states that it was the gradual intensification of "scientific management, . . . time-motion studies, reductive technologies and various schools of industrial psychology and human relations" that reduced the worker to "the commodity level of labor power." Under capitalism, early or *late*, labor power has always been a commodity. Marx spoke of alienated labor in the 1800's, and this concept is not a new feature of late capitalism.

8: Alienation and Humanization

In the transition from guild to factory system, Sipe states that the workers became "increasingly dependent upon the will of the capitalist class (this destruction of workers' subjectivity is central to mental pathology)." It is not possible to destroy a person's human subjectivity without completely destroying his or her brain. It is possible to modify it, influence it, confuse it, but not destroy it. Even psychotics have rational areas of human subjectivity. Human subjectivity may be an inanimate objective factor of production to the capitalist, but not to the worker. This is how the slaveholders felt about the human subjectivity of their slaves, but we all know of the heroic slave revolts and their associated passions, songs, loves, human suffering and joys. So with the struggles of the workers. It is fair to say that attempts were and are still being made to destroy the workers' human subjectivity, but workers have always fought against such efforts. If workers passively responded to the objective capitalist exploitative forces, why did the capitalists have to pass laws preventing the growth of unions and why are unions always struggling for shorter hours and more pay? Machines, which of course have no human subjectivity, never ask for raises, health benefits, pensions and holidays with pay. As intensification of exploitation occurred, an increasing resistance to it also developed.

When dealing with the problem of alienation, Sipe states, "All forms of alienation are forms of mental pathology and all forms of mental pathology are forms of alienation." Here again is a confusion of objectivity and subjectivity. Objectively, the worker is separated from his or her product, and thus relates to it as something alien from him or her. But objective economic factors in capitalist relations do not automatically make the worker himself or herself into an alienated or mentally pathological person. If one adheres to Sipe's formulation, then all workers have mental pathology. Marx spoke of alienation as an economic, not a psychological, force. Sipe and the colleagues he refers to appear to believe that one automatically leads to the other. Marx once commented that if objects and their subjective reflection were so related, so simple and direct, then if a person saw a bomb exploding in the distance, his head would blow off!

As alienation intensifies, reification sets in. Sipe states that "Reification is at the core of capitalist alienation . . . Reification is the individual's loss of subjectivity and consequent loss of human activity, or praxis." He believes that this economic fact of capitalism can best explain depression and schizophrenia.

He goes on to give a very good description of the various psychic phenomena that occur in the schizophrenic thought processes, concluding that "the subjective experience of these traits is a normal response to the reified nature of social relations in capitalist society . . . which most of us experience to some degree." Who says that this is a "normal" response? I believe that this is an *abnormal* response. Are we all more or less schizophrenic? Are only workers schizophrenic? What about middle class and upper class schizophrenics? Sipe hastens to say "I do not mean to imply that subjective factors are thereby reduced and determined by objective factors. Human behavior not only reflects the socioeconomic environment, but also has the capacity to change it." However, he does not show how or why this is so. What are the objective factors that lead to the opposite of alienation and mental pathology? Madness is not a rational way of surviving in an irrational world, but an *irrational* way of *dying* in an irrational world! We all have heard the expression, "He whom the gods would destroy they first make mad." The capitalists go mad, not the workers. Capitalists eventually go out of existence; the workers live on.

Sipe goes on to say, "The fragmentation of the personality system produces a mental pathos reflected in passive subjectivity among workers, which is necessary to the functioning of late capitalism." Again, workers are seen as puppets who do not respond to their oppression. Again, I must refer to the struggles of the working class from its inception. Sipe states, "The domination and redirection of the id, ego, and ego ideal of the worker's psychic apparatus" creates a social character among workers, channeling their energy and behavior into system-supporting outlets. So why have there been Palmer raids, Smith Acts, McCarthy periods, antistrike laws, the FBI, the CIA, etc. (and, incidentally, what is the id?)?

Sipe completely omits the mental effects of capitalism on its own ruling class. What about Forrestal, Nixon, Agnew, Mitchell, and all the corrupt, pathological ideation and practices among the leaders of our government and economic system? To the degree that subjective humanity is existent, it resides more in the struggling working class. If what Sipe says is true, the capitalist class would have no problems with workers, who are "increasingly unable to develop a critical consciousness and praxis as a revolutionary class."

This approach to "the one dimensional socialization process

of late capitalism" is itself one-dimensional. Sipe does a good job in describing the dehumanizing tendencies associated with the structure and direction of capitalist production and accumulation. He ignores, however, a fundamental Marxist understanding of the contradictions in capitalism itself. He points correctly to "social production" as a "central feature of capitalism." But this objective structure also affects the worker and leads to subjective reactions of solidarity, loyalty, one-for-all, comradeship — truly human qualities.

This is not to idealize the working class, but one cannot see it as dehumanized and stripped of subjectivity. The working class is in the process of a forward humanizing struggle, while the capitalist class is proceeding toward its own dehumanization. Workers don't adapt to their bosses; they learn to hate them. This is a subjectivity the boss can hardly eradicate, even with coffee breaks and Christmas gifts. Archie Bunker is not the typical worker. That is what corporate television would have us believe.

Marxism states that the ideology of the ruling class influences the ideology of the workers, and Archie Bunker may sound like General Brown in his racist remarks. Bunker takes himself seriously while people laugh; Brown laughed when people took him seriously. In other words, workers are not merely pressed into an alienated position, but into a contradiction between their class necessities and the pervasive ruling class ideology. It is such contradictions that probably cause more mental illness than "alienated labor." When a worker loses his job and says, "I can't believe it; this is the greatest country; maybe I don't have what it takes," he's in trouble. The laid off worker who resents the situation and fights along with his union and community for a full employment bill is less prone to a depressive reaction.

When I prefer the use of the term "imperialism" to "late capitalism," I also think of the working class in France, Italy, Portugal and Spain; the national liberation movements in Viet Nam, Angola, and South Africa; and of course the workers of the Socialist world. Are they apathetic? Stripped of subjectivity? Sipe understands the capitalist system well; he doesn't understand the dynamics of the working class. Marx has shown that the history of man to date has been the history of class struggle, and not of class accomodation. In using the term "imperialism," which describes a development of history following Marx's time, one has to include the application Lenin made of Marxism in the stage of "late capitalism." The Socialist world negates alienation.

Under capitalism, alienated labor loses its connection with its products, but laborers increase their connections with fellow workers, friends and family. The capitalists accumulate the fruits of labor, but increase their separation from fellow capitalists, friends and family. The capitalists must compete; the workers must cooperate. Competition breeds hate; cooperation breeds love. The capitalists have more money than love; the workers, more love than money. To the degree that schizophrenia is socially determined, alienated labor as an objective factor of capitalist relations probably breeds the schizophrenic dynamic in all classes.

It is commonly agreed to by most investigators that the recent burgeoning of the mystical movement — the Moonies, Jesus Freaks, Born Again Christians, EST, Rebirthing, etc. — is mainly found among the middle and upper sections of the white population. Think of the paranoid ideation in our ruling class regarding the U.S.S.R. Forrestal exclaimed, "The Russians have landed," and ended up by jumping to suicide.

Today, the so-called alienated workers are indeed "the spectre that is haunting" the capitalist world. It is the capitalists who are stripping themselves of their subjectivity and humanity, and the workers who, in their struggles, are maintaining and further developing the human qualities required for a sane society. The working class produces, of necessity, in a cooperative socialized way, and though alienated from its products, will transform them into its own products once again, and thus eliminate this economic and psychological contradiction — this is the "negation of the negation" which is occurring in our times.

It is true that in this struggle many workers will succumb to mental and physical pathology. They need to be helped as any wounded soldier in battle. Helped not to adapt to the system which produced their mental wounds, but to return to the struggle or to enter it. A rational, progressive, socially aware therapist with experience and training in the vicissitudes of mental illness can effect such healing.

Sipe's view that schizoid traits are "a normal response to the reified nature of social relations in a capitalist society" is similar to the view that madness is rational in an irrational world, held by R. D. Laing, David Cooper, et al. I recall a quote by Dr. Andrew Weil in *The Natural Mind*, referring to the positive potential of psychosis, "a potential so overwhelming that I am almost tempted to call psychotics the evolutionary vanguard of our species." I hear their distant chorus chanting, "Psychotics of the world, unite —

8: *Alienation and Humanization* 175

you have nothing to lose but your brains." I maintain that irrationality can be combatted only by rationality. As Marx put it, "Workers of the world, unite — you have nothing to lose but your chains."

PATHOLOGICAL ILLUSIONS AND COMMODITY FETISHISM

Francis H. Bartlett
Benjamin Rush Society

I agree with most of the criticisms brought against Dr. Sipe's paper, especially the charge that he does not allow for the social processes which counter fragmentation and generate struggle. Yet, like several other members of the Benjamin Rush workshop which discussed his paper, I am in wholehearted sympathy with any attempt to bring the unifying power of Marxist theory to bear upon a field which is so infinitely complicated. After many years of trying to become a better Marxist and a better therapist, I am keenly aware of the fantastic difficulties involved in trying to understand the connections between changing society and changing individuals. And yet, since I believe that that human nature which we study is the *ensemble* of our social relations, it still seems reasonable to me to expect some clarification to come from bringing together even an oversimplified Marxist understanding of capitalism with an oversimplified understanding of what we know about the participating individuals. Therefore, after great doubt and several attacks of anxiety, I decided that, instead of criticizing Dr. Sipe for making the mistake of oversimplifying the relation between the economic and the personal, I would rather repeat his mistake, but in a different form.

Like Dr. Sipe, I am going to assume a direct relationship between the macro and the micro which does not in fact exist, or rather, from which all the indispensible links are missing. I am going to try to get you to listen to and take seriously my attempt to bring into immediate juxtaposition two incomparables, to synchronize a sort of satellite telephoto shot of commodity production with a whispered, hardly audible tape of certain individual fantasies.

I now have to admit that I am not the sole author of this attempt. Some thirty years ago, I participated in a workshop for many months with a dozen other Marxists, some of whom know a great deal about what we were then calling schizophrenia. We tried to develop just such a theory as Dr. Sipe has attempted. So I was prompted to look back into those old yellowing files. There is much there to be critical of, but, if we make allowances, if we don't take it all too literally, there is something still there, I think, which may give us a glimpse of that unified view we need. Therefore, I decided to bring you a revised version of some of those old notes. The other authors will have to remain anonymous.

I plan to emphasize what Dr. Sipe introduces rather later in his paper, *commodity fetishism*. I am going to argue that if we truly understand what Marx meant by commodity fetishism, we will be able to understand also the social sources, the experiential roots, of some of the most frequently observed pathological distortions in individual consciousness.

As a change of pace, I am going to start at the microscopic end with certain individual illusions and fantasies. But first, one further hint: Back in those old musty pages, I came across a quotation from V. J. Jerome's pamphlet, *Culture in a Changing World*. It epitomizes the connection which Marx revealed between commodity relationships and the special kind of distortion in consciousness which grows out of them:

"Marx," wrote Jerome, "corrects the inverted appearance of 'people and their relationships' in the *camera obscura* of bourgeois ideology with its mystique of the transcendent individual, the cock who (in George Eliot's words), thinks the sun has risen to hear him crow.''

We liked that quotation then because it so happened that we had become accustomed to using the very word "transcendence" to identify a certain cluster of illusions characteristic of a large number of our patients. These illusions of "transcendence" are widespread, and I would not want anyone to become unduly alarmed if he should happen to recognize something of this outlook in himself. But, at that time, we were mainly concerned with what we were calling schizoid people, and it is in such people that we can identify most clearly as a characteristic mode of living and thinking what we call transcendence.

Such people tend to be more isolated than others, not necessarily in the sense that they are literally solitary, but in the sense that they keep a greater emotional distance from other people. They are more afraid, distrustful, elusive and uncommitted. They tend to avoid direct, plain intelligible relationships with others. They seem to want to keep "free" not only from entanglements with people, but from any obligations, requirements or regulations. They do not like to be bound even by their own promises to themselves. Now such a mode of living is the manifestation of a whole cluster of illusions which tends to be self-regenerating. Implicit in their actions and inactions, their expectations or indifference, in their disappointments and vulnerabilities, we find certain deeply engrained assumptions. These people develop the profound conviction that they really are disconnected from other people. The core of this illusion is that they can live in their heads, so to speak, that their minds, their imagination, their spiritual life is really independent of the material conditions of human life. Like Laing's "Divided Selves," they come to believe that their inner self, which they regard as "real" and special, is "free" from ordinary life, from time, process, change, cause and effect. They may even develop the secret conviction that they are immune from illness, aging and death. Even when they are atheists, their private illusions have more than a little in common with mystical and religious thought.

I may now have to remind you that such people are not so very different from you and me. They also know that they are not really invulnerable, omniscient and perfect. It is just that they have a harder time than most of us in keeping their illusions out of the act. In fact, their central problem in life, the theme of their development as seen in therapy, is the contradiction between their illusion that they are above it all and the continuing intrusion of the reality, which they cannot deny, that they are inexorably connected with the material and social conditions of human life. They *are* mortal; they *do* live in interdependence with other people. They need other people; they even yearn for intimacy. Even their precious "true" self starves without others to share with. The necessities of life, including their own changing bodily needs, are always demanding change, pressuring them to join with others, to struggle, to work, to learn, to change. The direction of their development depends upon the degree to which they are able to modify their stubborn insistence that they are isolated atoms and relinquish their illusion of "splendid isolation."

Now if anything is clear at all, it is that human beings are profoundly social, their achievements are collective, their most private thoughts are intimately connected with the lives of others, living and dead, that their personalities are the outcome of social history. How can it happen that individuals who draw their sustenance and their souls from their historical existence should come to believe, not in their heads but in their guts, that they are isolated atoms?

It may not surprise you that I am going to suggest that these deeply embedded individual illusions are generated out of the experience of living in a commodity society and are, in fact, one more example of what Marx called commodity fetishism.

In a commodity society, especially capitalism in decline, the social production presents a surface appearance which is deceptive, which is the diametric opposite of the underlying reality. Every society, in order to be a society at all, depends for its continued existence upon the collective performance of a total social labor. It is through the fabric of this interdependent productive activity that the society is constituted; it is by their participation in this collective activity that people bind themselves together and become human. In different kinds of societies and at different stages in the development of the productive forces, this total social labor is allocated in different ways to the individuals who do the work. It could be, in a small primitive community, a relatively simple division of labor, traditionally established or, in a large socialist society, the allocation of the necessary social labor could be according to plan. In neither case need there be any great mystery about the pooling and the exchange of the various tasks and services performed.

But in a developed commodity society, the situation is altogether different. The very activities which tie people together assume a form which separates them; the collective labor sets them at each other's throats. The cooperative labor assumes an individualistic form. The fact that the total social labor is already allocated and that the individual producers are in fact completely interdependent is not apparent to the participants. Their interconnection appears in the form of and only at the moment of the sale and exchange on the market of their products. The distortion is twofold; it lends a mystique to money, to the stock market, to the commodities themselves which, unknown to the naive observers, are the bearers of their human connections. The other side which I have been emphasizing is the atomized appearance of the human relations. The deeper social connections which constitute the productive forces cannot be directly percieved by the naive senses; to be grasped, they require a theory which makes the unseen connections. These connections are not a part of the everyday experience of the participating individuals. The individuals experience themselves and come to conceive of themselves as having

9: Pathological Illusions 181

no necessary indispensible connections, of being isolated atoms, because in a certain sense they really are. The surface appearance of isolation is not in itself an illusion; the individuals actually do lack plain, direct intelligible relationships with each other and with nature. There is a cash nexus, but not a human one. It is easy to see how individuals, experiencing this form of social relations without understanding it, could come to develop illusions. A capitalist might easily imagine that his wealth, power and freedom, actually sustained by the concealed exploitation of thousands of workers, are his by virtue of his inherent superior qualities. Instead of the recipient, he becomes the benefactor. Bourgeois ideologists would also see things upside down in their *camera obscura* and interpret history as the lengthened shadows of great men. It was such distortions, among many others, that Marx called commodity fetishism.
characteristic of certain patients whom we see in psychotherapy are just such distortions. They are perfect examples of commodity fetishism. The surface atomism of capitalism penetrates everywhere; it seeps into families, poisons loving couples, sets the rules for children's games. It infuses all ages and phases of life. It is one of the deepest and most persistent of all experiences. Is it any wonder that such a widespread experience should for many become truly pathological? Some individuals may find themselves members of a family in which the atomism of the society has been cultivated over generations to such a fine point that the members hardly ever have direct intelligible relationships with each other. I am not saying that the individuals have this atomism stamped upon them as if they were themselves commodities. No. They participate actively in the process. They themselves begin early to cultivate the distance, to declare by word and body language that they have no necessary relations with any others. They participate in the cultivation of their own mystique of transcendence.

Since the experience of being an atom is an illusion, the individual who cultivates that illusion also has the possibility of undermining it, of struggling for a truer experience of himself as a human being, as a participant in history. He is not alone. He is not doomed to an existentialist fate. Whatever the appearances, people are engaged in collective human efforts. Sometimes these can even be found in work, in spite of, in the very midst of alienating conditions; sometimes they take the form of struggles to change the conditions of work. In everyday life, it is the ever-present necessity and possibility for taking concerted action to meet mutual needs which forms the social basis for therapeutic as well as social change. The possibilities are not easily discerned. The same conditions which give rise to commodity fetishism in the first place continue to operate. Even for the industrial working class where the necessity and possibility for concerted action are greater, much remains potential. For other sections of the population, the ways and means of implementing interconnections are even less apparent. It is difficult to struggle for a healthier and more human life.

I told you I was going to repeat Dr. Sipe's mistake of uniting incomparables. There is an obvious difference in level, a difference in kind, between the apparent unrelatedness of commodity producers and the mutually distancing, depersonalizing activities which go on between the members of a "schizophrenogenic" family or the carefully separated workers in an electrical plant or the frantic participants of the stock exchange on a bad day. And yet, though all the real scholarly work still remains to be done, I still believe that it is not altogether useless to sketch out such an oversimplification.

IV:
CULTURE
POLITICS AND
TECHNOLOGY IN
CAPITALIST DEVELOPMENT

BILINGUALISM AND THE LIMITS OF THE MELTING POT

Lajos Biro

1.

The question of bilingualism and bilingual education has become one of the most hotly debated issues in the present crisis situation confronting the U. S. The rising national consciousness of linguistic minorities has forced the ruling class to admit that a nationality problem exists in this country. Legislative measures based on academic theories are put into action to "solve" this problem within the existing social order. The major flaws of the present theories and official measures concerning bilingualism in the U. S. were quite well captured by Lewis in the following statement:

> Language planning has to do with how people are educated, with the choice of instrument for education and with how the chosen medium can be made more efficient, which includes enabling it to deal with information more adequately along a 'rating scale of intellectualization.' Bearing these aspects of language planning in mind the educator or planner who proceeds without specific regard to the economic, social and practical considerations is likely to put the relevance of his work at risk. Innovation whether in linguistic theory or practice is never without its impact upon the organization of society, which is an aspect of political theory. In most countries [i.e. capitalist — L.B.] perhaps, the political consequences are subordinated to more theoretical or academic considerations, or more usually are left to take care of themselves.[1]

While the solution of the nationality problem within capitalist society seems remote, the present interest in this question offers an opportunity for Marxists to present the socialist approach to bilingualism. In view of the large number of readers who are not familiar with the dialectical materialist approach in social sciences this paper will offer explanations which Marxists may consider self-evident. However, we will seek to explore the question of bilingualism on the basis of the strikingly original but relatively unknown analysis of languages in general, and in function of the social analysis of languages as part of the superstructure, as provided by the Marxist linguist, Lev Semonovich Vygotsky. By this means we hope to accomplish the following objectives:

1. To present the non-Marxist with an insight into the dialectical materialist concept of society through the Marxist approach to bilingualism.
2. To establish a system of contrasting pairs of concepts used in bilingual situations on the level of the superstructure and to prove that many of these contrasts ultimately can be traced to contrasts in the economic basis.
3. To demonstrate that the linguistic conflict between Anglos and Mexican-Americans was preceeded by an economic conflict historically in which the Anglos occupied the land of the Mexican-Americans, and to show how the linguistic difference was used for the economic exploitation of the Mexican-Americans.
4. To analyze the "melting pot theory" in the U.S. and to show the reactionary character of a total rejection of this theory when it is used against the integration of minorities.
5. To demonstrate that the struggle for symmetrical bilingualism and bilingual education can raise the class consciousness of minority people.

2

In his carefully researched experimental book, *Thought and Language*, Vygotsky elaborates a definition of verbal thought (language) that provides an appropriate basis for a Marxist approach to bilingualism. Says Vygotsky:

Verbal thought is not an innate, natural form

of behavior but it is determined by a historical-cultural process and has specific properties and laws that cannot be found in the natural forms of thought and speech. Once we acknowledge the historical character of verbal thought, we must consider it subject to all premises of historical materialism which are valid for any historical phenomenon in human society. It is only to be expected that at this level the development of behavior will be governed essentially by the general laws of the historical development of human society. The problem of thought and language thus extends beyond the limits of natural science and becomes the focal problem of historical human psychology, i.e. social psychology.[2]

If we assume with Vygotsky that language is subject to all premises of historical materialism, then bilingualism as a variation of verbal thought must be analyzed within this context.

In a critical analysis of bilingualism we have to concentrate on the reconstruction of the social process which produced a specific bilingual situation. Most of the studies in bilingualism are engaged in the description, classification and analysis of linguistic particularities of certain bilingual groups or individuals within a group.

The importance of the economic and historical factors in bilingualism is recognized by many non-Marxist authors, but they fail to give these factors the preponderant importance they merit. Joshua A. Fishman, perhaps the best known American expert on bilingualism, clearly states the necessity of historical analysis in the remark that "the appropriate designation and definition of domains of language behavior obviously call for considerable insight into the socio-cultural dynamics of particular multilingual settings of particular periods in their history."[3] We delineate particular historical periods for bilingual settings, following the *assumption* that those periods signify qualitative changes in those settings. The closing of one period represents the end of one era and the beginning of another qualitatively different one.

Two other assumptions derived from Vygotsky are of central importance in applying his Marxist approach to the particular problem of bilingualism. First, since bilingualism in a given setting was preceeded by monolingualism of two or more groups of people who became bilingual (or multilingual) through extended contacts, it follows that *contact* between language groups is a prerequisite in establishing a bilingual situation.

The second assumption refers to monolingual groups and demonstrates the materialist explanation of the origin of languages in very broad terms. This assumption is stated as follows: "Where in any land different languages are spoken in different parts, those parts are not isolated because the people speak a different language, but they speak different languages to the extent that they are isolated."[4]

From these interrelated assumptions we have to conclude that contact between linguistic groups is the crucial factor in bilingualism, and from the Marxist viewpoint we have to look at how this contact is manifested on the economic level in the first place. Once we have succeeded in establishing the quality of economic contact between various linguistic groups, we can then proceed to analyze the cultural, psychological and linguistic differences between the groups in question.

Usually the quality of economic contact can be defined by determining whether a conflict exists between the linguistic groups on the economic level and how this conflict is manifested on the linguistic level. Of course, conflicts between groups of people in contact are not always expressed in linguistic terms, but linguistic differences often are the signs of more deeply rooted economic conflicts.

When bilingualism does not represent a conflict situation between two groups speaking different languages, then we are confronted with a "symmetrical bilingualism," as for example in Switzerland where three different language groups have relatively equal status. In contrast, according to Theodore Andersson, "asymmetrical bilingualism" represents a conflict situation in which two groups of people speaking different languages are polarized:

> ... The problem arises only when a population through emmigration or conquest becomes a part of a community where another language is spoken and this language is imposed on them through the school system or by authorities.[5]

Andersson's description contains a brief but essentially correct description of the most probable processes in the development of problem settings in bilingual situations. Here we have to note the primacy of conquest or emmigration and the fact that these acts have little to do in themselves with language differences. Discrimination based on language differences by the people involved in acts of conquest or emmigration *follows* the acts. At the same time, however, we have to recognize that once a contact situation is established between linguistic groups, whether through conquest or peaceful emmigration, the linguistic difference can acquire central importance in a conflict situation at certain historical stages. In the case of conquest, for example, the primary aim is to acquire territory and natural resources, to exploit labor, etc., in other words, to achieve economic goals. After the actual conquest, however, the conqueror will emphasize non-economic factors, such as the alleged lower cultural level of the conquered and differences in religion or language, as the reasons for subjugating a people. With the passing of time, the economic rationale may fade in the consciousness of both sides involved in a conflict situation and the focus shifts to cultural, religious or linguistic differences.

Studies in bilingualism provide adequate demonstrations of the social polarizations on linguistic grounds even when they look at the questions strictly in "pure" linguistic terms. Delineations, such as given by Andersson in his definition of symmetrical and a-symmetrical bilingualism, can be supplemented by several contrasting pairs used by various other authors. Contrasts referring to bilingual settings, or to behavior development in bilingual situations, can clarify for us the social nature of bilingualism through the dialectical process. The following list of contrasts represents meaningful concepts for a dialectical analysis of bilingual situations:

a) dominant language — dominated language
b) assimilating language — assimilated language
c) elite bilingualism — common bilingualism
d) dynamic bilingualism — static bilingualism
e) ethnicity acceptance — ethnicity rejection
f) language maintenance — language shift

By themselves these contrasts do not represent necessarily conflict situations in any bilingual setting. For example, using the expression of "dominant language" and "dominated language" for a given bilingual setting does not necessarily reflect a conflict between two linguistic groups. The numerical dominance of the speakers of one language over another does not necessarily represent a conflict situation in the socio-economic conditions of the two groups. The problem arises only when the language difference is used to promote ot to maintain socio-economic differences in a bilingual society. In the literature on bilingualism, for reasons of expedience, the term "dominant" is restricted "to languages in contact situations where the difference in other tongues is coupled with a significant difference in social status."[6]

If we discover that the dominant language of a bilingual setting represents more than the numerical plurality of speakers of one language group over another, then the socio-economic conditions of class structure and the distribution of wealth according to language groups should receive the major attention of a critical analysis. At the same time, detailed studies of linguistic and cultural differences can illuminate how the process of socio-economic differentiation evolved and how differences were shifted to the level of superstructure, namely to differentiation based on language.

When there are no socio-economic differences involved in a dominant and dominated language situation, the numerical plurality of the dominant language represents a "non-conflict" advantage for its use in all spheres of communication. This advantage is an objective condition and it has to be recognized as such, "for no matter how much official pronouncements emphasize the equality of all languages in a multilingual state, not all languages are equally competent to fulfill a particular individual's diverse needs at any one time, when several languages are available."[7]

The validity of this statement can be demonstrated by the "melting pot theory," which has a certain validity in spite of the objections raised against it presently on cultural and linguistic grounds. Indeed, historical analysis reveals that the melting pot phenomenon worked remarkably well for vast numbers of the population in terms of socio-economic conditions as well as on the level of linguistic integration. Millions of European immigrants were integrated linguistically into the English speaking population, and, by and large, they were on their way toward economic integration also, although, of course, within the confines of the capitalist society. Here we are not ignoring the economic hardships, exploitation and prejudices suffered by the newly arrived immigrants, but the language situation of these people represented a dynamic bilingualism whereby they perceived a better future for their children through acquiring fluency in English. English became the language of these masses not because it is beautiful or divinely preordained but because it was accepted by the numerical plurality of its speakers as the best medium of communication. The challenge to the melting pot theory for purely linguistic and cultural reasons represents an incomplete analysis of the problem, and, in a sense, it can even contribute to the maintenance of socio-economic discrimination against one segment of the society. In relation to the melting pot theory the following general questions are relevant to the issue of bilingualism:

1. Assuming that the melting pot phenomenon worked for a great number of European immigrants, what were the economic and cultural factors enhancing this process?
2. In the analysis of these factors, can we establish the value priority for any of them?
3. How do these factors correspond with the same factors in reference to minority groups (Blacks, Hispanos, Indians) which were excluded from the melting pot?
4. What proportion of a minority group has been integrated?
5. Can we state categorically that linguistic, racial or cultural differences are the primary reasons for acceptance or rejection of one group of people by another?
6. If there is a segment of the minority population which adapted by and large, to the values of the majority population, what is the socio-economic status of this group?

To find the answers to these questions we do not have to search for new data, since the existing literature provides adequate material for a critical analysis which will yeild a comprehensive picture of the social realtiy in a bilingual situation.

3.

As a case in point, let us take the most widely studied bilingual problem in the U.S.: the case of the Mexican-Americans as it is presented in the literature dealing with bilingualism. As an introduction, we should remark that credit is due to most of the authors on this topic for their meticulous work and good intention toward the solution of the problem.

In reconstructing the historical past, most of the authors would agree with Clark S. Knowlton's observation concerning the origin of the conflict between Anglos and Mexicans:

> many hard fought battles over land, water and dominance took place between the

to their understanding of the feelings of their co-national workers and attempt to convince them that they are better off "spiritually," even if the wages are just as low as those paid by Anglo employers. Studies in bilingualism deal extensively with the psychological aspects of assimilation and acculturation processes. Vague references are made to the polarization process in assimilation, as we can see in Weinreich's observation:

> The more realistic members of an objectively dominated group may attempt to better their lot by associating themselves with the dominant group. The way in which the dominated group splits can sometimes be explained by its internal make-up.[11]

In a critical analysis, the splitting of the dominated group is not of marginal importance. It should be pursued in every study of bilingualism that seeks to understand the social reality of the situation. By neglecting to keep our attention constantly on the socioeconomic conditions while analyzing the linguistic, cultural or psychological aspects of a bilingual setting, we can find ourselves in open contradiction. In order to illustrate this kind of contradiction one can analyze Knowlton's article, which was already quoted in this paper. Paraphrasing the quotation we find that the primary aim in the contact between Anglos and Mexican-Americans was to acquire the territories of the present Southwest of U. .S. Through conquest the Anglos expropriated most of the land, and, as a bonus, the native Mexican-Americans became a cheap source of labor. If this statement is an accurate description of the original contact, then all other factors which emerged during the period after the conquest should be viewed from this basic motive on the part of the conquerors. However, Knowlton is not satisfied with his own findings, and he discovers a more important factor than the economic interest in the conflict. Thus, on the very same page where he states that the purpose of the conquest was to acquire land, we find this categorical statement:

> The American conquest of the Spanish speaking people in the Southwest must be understood primarily in psychological terms, all the more so because they had not put up a real struggle.

Placing this statement beside the description of the motives of the conquering Anglos, we will find that the conflict between the two groups did not originate primarily from the psychological make-up of the Spanish speaking people. The presumed fact that they did not put up a struggle does not change the purpose of the conquest. Rather, we can assume exactly the opposite: the conquest determined the fate of the conquered Spanish-speaking people for the coming times. There was nothing Hispanic in not resisting the Anglos. There could have been many reasons for it: for example, that the Spanish-speaking population recognized the futility of a fight against the overwhelming power of the Anglos. And we venture to go further by stating that all the linguistic and cultural attitudes of the Spanish-Americans were determined to a great extent by their exploited status within the majority population. As far as the manifestations of these particular attitudes are concerned, it is irrelevant whether they are expressed in turning inward maintaining old customs, or in trying to better their lot by assimilation.

4

When we state that the attitude of the Mexican-Americans can be traced to their exploited situation, we do not try to negate the existing cultural and linguistic differences, but we place these differences within the context of the broader social reality. In this social reality the existence of the Mexican-Americans is primarily determined by the Anglo dominated socio-economic system. Whatever decisions the Mexican-Americans make individually or collectively, the outcome of the decisions ultimately will depend on the attitude of the power-holding Anglo majority. At this point we can look at the questions of assimilation as one of the options of the Mexican-Americans. Several authors remarked that few Mexican-Americans have been assimilated into the American society, and most of the explanations for this phenomenon dwell on particular Hispanic traits or psychological inhibitions on the part of the Mexican-Americans. Fishman, however, provided an observation which enhances the Marxist explanation of assimilation:

> The underlying assumption is that assimilation, unlike acculturation, ultimately hinges upon the consent of the dominant society, even though the minority group may desire to be assimilated.[12]

Describing the present conditions of the majority of Mexican-Americans we can accept Hayden's statement as it is quoted by Fishman:

> By far the largest number of Mexican-Americans continues to constitute an exploited and underprivileged group, engaged in low-level service occupations, in agricultural labor or in other unskilled occupations. The latter live in an area geographically and materially distinct from that inhabited by most of their more fortunate compatriots, Hispano or Anglo.[10]

The last sentence in the passage cited gives important clues for further analysis. In the first place, it reinforces our previous statement about the role of isolation in the development of linguistic and cultural differentiation. The factor of isolation is presented in the most relevant manner, whereby we see that occupational and economic differentiation is concomitant with geographic and material isolation.

The second clue in the passage is the reference to the "more fortunate compatriots, Hispano or Anglo" as the opposite pole to the majority of Mexican-Americans. When the author designates the general category of "more fortunate compatriots" we assume that he speaks about economic fortune. Where there is economic advantage the linguistic and cultural differences between the Anglos and "fortunate" Mexican-Americans seem to diminish into insignificance. Here we are admitting that not all Mexican-Americans seem to diminish into insignificance. Here we are admitting that not all Mexican-Americans suffered equal misfortune after the conquest of the Southwest; and according to the accepted myth in the American dream, one would say that those of them who live in better economic conditions "pulled themselves up by their bootstraps." The Marxist approach does not deny the possibility that certain individual members of an oppressed group of people may have access to a limited mobility within their own group, or even upward movement into the oppressor's group. The crucial task, however, should be directed to the explanation of the economic effects of this limited mobility for the oppressor, as well as for the oppressed group as a whole. At the level of production, for example, employers need reliable people for supervision from

10: Bilingualism and the Melting Pot

the ranks of the workers, and these are necessarily better treated and better paid than the rest of the workers. In the case of a linguistically different workforce the supervising foreman needs the added skill of a degree of bilingualism to understand and transmit the employer's order. By being in a relatively better economic condition, a bilingual foreman can secure the same or better position for his children. After a few generations some of his offspring could, indeed, become owners of the means of production, be it the land or a factory. The mobility of a limited number of individuals from an oppressed group can serve the interest of the oppressors in several ways. First, the employer gains a reliable ally who will play the middle man in the achievement of economic goals. Second, by splitting the workers into less and more advantaged groups the employer can shift the attention of workers from the fact that s/he benefits most from their labor, to the foreman who is visible every day. Third, the more advantageous position of the foreman gives some workers the false hope that one day they will "make it by pulling themselves up by their bootstraps."

The level of communication between management and labor depends on the level of sophistication of the tasks performed by labor. Work requiring higher intellectual or technical skills requires more communication between management and labor. Even in a monolingual setting, however, there is a language difference between management and labor, whereby the interest of management dictates the use of a language which is hard to understand by ordinary workers, especially in topics regarding the profit arrangements of the enterprise. In an asymmetrical bilingual setting the employer has the added advantage in the form of a "natural" language of management, especially in the case of agricultural labor, which is based on traditional skills and a strong back, and therefore little communication between management and labor for the actual physical performance of the necessary tasks. We do not have to be too imaginative to recognize that the interest in cheap labor is equally important for the Anglo as it is for the few Mexican-American employers. Of course, the language difference can be used in different ways by Anglo and Mexican-American employers respectively. Anglo employers can justify the low wages paid to their workers with the excuse that the Mexican-Americans do not understand directions given in English and that their cultural patterns of siestas and lack of punctuality are hindrances for productivity. Mexican-American employers can always appeal

> Spanish speaking groups and the Anglo-Americans. Few segments of the U. S. experienced as much bloodshed as, the Southwest. The memories of the past conflicts still preserve as harsh memories of past injustices among the minority groups of the Southwest.[8]

In this account we find land and water, the most basic means of production, mentioned as the reasons for the conflict, while language and culture are completely missing from the account; yet, the two groups in conflict represented two distinct linguistic cultures. The question of language differences is not mentioned at that stage of the conflict since the economic factors were in the foreground. In a Marxist analysis we have to proceed from these factors and show how they influenced the attitudes of the people in conflict; we have to unearth how the language difference was used after the conquest of the Southwest to keep the Mexican-American population in subjugation.

Other authors writing about the beginning of the conflict between Anglos and Mexican-Americans have found that language became an issue soon after the conquest. Fishman, for example, gives an accurate picture about the very close connection between economic exploitation and linguistic discrimination.

> Economically, too, the conquest was obvious from the beginning. Land that had been used for generations by Spanish-speaking people was suddenly pre-empted by Anglos. Those who spoke Spanish usually found themselves in the poorest jobs at the lowest wages. Social discrimination was closely connected to economic disadvantage. Housing, services and schools were nearly always the poorest available. The Anglos had unexpectedly stumbled onto a source of cheap labor in their frontier march, and they had no intention of giving it up.[9]

Here we have the blunt description of the most significant factors in the development of the conflict situation between Anglos and Mexican-Americans in the U. S. Southwest. We can see the priority of the economic factors and how the linguistic difference served as an excuse for maintaining economic inequalities. The particularities and variances in linguistic and cultural matters became criteria for discrimination against the Mexican-Americans by the Anglos only after their subjugation, as a means to justify using the Mexican-Americans as a cheap source of labor. This does not mean that there were no particularities in the behavior of the Spanish-speaking population, but the essential point is that only later did the particularities become an excuse for maintaining the socio-economic relations established at the time of the conquest. The language difference became one of the main instruments for conserving the status quo. An asymmetrical bilingualism developed whereby the dominant language became the symbol of progress and status, and the members of the dominant language group did not even consider it worthwhile to learn the language of the allegedly inferior dominated group. At the same time, the dominated group was forced to learn a minimum amount of the dominant language in order to survive in their everyday struggle to maintain their low paying jobs. The entire social structure was, and is still, based on unequal terms between the dominated and dominant groups whereby there is a great deal of segregation between groups as far as housing, occupational opportunities and schooling are concerned. Here we have to refer to our previous remark that different groups speak different languages to the extent that they are isolated. In contrast to other bilingual situations in the U. S., the isolation of the Mexican-Americans has been maintained to the present time. The English speaking population did not offer a comparable resistance to the economic and linguistic integration of other nationality groups with which contact was established through the acquistion of new territories. As a case in point, the French speaking landholders of Louisiana were accepted and integrated by the Anglos without significant difficulties, in spite of the linguistic differences, since their major economic interest, the slave-holding land tenure system, coincided.

At the time of the conquest of the Southwest by the U. S., the victorious Anglos did not find such a well established labor pool as the Black slaves represented in Louisiana. The Mexican-American population became the only available source of labor for the newly acquired, vast agricultural lands (which offered great economic opportunities through irrigation). The history of the Spanish speaking people in the Southwest shows that their exploited status basically has not changed since the beginning of the Anglo contact.

The crucial part of this statement is "the consent of the dominant society," which has to be viewed within the economic context of the language groups in contact. Since the economic interest of the dominant group in the Southwest is to have plenty of cheap labor available for seasonal work, and since the Mexican-Americans represent the bulk of this labor force, any attempt for assimilation on their part runs into more difficulties than other language groups have experienced in assimilating into American society. The majority of non-Anglo-Saxon immigrants entered an industrial sector of the economy which provided year-around steady jobs. The performance of the jobs required higher skills where a degree of proficiency in English was a basic necessity. By the second generation, the bilingualism of the first generation immigrants gave way to linguistic and cultural assimilation in the industrial sector of the American economy. In contrast to the European immigrants, the majority of Mexican-Americans were relegated to seasonal agricultural labor with little or no language requirement for the performance of the jobs. The position of the Mexican-Americans within the economy leads to a vicious circle whereby their limited knowledge of English serves as an excuse to exclude them from social mobility and to maintain their isolation within the Anglo society as a cheap labor pool. In contrast to the static bilingualism of the Mexican-Americans stands the dynamic bilingualism of other language groups: "the bilingualism of peoples on the move socially and geographically which provides for a greater tendency towards assimilation."[13]

The isolation of an oppressed group in order to prevent its social mobility or assimilation, does not necessarily represent the use of force or overt discrimination by the oppressor. Quite often the oppressed group helps involuntarily to perpetuate their exploited status by perceiving the cultural aspects of their lives as the crucial factor in their existence, even when they are deeply dissatisfied with their socio-economic conditions. In a conflict situation the false consciousness of perceiving the linguistic and cultural differences as the cause of inequalities between the antagonistic groups could result in the maintenance and widening of the socio-economic differentiation. Often the dominant oppressor group depicts the cultural traits of the oppressed group in a seemingly positive, but basically paternalistic way, by asserting that the oppressed group by its "good nature" and "simple life style" inherently rejects economic advantages for themselves in favor of enjoying their cultural particularities. And, indeed, the isolation

10: Bilingualism and the Melting Pot

and the frustrations of the exploitative working conditions often leave no other alternatives for the oppressed group but to try to find a psychological escape mechanism which is available to them in their own culture. The escape into one's cultural particularities as a source of self-esteem and pride, however, does not mean that a person willingly accepts the economic exploitation or that s/he is unable to cope with, and to appreciate intellectually, more complex and better paying but less alienating work conditions. As a matter of fact, the success part of the melting pot phenomenon, and we cannot deny that it was somewhat successful for many people, was primarily due to the economic opportunities in the U. S. within the limits of capitalist society. Fishman gives a long list of factors for the success of the melting pot theory:

> The Americanization of the immigrants has been explained on the basis of irresistable mass culture; industrialization and urbanization; reward system through public education to social mobility; youth culture; etc.[14]

The marxist analysis using this list concentrates on establishing an order of importance among the factors contributing to the success of the melting pot phenomenon. Using the dialectical method, we have to ask questions such as: Did the mass culture produce industrialization or did industrialization lead to mass culture? How did these factors work in the U. S. Southwest, where the melting pot had no effect on a segment of society? What was the ratio of industrial workers to agricultural laborers in the Southwest compared to other parts of the country? Did the availability of cheap labor favor a different type of agriculture from other parts of the country? How did the natural conditions (soil, climate) coincide with the availability of labor for certain types of agriculture? How did the industrial development influence the agricultural conditions and what were the effects of industrialization on the local labor market? What chances had the Spanish-speaking people for employment in industry?

Answers to these questions require an in-depth analysis of the available economic data during the historical development of the Southwest through which we can identify the basic socio-economic conditions of the Mexican-Americans. Once we have succeeded in establishing the socio-economic profile of a linguistic minority tonation itself; and the radioactive contamination is not spread over large areas, but remains local and concentrated within a range of approximately one to two miles. The human casualties within this area, however, are by no means less. Only instead of an immediate and massive extermination as with the A or H bomb, most of the neutron bomb victims would die a gradual death, as a result of massive radiation exposure, sometimes with the first symptoms only appearing after a few days. The neutron bomb could kill without the victim's knowledge of having been exposed to its death rays, which can reach even as far as two to three miles away from the center of the blast. The killer rays penetrate buildings, and even go through concrete walls like dust blowing through a fence. Given the horribly agonizing death of radiation victims,[2] we might even consider fortunate those who would be killed by the initial blast.

Thus, we can discredit some of the often heard arguments in support of the neutron bomb. The "clean" weapon in fact is the dirtiest and most vicious invention of scientifically designed genocide. The devastating effects of conventional A and H bombs prohibit their use for fear of retaliation. The different effect of the neutron bomb however would diminish this fear of retaliation, thus making an aggressive nuclear war only more probable, particularly since the weapon is not in the hands of the Soviet Union. To call the neutron bomb "safe" is but another expression of cynicism on the part of its proponents in political, economic and military circles. Nor is the neutron bomb a "cheap" weapon as is so often stated to the U. S. public, in the sense of the number of people killed per million dollars of the military budget.[3] In view of these facts, how can anyone support the development and use of nuclear weapons?

We have to understand that the decision about mass production of the neutron bomb is not the dream of psychopaths, but part of a calculated scheme. It has always been an interest of the U. S. to find a way of using nuclear weapons without facing the disastrous consequences. As early as 1951 J. Robert Oppenheimer, one of the "fathers" of thermonuclear weapons, stated: "Only if the atomic bomb can be made useable insofar as becoming a tool for conventional military operations, will it really be of major importance in the actual fighting of war instead of merely as warning and deterrent."[4]

The same strategy of "flexible response" was also formulated by Henry Kissinger in 1957, for whom violence and aggression have their place in diplomacy if they can be kept to a less than catas-

trophic level, i.e., slightly short of thermonuclear war.[5]
The neutron bomb, the "enhanced radiation weapon," is the answer to such desires. Its "collateral damage," i.e., its undesired material loss and human casualties, is considered small compared to a thermonuclear weapon.

2.

We don't want to deal with the question whether it is more "humane" to commit instant or gradual genocide. Many individuals and groups have pointed out the contradiction between the stated U. S. commitment to detente as the basic principle of its foreign policy and the further escalation of the arms race which is embodied in the neutron bomb, cruise and MX missles and other weapons. This contradiction is a very real one, and can only be understood if one recognizes how each of these developments, detente and arms escalation, fits into the overall continuous pattern of U. S. foreign policy.

This policy has had one continuous thread of development since 1917, when the October Revolution brought the first Socialist country into existence. The thread has been an underlying hostility to the Socialist countries, which finds its most virulent expression in the ultimate aim of "rolling back" socialism, or even totally destroying it.[6] In the early years this included direct U. S. military intervention in the Soviet Union on behalf of various counter-revolutionary forces. Even during World War II, when the U. S. and the Soviet Union were allies in the great war against fascism, General Leslie R. Groves took over the Manhattan Project to develop the atomic bomb with the express understanding that "the Russian is the enemy."[7]

From the days of the Cold War following World War II up to today, U. S. foreign policy has changed its face many times under the influence of such personages as John Foster Dulles, George Kennan, Zbigniew Brzezinski and Henry Kissinger, not to mention David Rockefeller's Trilateral Commission. But these changing faces of U. S. foreign policy have not meant any real change in the basic hostility toward the Soviet Union and the Socialist countries. They have only been changes in response to the real change in power relations between the Socialist and Capitalist countries. As the Socialist countries grew stronger, approaching parity with the Capitalist countries,[8] the policy of direct confrontation became

THE NEUTRON BOMB AND THE CRISIS OF U.S. FOREIGN POLICY

Georgia Stevic

The neutron bomb is a weapon of mass destruction designed to selectively annihilate all living things while leaving inanimate structures intact. This standard description might be encountered even in the conservative mass media. But it does not explain that the neutron bomb is the culmination of long term efforts by the United States to develop nuclear weapons for conventional battlefield use. This cynical attempt to push nuclear weapons into the arsenals of regular combat units poses a serious threat to all attempts to limit the proliferation of nuclear arms, and also lowers the threshold which might trigger a nuclear holocaust. The analysis presented here is intended to show further that the neutron bomb is one reflection of the military and foreign policy crisis on the U. S. and its NATO alies.

1.

The neutron bomb as a nuclear weapon of mass destruction has some aspects in common with atomic and hydrogen bombs; other aspects, however, are different. According to the description by British nuclear physicist Prof. Eric Burhop, participant in the U. U.S. atomic bomb project during World War II, the degree of lethal action on human beings is very similar with all types of nuclear weapons. But the distinguishing feature lies in the release of unusually large quantities of lethal radiation without a massive destructive detonative blast.[1] Thus, buildings and living matter are not destroyed immediately, except at the very center of the de-group as fully as possible, then we can proceed to investigate its linguistic and cultural particularities. The Marxist analysis treats the linguistic and cultural characteristics of a people not as static phenomena, unrelated to that people's economic conditions, but as the manifestations of the superstructure of the entire society.

When the dominance of linguistic differences is in the center of the consciousness of the people involved in a conflict situation, then the language problem should be approached on its own merits by examining how the members of one linguistic group are placed in a disadvantageous position compared to the other group in occupations, housing, education, etc. The result of a critical analysis of a bilingual setting should culminate in the recognition that a conflict situation based on linguistic differences cannot be eliminated through changes on the level of the superstructure alone, i.e. through language or educational policies. At the same time we have to recognize that a change in the superstructure, such as introducing bilingual education for a linguistically oppressed group could enhance a movement toward a change in the economic basis.

The case of the Mexican-Americans shows that this particular bilingual situation emerged during the territorial expansion of the U. S. and the linguistic difference was successfully used for more than a century to keep a people in subjugation. Focusing on the linguistic difference between Anglos and Mexican-Americans those who made great fortunes in the Southwest succeeded in distracting attention from the class conflict between the propertied class and the rest of the population. The rising national consciousness of the Mexican-Americans can be viewed as an example of increasing class struggle in the U. S., and the question of bilingualism and bilingual education can have an important role in this struggle. If the question of bilingualism is approached from a narrow nationalistic view by the Mexican-Americans they could retard their own liberation, but if they recognize the necessity of international solidarity of all oppressed people, they will be a force in eliminating the injustices of capitalism while retaining the progressive elements in their culture.

Notes

1. Glyn E. Lewis, *Mutilingualism in the Soviet Union* (The Hague: Mouton, 1972), p. 286.
2. Lev Somonovich Vygotsky, *Thought and Language* (Cambridge, Mass.,: M.I.T. Press, 1962), p. 52.
3. Joshua A. Fishman, *Language Loyalty in the United States* (The Hague: Mouton, 1966), p. 231.
4. Lewis, p. 286.
5. Theodore Andersson and Mildred Boyer, *Bilingual Schooling in the United States* (Washington: U. S. Government Printing Office, 1970), p. 9.
6. Uriel Weinreich, *Language in Contact* (New York: Columbia U. Press, 1953), p. 98.
7. Lewis, p. 54.
8. Clark S. Knowlton, *Spanish Speaking People of the South-West* (El Paso: University of Texas, 1967), p. 1.
9. Fishman, p. 286.
10. Fishman, p. 191.
11. Weinreich, p. 101.
12. Fishman, p. 188.
13. Lewis, p. 276.
14. Fishman, p. 29.

simply a policy of containment. Further, as the war in Vietnam drained more and more U. S. resources and the ensuing domestic unrest became a factor, containment changed to coexistence, and finally to detente and economic cooperation. But the fact that even such apparently peaceful policies as detente and economic cooperation could be made to serve the interests of aggresively hostile forces in the U.S. becomes clear when seen in the context of Carter's human rights policy, U.S. SALT strategy and U.S. military policy.[9]

Open hostility toward the Socialist world was clearly unacceptable in the early 1970's, especially considering the genuine disillusionment of the American people with such policies in Vietnam. The peace movement in the U. S. played an important role in forcing first withdrawal from Vietnam and then the actual beginning of the Strategic Arms Limitation Talks (SALT). The policy of detente was developed at the time to restrict the real conflict between the Capitalist and Socialist systems to the ideological level, and the Soviet Union was even proclaiming the possibility of mutual reductions in strategic forces based on positions of equality. At the same time, however, the U. S. military-industrial complex was proceeding at full speed with the technological developments which would eventually lead to a further qualitative escalation of the arms race and to an imbalance in strategic forces between the U. S. and the USSR.[10] The SALT I agreement, signed in 1972, placed quantitative limitations on strategic arms, but no limitations on qualitative "improvements."[11] Clearly the U. S. military intended to keep a free hand to maintain the strategic military upper hand by means of technological advances. This can only be understood as a basically hostile attitude towards the Soviet Union; it reflects a desire to keep open the possibility of military aggression.

Jimmy Carter's "human rights" campaign came at a time when the Cold War rhetoric had completely lost its credibility. But the fact that this campaign for "human rights" could be directed againt the Socialist countries was not lost on Rockefeller's Trilateral Commission, which threw its support behind Carter's candidacy. Indeed, the "human rights" campaign served very well to maintain hostility toward the Soviet Union and to justify U. S. drums about the Soviet menace in Central Europe. This all set the stage to undermine the SALT II negotiations. Thus, Cyrus Vance traveled to Moscow in March, 1977, with new U.S. proposals for a

SALT II agreement which could only be understood as a U. S. effort to gain unilateral strategic advantages. Carter skillfully gave the appearance of a genuine interest in peace and disarmament when he decided not to go ahead right away with production of the B-1 strategic bomber. But at the same time, the proposal he sent to Moscow excluded from any SALT agreement the even more insidious cruise missile, which is even better able than the B-1 to penetrate undetected through Soviet air defenses with a nuclear warhead. This proposal also represented a distinct departure from the Vladivostok accords of 1974, and called for the Soviets to forego many planned strategic developments, while only calling for a virtually unenforcible range limitation on U. S. cruise missiles.[12] Thus the "sacrifice" of the B-1 bomber program was no sacrifice at all, but a recognition that the cruise missile was a more effective weapon and could be used to circumvent and undermine any SALT agreement.[13]

The neutron bomb has the same sort of effect on the militarization of Central Europe as the cruise missile and other systems such as MX missile and Mark 12A warhead have on the international strategic balance. The neutron bomb, as will be discussed in the following section, represents a substantial escalation of the aggressive posture of the NATO forces in Western Europe.

All these developments must be understood as an attempt by certain forces of the military and monopoly capital to redirect the conflict between the Capitalist and Socialist systems along more hostile lines. Certainly, as indicated above, a policy of detente was a necessary expedient at a certain time, even for the forces of monopoly capital. The anti-militarist and peace forces dictated such a policy, as did the balance of world power. But the contradiction between the two systems became too obvious. The fact that the Socialist countries continued a pace of steady economic growth, while the Capitalist countries have been increasingly unable to solve their own economic crisis, made a continued policy of detente too dangerous to the interests of monopoly capital. The benefits of Socialism might become too clear to the multitudes of unemployed, underemployed, underpaid and oppressed in the Capitalist countries. The continued general crisis of Capitalism is calling forth an entire new wave of U.S. militarism.

3.

Since the neutron bomb is meant to be deployed in Europe according to the current NATO concept of "Forward defense," it is mostly the task of the European countries to prevent that deployment. Since the first announcement of the planned deployment by the U. S. in July 1977, the opinion of West German politicians, political analysts, civic and church leaders, women's groups, editors of major newspapers, the armed forces and industrial leaders has varied from full support to violent opposition. The majority of the voices against the neutron bomb put the weapon in the same category with previous genocidal atrocities such as Auschwitz, Hiroshima and the Napalm drops over Vietnam. On the extreme other side, the defenders of the neutron bomb try to belittle its horrible effects by saying that the architectural beauty of Bavaria would survive its use. The supporting arguments for the neutron bomb substantially outnumber the opposing voices in the West German bourgeois press. One wonders why there is such support, so obviously violating and challenging all humanitarian beliefs and the hopes of human kind for peace and survival.

Since joining NATO in 1955 the FRG has been in agreement with the long-range foreign policy decisions of the U. S. Following the establishment of the two German states in 1949, the Bonn government, under the leadership of the Christian Democrat Konrad Adenauer, pursued an aggressive policy aimed at changing the borders drawn after WWII. "Freeing our brothers and sisters beyond the iron curtain" was the going slogan during the 50's and early 60's. But since open and direct military intervention to roll back Socialism was out of the question for the FRG, the government resorted to a policy of political intervention, namely the so-called "Hallstein Doctrin" (similar to the Jackson Amendment today). According to this doctrine the FRG broke off diplomatic relations and stopped economic assistance to any country recognizing the GDR. This policy only proved effective for a short while and resulted ultimately in a self-imposed blockade on the side of the FRG[14] The "Hallstein Doktrin" is but one specific example of a general strategy which became unworkable. The Western powers, the FRG in congruence with U. S. policy, started to develop a new concept in foreign policy, designed to take the growing economic and political strength of the Socialist countries into account.

ski et al. in the mid-sixties, [15] were characterized from the very beginning by a Janus-faced quality. Coexistence instead of direct cold war meant that the former antagonisms were not solved, but merely placed into the ideological realm. The final aim, however, the changing of the *status quo*, remained the same. Only the means for achieving it were changed.

These aims were also central in 1966 in the program of the West German politician Franz-Josef Strauss, who was long-time defense minister under Adenauer, leader of the strong reactionary opposition party — the Christian Democrats (CDU/CSU) — and recently best known for his friendly visit to Pinochet. But the Strauss program *excluded* the U. S. from the position it had traditionally held in Europe, namely as chief executor of such policies. Certainly this concept of a strong, independent West Germany did not find positive response among its partners in Europe nor with the U. S. Furthermore, the U. S.' own policies of a "soft," more refined kind of containment and final dissolution of Socialism under the name of detente in the late 60's was in line with the general political sentiment here and abroad. It is therefore no coincidence that the Social Democratic Party (SPD), in coalition with the Free Democratic Party (FDP), and under the leadership of Willy Brandt, could win the elections in West Germany on the platform of peace and reform politics. Their concept of "democratic socialism" coupled with a policy of detente toward the Socialist countries created the mass base that has since kept the coalition government in office.

When it became clear to the U. S., however, that the policy of detente with its anticipated goals of weakening the Socialist countries was failing, the "indirect strategy" was gradually reversed.[16] Gerald Ford's phrases, the "End of Detente"[17] and "policy of peace through strength" constituted but one indication of this changing policy. The change was, of course, heralded by the reactionary Christian Democratic Party. That it was also received quite favorably by the Social Democratic Party is a cause for concern and investigation, since the SPD was elected on the ticket of peace and detente. The question, therefore, is what makes the SPD support a policy that in the long run might be suicidal to its own political existence.

It is a fact that West Germany, with its relatively stable economy, is one of the strongest members of the European Community (formerly known as the Common Market). That position of strength, of being "Europe's paymaster," has afforded West

Germany the power to attach political conditions to its economic assistance. In very concrete terms this means that West Germany can exercise imperialist power, which ranges from Helmut Schmidt's "friendly advice" to the Portuguese, to direct threats of cutting economic assistance in the event the left had come to power in Italy after the last election.[18]

Along with this economic dominance of Europe, the Christian Democrats would also like to see West Germany replace the U. S. as the dominant military force in Western Europe. This goal is certainly consistent with the goal of economic hegemony in Europe. As part of this new military role in Europe, the Christian Democrats feel it should be "up to us" (as Strauss puts it) to take aggressive steps. The goal of West Germany having control over its own nuclear weapons is one aspect of this aggressive program. Any continuations of U. S. detente policy would only maintain the *status quo* and threaten the ideological platform for increased weapons' production by big West German industries. The "soft approach" of the U.S. detente policy and the "Ostpolitik" of the FRG were plainly bad business in the eyes of the CDU/CSU.

No wonder that in spite of Strauss' general anti-U. S. stance the planned deployment of the NB found wide support among his political cronies. Even though the new U. S. anti-detente policy is *not* in full congruence with Strauss' own policy for West Germany, namely equipping West Germany with its own nuclear weapons, it is certainly closer to his goal. Operating under the assumption that second best is better than nothing, the deployment of the NB would bring West Germany into the new position of almost having trigger control over nuclear weapons.[20] In addition, the NB, through its construction, military function and effect, is an expression of a real commitment on the part of the U. S. to become aggressive again toward the Socialist countries. The NB would be one of Jimmy Carter's trump cards for continuous blackmail and threat in case of Soviet "imprudence." It is therefore no contradiction that Strauss himself in an interview with the reactionary daily *Bayernkurier* of April 30, 1977, spoke in favor of closer, co-ordinated ties in matters of U. S. and West German foreign policy. Clearly on the basis of his previous position he does not speak out of conviction but out of political pragmatism and necessity. But when his ultimate fear of seeing Europe move toward Socialism becomes more real, even the U. S. becomes acceptable as a partner.[21]

The matter is slightly different with the Social Democratic Party. They have come to power with a policy different from the

Christian Democrats', namely peace and co-existence. The expressed agreement of the SPD to the deployment of the neutron bomb could therefore undercut its own political powerbase and be in the long run suicidal. While this seems contradictory, there are many opposing forces at work. First of all, one should not forget the already existing close ties of the monopoly industries to the West German government. Secondly, voices from within the West German armed forces are strongly in favor of the deployment of the neutron bomb. And finally, the SPD has a long tradition of unity with U. S. foreign policy decisions even if this involves changing its own positions. But that does not necessarily mean that West Germany feels compelled to accept an automatic transfer of U.S. foreign policy. There is precedent for separate and even competitive agreements with Third World countries on economic matters, with the U. S. not being able to stop West Germany from pursuing a policy contrary to U. S. interests. But this competition between U. S. and West German monopoly capital does not extend beyond certain economic and political spheres. When it comes to facing the common "enemy," they stand shoulder to shoulder.

The imperialist aim of West German policy was not curbed by the development of the atomic bomb with its potential for global devastation. The possibility of any war becoming a holocaust did not affect their thinking in general, just the risk calculations.[22] With the introduction of the neutron bomb the risk seems small enough to take. However, the continued presence and domination of the U.S. in Europe in the military and political arenas would weaken the West German national position and its goal of expanding its leadership in Europe.

The political difficulties of the West German government in openly supporting the neutron bomb are further compounded by strong anti-American sentiments resulting from the presence of U.S. soldiers in the FRG, and the tradition of anti-imperialist demonstrations during the Vietnam War. Any demonstrations against the neutron bomb could build on this sentiment, and easily develop into an anti-American campaign or an even more dangerous anti-imperialist movement. To this foreign secretary Genscher alluded involuntarily when he warned that actions against the neutron bomb should not take an anti-American twist.[23]

This new concept, recognizing the new global structure, was different from the old direct offensive posture toward the Socialist countries. In that its aim was the gradual disintegration of the Socialist countries. The policies of detente, developed by Brzezin-

4.

The struggle against the neutron bomb, and against militarism and war-mongering in general, can take place on many levels. The specific struggle against the neutron bomb has probably attracted more popular support in Europe than any movement since the "Ban the Bomb" campaign of the 1950's and '60's.

The strongest resistance to a unified campaign for peace, detente and disarmament will come from the monopoly bourgeoisie, especially from those sectors which profit from the arms business. These most reactionary representatives of the monopoly bourgeoisie have great political and economic power. But it is false to conclude from this that disarmament is an impossibility, without considering that Capitalism can be forced to adapt to new conditions under the pressure of anti-militarist forces and the influence of new power relations on a world scale.

A peace campaign within the U. S. will have to counter all of the usual ploys used to argue for ever-expanding military outlays. This includes those who cry out about the "Soviet menace," those who claim that building weapons makes jobs and the more subtle proponents of the "bargaining-chip ideology" of strategic arms limitations. Each year, when the military budget is being debated, we are bombarded with the latest "official estimates" of the Soviet military threat. Statistics showing supposed Soviet superiority in conventional forces never contain any analysis of the Soviet military situation. It is never recognized that while the U. S. has no borders with hostile countries, the Soviet Union must maintain large armies along its thousands of miles of borders with China and Iran, the major recipient of U. S. arms exports. What's more, if they were to balance the entire NATO forces against the entire Warsaw Pact forces, this supposed conventional superiority of the Soviet Union would evaporate. And every year, we learn that the U. S. has not only maintained its strategic and technological lead over the Soviet Union, but even further widened its advantages with such new items as the neutron bomb and the cruise missile. But by this point the die has been cast, and the next round of arms escalation has been guaranteed. As Herbert Scoville, former Deputy Director of the CIA, has said, "Duplicating a Soviet counterforce capability would be a hazardous response even if the Soviets were to achieve it, but to match it *in advance* will insure only that the Soviets acquire such weapons."[24]

It is true, as Scoville says, that the Soviets cannot accept a position of military inequality and will continue to match U. S. military initiatives. One aim of this policy is to force the Soviets into ever higher military expenditures. These expenditures are supposed to destabilize their planned economy, make them less able to meet the demands of their citizens and make them less able to give support to Socialist, national liberation and other progressive forces around the world. While the arms race has certainly diverted substantial wealth from meeting real needs in the Socialist economies, the history of the past thirty years clearly demonstrates the futility of these attempts. While the Socialist economies have continued steadily to grow and prosper, it is the Capitalist countries which are plunging deeper and deeper into economic crisis,[25] and the various progressive forces in the world continue to shrink the Capitalist sphere.

Those who argue that increased military spending not only keeps America strong, but makes more jobs for the American people probably mislead the largest numbers, especially among those directly employed by the military-industrial complex. That these arguments are patently false has been shown most recently by a U. S. study,[26] which concluded that a billion dollar expenditure would create:

22,000 jobs if spent on B-1 bomber projects;
58,000 jobs if spent for military personnel;
73,000 jobs for firemen;
76,000 jobs for teachers;
85,000 jobs for nurses;
145,000 public service jobs.

The final, and perhaps most subtle, position can be called the bargaining chip approach to disarmament. This is the position taken by those supposedly more liberal elements who proclaim an interest in disarmament and peace, but insist on "negotiating from a position of strength." This bargaining chip approach, exemplified by placing the neutron bomb and the cruise missile on the SALT bargaining table and demanding concessions, is responsible for the currently stalled talks. The continual process of "ante-uppong," by bringing new weapons developments into the negotiations, makes the actual conclusion of any agreement nearly impossible. While Jimmy Carter has certainly "laid all the cards on the table" at the SALT talks, he has deliberately attempted to stack them in favor of the U.S.

Public education and agitation against all of these usual tactics of the military-industrial complex can be very successful, but the strongest movement is one which appeals to the immediate interests of the people. The campaign for disarmament and peace is just such a movement, because it goes hand in hand with a campaign for jobs and economic rights for all citizens. In the last two decades, both social and military expenditures have increased dramatically in the Capitalist countries. The high level of these governmental expenditures has lead to rapidly mounting deficits. As of 1975, the accumulated U. S. national debt amounted to a staggering 51% of the gross national product. The phenomenal increase of these deficits can be directly related to the crisis of unemployment and inflation in the U. S. Without controlling these deficits it will be impossible to solve these economic problems within the current system. Eight percent of the 1978 budget ($49 billion) will pay the interest on the national debt and enrich the finance capitalists, with 24% (approximately $125 billion) additionally being spent on the military (not including such items as the CIA and the neutron bomb which are hidden elsewhere in the budget). Aside from creating very few jobs, none of these expenditures benefits the people. It is here that spending must be cut. For the Capitalist countries, the continued increase of both social and military spending will spell intensified inflation.[27] It is apparent from Carter's "welfare reform" proposals that he intends to control inflation by reducing social expenditures, not by reducing military outlays. As shown by the previously cited study on jobs, this will mean not only a decrease in social welfare, but a rise in unemployment. The struggle for jobs and economic welfare, then, translated directly into a struggle against the economic crisis and against militarism and military spending. An important and precedent-setting struggle is that for the *Transfer Amendment*.[28]

Around the world, protests against the neutron bomb have gathered very broad support based on the argument that the neutron bomb is, after all, a nuclear weapon. The point is that there is no such thing as a so-called "tactical nuclear weapon," and first use of any atomic weapon will dramatically escalate the probability of a global nuclear war. This line of reasoning has received support, even from widely respected Western military authorities. West German General Johannes Steinhoff,[29] former leader of the NATO Nuclear Planning Group, agrees with Herbert Scoville that

"The neutron bomb does not make atomic war more humane, only more probable."[30] In the U.S., the Pentagon is attempting to suppress a report by the U.S. Arms Control and Disarmament Agency which warns that the neutron bomb "will increase the chances for a full scale nuclear war." The report also states that to proceed with production of the neutron bomb "might be viewed by other nations as running counter to the disarmament goals announced by the Carter Administration."[31] Such a sober, albeit somewhat limited, analysis is already seen as a grave threat by the agents of the military-industrial complex.

On another level, the struggle against the neutron bomb is highly moralistic, emphasizing the inhumanity and cynicism of the neutron bomb. The struggle on this level can have the broadest appeal. A person such as Egon Bahr, Secretary of the ruling West German SPD, can write, "it is a question of humanity. . . . Here the scale of all values is turned on its head. The goal has become the preservation of material things; the human being is secondary. . . . This is claimed to be the ultimate progress? Is humanity going insane?"[32] While arguments such as these are correct, they are easily subverted to make new arguments for the neutron bomb. For example, one West German account indicates that if the neutron bomb rather than incendiaries had been used on Dresden in World War II, then "Dresden could have been preserved in all its beauty despite the mass murder of citizens and refugees."[33] Others have argued that such moralistic positions as Bahr's present no alternatives because all war is inhuman.[34]

At a somewhat higher level of synthesis, the militaristic-confrontational strategies of the Western Capitalist countries can be analyzed in terms of international class struggle. Such an analysis recognizes that new military escalations, such as the neutron bomb and the cruise missile, are directed specifically against the Socialist countries as one of the strongest links in the international working class movement. The maintenance of peaceful relations directly aids the building of Socialism, and furthermore promotes the specific national interests of the working class and all oppressed groups.

The possibilities for overcoming the opponents of detente are greater now than ever before. Today, the possibility exists for the anti-militarist struggle to build coalitions which extend even into the ranks of the bourgeoisie. In these times of economic crisis, even the monopoly bourgeoisie is divided by conflicts of interest in the question of armament/disarmament. These conflicts of interest arise both from a struggle for government financial support between the military and non-military sectors, who are being threatened by the crisis, and from the desire of many companies to seek new markets in the Socialist countries.[35] The very factors which lead the military-industrial complex to beat its war drums the loudest also mean that the time is ripe for a strong and consequential movement for peace and detente.

Notes

1. *Neutron Bombs — No!* (Helsinki: World Peace Council, 1977), pp. 12-13.
2. *Neutron Bombs — No!*, p. 17.
3. Fred M. Kaplan, "Enhanced Radiation Weapons," *Scientific American*, 238, No. 5 (1978), pp. 44-51.
4. J. Robert Oppenheimer, "Comments on the Military Value of the Atom," *Bulletin of the Atomic Scientists*, 27, No. 2 (1951), pp. 43-45.
5. Josef Rodejohann, "Entwicklung, Wirkungsweise und Gefahren der Neutronenbombe," *Hefte zu politischen Gegenwartsfragen*, No. 31 (1977), p. 53.
6. Ellen Weber, *Imperialismus in der Aupassung*, Reihe Marxistmus Aktuell, No. 45 (Frankfurt/Main: Verlag Marxistische Blatter, 1972), pp. 5-37.
7. Marilyn Bechtel, "U. S.-Soviet Relations: Detente is the Key," *Political Affairs*, 56, No. 11 (November 1977), pp. 28-29.
8. Erwin Marquit, *The Socialist Countries, Studies in Marxism*, Vol. 3 (Minneapolis: Marxist Educational Press. 1978).
9. Bernd Griener, "Konturen der Aussenpolitik Prasident Carters," *Blatter fur deutsche und internationale Politik*, 21, No. 8 (1977), p. 949.
10. G. Arbatov, "Soviet-USA Relations Today," *Reprints from the Soviet Press*, 25, No. 5 (1977), pp. 33-34.
11. "SALT: A Race Against the Arms Race," *The Defense Monitor*, 6, No. 5 (July 1977), pp. 1-8.
12. Marilyn Bechtel, "Of SALT, Sand and Jimmy Carter," *New World Review*, 45, No. 4 (July-August 1977), pp. 1-5.
13. George Kennan (former U.S. ambassador to the USSR) himself has said that the Pentagon is specifically responsible for the current deadlock in the SALT negotiations. See Edmund

Stevens, "The Arms Race, Not a Russian Blitz on Europe, Is the Real Threat," *The Times*, Jan. 26, 1977, p. 14, cols, 1-6.
14. Reinhard Opitz, "Die Neutronen-Bombe, die BRD und Europa," *Blatter Fur deutsche und internationale Politik*, 21, No. 9 (1977), p. 1054.
15. *Ibid.*, p. 1054.
16. *Ibid.*, p. 1059.
17. *Ibid.*, p. 1059.
18. *Ibid.*, p. 1061.
19. "SALT: A Race Against the Arms Race,", p. 1.
20. Opitz, p. 1064.
21. *Ibid.*, p. 1066.
22. *Ibid.*, P. 1072.
23. *Ibid.*, p. 1073.
24. "The Soviet Threat: Is There a Present Danger?" *The Defense Monitor*, 6, No. 2 (February, 1977), p. 1.
25. Jurgen Kuczinski, "Rustung, soziale Sicherheit und Inflation," *Marxistische Blatter*, 14, No. 5 (1976), p. 19.
26. Marion Anderson, *The Empty Pork Barrel: Unemployment and the Pentagon Budget* (Lansing: Public Interest Research Group in Michigan, 1978), p. 1.
27. Jurgen Kuczinski, p. 20.
28. *Transfer From Military Spending to Human Needs, Priority Action Guide*, (Washington, D.C. : Coalition for a New Foreign and Military Policy, 1978).
29. Johannes Steinhoff, "Die Neutronenwaffe gehort nicht auf Gefechsfeld," *Hefte zu politischen Gegenwartsfragen*, No. 31 (1977), p. 45.
30. "They have said . . . ," *World Trade Union Movement*, 9 (September, 1977), p. 5.
31. Richard Burt, "Neutron Bomb Study Irks Pentagon Aids," *New York Times*, Feb. 1, 1978, p. 3.
32. Egon Bahr, "Ist die Menschheit dabei, verruckt zu werden?" *Hefte zu politischen Gegenwartsfragen*, No. 31 (1977), p. 9.
33. Herbert Kremp, *Die Welt*, July 14, 1977, cited in Martha Buschmann, "The Neutron Bomb — An Affront to Humanity," *World Marxist Review*, 20, No. 10 (1977), p. 105.
34. Christian Potyka, "Einsame Stimme der Moral zum Wettrusten," *Suddeutsche Zietung*, July 19, 1977, p. 4.
35. Fred Schmid, "Ist Abrustung im Kapitalismus moglich?" *Marxistische Blatter*, 4 (1977), pp. 58-64.

THE IDEOLOGY OF AUSTERITY: A CRITIQUE OF FUTURISM

David L. Morgan and Dan G. Rebik
University of Northern Iowa

1. Introduction

To paraphrase Marx and Engels, a spector is haunting monopoly capitalism — the spector of the future, a future without capitalism! Its ghostly presence frightens those who have a stake in the existing order. To exorcise this spector, an often-tried means is ideological cooptation. Such cooptation can involve racism, national chauvinism, and anti-Communist propaganda. Sometimes it takes highly irrational forms, while at other times it wears a rational mask. A currently popular form of supposedly "rational" cooptation is *futurism* or *futurology*.[1]

Futurism purports to be an attempt to forecast the future scientifically and to shape the future rationally. It is an extraordinarily diverse phenomenon involving the efforts of journalists, scientists, computer experts, fiction writers, sociologists, philosophers, and others. It is highly organized and institutionalized. Among the better known futurists are Alvin Toffler, author of the best-seller *Future Shock*; Marshall McLuhan, whose conceptions of the contemporary and future role of communication media have evinced much discussion; Paul and Anne Erlich, who have investigated the effects of population growth on the environment; Donella and Dennis Meadows and their associates, who have used computer projections to forecast the future; and Barry Commoner, long active in documenting the effects of technology and industry on ecological systems.[2] Among the institutionalized forms of futurism one can cite The Commission on the Year 2000, whose chairperson is the well-known sociologist Daniel Bell; the Hudson Institute, presided over by Herman Kahn; and the World Future Society and its magazine, *The Futurist*.[3]

As we shall try to show, the projections of the futurists vary, although in recent times they have manifested a growing tendency to project visions of a future of sacrifice and austerity against a background of diminishing resources.[4] It is this tone which, with its supposedly scientific basis, has become a significant ideological theme in the present period of capitalist crises, a theme with the potential for diverting the struggle for progressive change away from a consideration of the weaknesses of capitalism. More specifically, the austerity theme provides a rationale for present and contemplated cutbacks in the standard of living, especially for the working class.

The diversity of method and theme creates some difficulty in defining futurism, but the following passage from Toffler's *Future Shock* is suggestive:

> Previously, men studied the past to shed light on the present. I have turned the time mirror around, convinced that a coherent image of the future can shower us with valuable insights into today. We shall find it increasingly difficult to understand our personal and public problems without making use of the future as an intellectual tool.[5]

For futurism a conceptualized image of the future is to be a primary guide to action and thought. It is this emphasis on the *image* of the future which unites futurists regardless of their outlook, be it optimistic or pessimistic. A secondary focus of many futurists is the role of technology, be it positive or negative.

Marshall McLuhan and the early Alvin Toffler are examples of writers who portray a technologically rich future. Automation, they tell us, will eliminate jobs as we know them. In McLuhan's view, the growth and integration of the communications media will revolutionize learning so that it becomes "the principal kind of production and consumption." Unemployment, he maintains, is to be welcomed as the harbinger of a new media-rich age.[6]

On the other hand, Barry Commoner, Paul and Anne Ehrlich and the Meadows group generally tend to be wary of the effects of technology and less confident of the prospects for a comfortable future. In *The Power of Poverty*, Commoner suggests that new "energy-intensive" production techniques and the wide use of non-biodegradable materials spell ecological disaster. Commoner recommends easing off of such technologies, but holds some form of socialism to be necessary for achieving a favorable result. The Ehrlichs see technology as interfering with the "intricate web" of physical relationships in the biological community. Such innovations as pesticides, herbicides and chemical fertilizers can lead, in their view, to an upset in the balance of nature and the consequent annihilation of humanity. As a solution they recommend mandatory birth control and a cutback in technological systems. These goals can be accomplished by such mass pressure as letter writing to government officials. In their influential book, *The Limits to Growth*, the Meadows group uses a series of computerized projections to assert that an unmanageably large population, diminishing resources, environmental pollution, and food shortages will produce disaster around the year 2050 unless efforts are made to reverse the trends they observe, What is needed in their view is the creation of a global no-growth system, the sooner the better.

Writers like Commoner, the Ehrlichs, and the Meadows group develop their views with a fair degree of care and attention to detail. Others, like McLuhan and Toffler, leave much to be desired, despite the wide circulation of their works. Toffler's *Future Shock*, for example, has sold over 6 million copies in 50 countries and has been translated into about 20 languages.[7]

By playing on the obvious distortions of technology under capitalism and on legitimate concerns regarding the environment and resource allocation, futurism can give itself a certain seriousness and a progressive thrust. And by making use of the pro-imperialist and anti-Communist distortions of the mass media, it can paint a picture of the human condition as being above the class struggle and the particularities of given socio-economic or political systems. The futurists can even appeal to certain "left" trends. For example, the Maoists' well-known support for certain primitive methods of production evokes a "socialist" austerity markedly similar to certain themes in Western futurism. One can thus see in futurism a familiar type of effort, that of seeking a "third path" between outright support of capitalism and identification with the Marxist analysis and reality of class struggle. In what follows we shall try to analyze some of futurism's key assumptions and its relationship to the the present general crisis of capitalism.

2. From Leisure to Austerity

When an attempt is made to survey futurist writings over the past 15 years, an important trend emerges. Whereas many writings of the early sixties projected a generally optimistic view of society, with technology and industry engendering a high standard of living and a move away from brute manual labor, more and more in recent years the austerity theme has taken over.

Typical of the rosier views of the future to be found in the earlier period is a collection of essays by staff members of the *Wall Street Journal* entitled, "Here Comes Tomorrow."[8] The authors paint a gaudy picture of a world super-rich in commodities and services. Food, both natural and artificial, will be more plentiful than ever, although some problems may exist in underdeveloped countries.[9] Energy use will expand and diversify, but, significantly, the authors foresee no problems whatsoever with shortages.[10] For the U. S. military it will be business as usual! The Marine Corps will be able to use Saturn-type rockets to ship batallions of over 1000 men to such "trouble spots" as Africa in a matter of minutes. No such irritations as a staggering military defeat in Indo-China or pressure for disarmament are expected.[11] Educational enrollment will rise at all age levels, and in a few years, according to a Ford Foundation expert, the U. S. will be founding new colleges at the rate of one per week. The educational cutbacks of the present seem far away![12]

Alvin Toffler, the originator of the term "future shock" reflects in his own writings the shift from leisure to austerity and from optimism to pessimism. In an article for *Horizon* (Summer, 1965), Toffler, using the term "future shock" for the first time, waxes eloquently on the marvels of technology. He quotes another futurist, Kenneth Boulding, to the effect that we will shortly be able to produce all the food we need with the efforts of less than 5 percent of the population. Toffler goes on to tell us that manual labor will be eliminated by the year 2000 and that by that time the work week which, he claims, has already been cut in half since 1900 will probably "be slashed in half again by 2000." There will be difficulty in determining "a man's" esteem since labor will become less central. It will no longer be possible to know which occupations will exist "when a boy becomes a man."[13] The problem, as Toffler sees it in 1965, is whether or not people will be able to adjust to this highly automated, fast-paced world; hence the term "future shock."

Five years later, Toffler has expanded his vision. He continues

12: The Ideology of Austerity

to speak cheerfully of a leisure society, but his writing is somewhat more sober. He stresses the *ifs*, *ands* and *buts* of his forecasts while previously he had warned against *underutilizing* our ability to predict.[14] Yet just one year later, Robert Sklar noted how far-fetched Toffler's visions seemed in view of the economic recession with its accompanying lay-offs, particularly in the technical professions.[15]

By 1972, Toffler has become more grim. Thus he introduces *The Futurists* by noting that while those who do not learn from history are compelled to relive it, "If we do not change the future, we shall be compelled to endure it. And that could be worse."[16] The first article in *The Futurists* lays out a dreary scenario penned by Paul Ehrlich entitled "Eco-Catastrophe," according to which the death of the ocean is forecast for the summer of 1979 with other disasters wrought by both the U. S. and the USSR shortly to follow.[17]

Finally, by 1975, Toffler reaches a hysterical tone in his *Eco-Spasm Report*. So cataclysmic is the impending economic collapse, that no economic strategy and no political outlook from left, right, or center can cope with it. Rather, what is called for is a "super-industrial" approach that eschews reliance on the nation state. While multi-national corporations must "wake-up to their own interests" by curbing their greed, the unemployed must do their part by setting aside their cravings for material goods, seeking instead to create their own service jobs such as running day-care centers, transporting the elderly and the handicapped and setting up non-profit companies to do household repairs. The basic employment practice recommended is "to provide the most jobs, and the most services, for the least money."[18]

Lest one take Toffler's nonsense as mere journalistic hype, it can be noted that at key points his conclusions jibe with many of the more "scientific" projections Commoner, the Ehrlichs, and the Meadows group have made during the past few years. There are limits to growth we are told. Modern technology-rich production wastes energy and other resources while polluting the environment. Our material comforts come at too high a price, and too many people are clamoring for too much. But except for Commoner the leading futurists do not propose the nationalization of resources under democratic control. Almost all either ignore or denigrate the Marxist tradition and the experience of existing socialism. They accept without analysis the view promoted by the mass media and professional cold-warriors that socialist countries like the Soviet Union are, like the U. S., plagued by heartless technocrats, rampant pollution, gaudy consumerism, and the waste of material resources.

But Marxism and socialism are not the only items overlooked by the futurists. The period from the early 1960's to the present was one of great democratic upsurge in the U. S. and abroad, highlighted by the civil rights and anti-war movements at home and the stupendous defeat of U. S. imperialism in Indo-China. It was also a period of worldwide anti-colonial struggle and of the deterioration of the economic stability of international capitalism. One might think that the defeat of colonialism, a lessening of the Cold War, and significant strides against racism and male supremacy might be cause for optimism in the futurists' projections but such is largely not the case. Instead, it appears that the vision of happy leisure so assiduously promoted a few years ago was more a product of U. S. capitalism's one-time arrogant self-confidence than of humanist values and scientific commitment. Indeed one looks largely in vain for a futurist discussion of the achievements of the anti-colonialist and anti-imperialist movements of the past thirty years, or for recognition of the fact that the emergence of dozens of independent nations was the result of determined struggle against the colonizing powers, a struggle which of necessity affects colonizer and colonized alike.

Paul and Anne Ehrlich, for example, list the entry "morning-after pill" in their index but not "imperialism." For them it seems that "imperialism" is mainly a propaganda term invented by the Soviet Union, which serves to cover up an essential parallelism between U. S. and Soviet policies.[19] Both "developed" and "underdeveloped" countries are to be blamed, the Ehrlich's claim, for the exploitation and underdevelopment of the Third World. The underdeveloped countries, in their view, are unable to use the commodities they produce, and even if the developed countries did not encourage exploitation, the lack of "cultural conditions" for industrialization would likely keep such countries at a low level of development.[20]

Futurists mount similar chauvinist attacks on those Third World countries that *do* manage to exercise some prudent control over the exploitation of their resources. For example, Toffler attempts to blame high fuel prices on the efforts of the Organization of Petroleum Exporting Countries to gain a more equitable deal on their oil sales.[21]

It must be said that those who attack modern technology and urge a return to more primitive forms of labor, regardless of their

12: The Ideology of Austerity

intentions, condemn Third World countries to a permanent impoverished status. Thus Barry Commoner, while making a sharp attact on colonialism, states the view that the production of synthetic fibers drives out the production of natural cotton and rubber and thus deprives "impoverished developing countries," which are "well suited" to produce such natural materials, of an opportunity to attain stronger trading positions.[22] Yet implicit in this view is the idea that labor-intensive, back-breaking production is somehow the permanent lot of such countries, their being "well-suited" for such production. Commoner, it should be said, is generally against all production of synthetic fibers.[23]

Typical of futurism's abstract conception of democracy and its isolation from real social movements is the following passage from Toffler:

> Democratic political forms arose in the West not because a few geniuses willed them into being, or because man showed an "unquenchable instinct for freedom." They arose because the historical pressure towards social differentiation and towards faster-paced systems demanded sensitive social feedback. In complex, differentiated societies, vast amounts of information must flow at ever faster speeds between formal organizations and sub-cultures that make up the whole . . . . Political democracy facilitates feedback.[24]

Toffler tells us that "feedback" is necessary "to assume control over accelerant change."[25] Nowhere in this analysis does there seem to be an awareness of the role of mass struggle and what Marx called "revolutionary practice" in shaping democracy.[26] Indeed the movement of history seems separated from the movement of human beings. It is thus no wonder that when mass democratic movements such as those of the 1960's develop the futurists are caught napping.

The lack of attention to real social processes not only accounts for futurism's sterile view of democracy and its distortion of the class struggle, it also lies at the base of the movement from *leisure* to *austerity*. These concepts, although seeming to be opposites, share a common lack of appreciation of the creative role of labor so central to Marx's understanding of the productive process. The failure to take into account the productive process in all its richness and diversity is the hallmark of philosophical idealism.

3. Idealism and Shades of Malthus

One recognizes in futurism the influence of major contemporary bourgeois philosophical trends, especially the conception of science which these trends encourage. Both the neo-positivist analytic school and the existentialist-phenomenological school deny that science uncovers objective truth about the material world. For the first school, science is essentially a process of describing, inferring, and testing in order to arrive at a body of interconnected statements, including those articulating scientific laws. Such statements are usually construed as denoting "sense data" composed of atomistic parts. Material objects are, at best, constructions of "sense data." Knowledge of a "real" world beyond sensations and independent of them is viewed to be beyond the limits of experience.[27] In many ways the contemporary "analysts" follow Kant in erecting a wall between the world as experienced and the world as it actually is. For the existentialist-phenomenological school, the generalized statements of science involve assumptions and linguistic constructions which fail to reflect the unique particularities of individual conscious experience.[28]

Despite their differing approaches, there is no room in either of these schools for viewing science as an activity that unites the individual with the objective world in a dialectical manner, an activity which is equally the development of *scientists* and their capacities as well as the development of descriptions and laws concerning the physical universe. For much of contemporary bourgeois philosophy, scientific knowledge is mainly composed of rigid, highly formalized conceptions. The substitution of concepts for material content puts the trends we have discusses squarely in the camp of idealism.

Dialectical materialists recognize that ideas are not absolute, but that they are partial reflections of the material world, reflections which must be constantly refined in order to move closer to the realities of that world. For Marxists, science is an activity directed towards approaching and understanding the infinite richness of matter and its interactions. There are no unbridgeable dualisms, no absolute barriers between consciousness and material reality. Understanding scientifically the interconnections in the material world is distinct from passively hooking together separate

12: The Ideology of Austerity

absolute ideas or "sense data."

The Marxist conception of science is drastically different from that of the futurists. Futurism begins with "atoms" of the present, for example, the Meadows group's conception of usage rate trends. These "atoms" are separately projected into the future by mathematical processes and then passively hooked together creating a future of fixed ideas. Out of such projections comes the Meadows group's conclusion that there will occur a general catastrophe around the year 2050.[29]

It is precisely the scientific and pseudo-scientific content of these writings which infuses them with much of their persuasive power. The fact that even idealist approaches are influenced by the development of science was noted by Engels in his remark that "idealist systems" are forced to fill themselves "more and more with a materialist content."[30] But this content remains devoid of the recognition of the role of ongoing material processes including the productive activities of human beings. The separation of science as abstract product from science as human activity results in the further separation of scientific and technological propositions from the concrete human resources and potentials which form an essential component of the knowledge of such propositions described. These separations distort one's understanding of both the propositions and the human resources involved; they are highly evident in the futurists' widespread adoption of Malthusian conceptions of population growth and of other matters.

Thomas R. Malthus argued that population expands at a geometric rate while the means of subsistence expands at a mere arithmetic rate. He thus urged a cutback on charity to stem the ability of what he called the "surplus population" to reproduce.[31] This conception of a surplus population was thoroughly criticized by Marx and Engels. Engels, for example, pointed out that Malthus confused the *means of subsistence* (one's actual capacity to produce for basic survival) with the *means of employment* (the given relations of production in a given socio-economic system such as capitalism). Every grown person, Engels argued, is *capable* of producing more than he consumes, else humankind could not multiply. Engels also challenged Malthus' claim that while population increases geometrically, the productive power of the land (an essential part of the means of subsistence) increases only arithmetically. Even if population growth is not always matched by a growth in *labor-power*, the growth of science "whose progress is as unceasing and at least as rapid as that of the population" makes up for such shortcomings.[32] When one considers the enormous productive potential of the ocean, and the energy potential of the atom, Engels' remarks would seem to be equally valid at the present time.[33] On the other hand not every potential increase in the means of subsistence will be realized if it is not dependent on comparable increases in the means of employment as they exist under capitalism. Engels observes that:

> Only in their end-result are the means of employment increased by the increase in machine power and capital. The means of subsistence increase as soon as productive power increases even slightly.[34]

Thus, through the restrictions it engenders in attempts to increase the means of employment, capitalism may well restrict immediate growth of the means of subsistence, but it cannot restrict the potential growth of those means of subsistence dependent upon science. Malthus, however, employs the economic limits of capitalism to define supply and demand and to characterize the unemployed population as surplus. Engels continues:

> The economist's "demand" is not the real demand; his "consumption" is an artificial consumption. For the economist, only that person really demands, only that person is a real consumer, who has an equivalent to offer for what he receives. But if it is a fact that every adult produces more than he himself can consume, that children are like trees which give superabundant returns on the outlays invested in them — and certainly these are facts, are they not? — then one ought to believe that each worker should be able to produce far more than he needs and that the community, therefore, should be very glad to provide him with everything he needs.[35]

It may be asked why capitalism cannot make greater use of the "surplus population" in order to expand production and the means of subsistence. Marx answers this question on Volume I of *Capital*, where he describes the basic features of capitalist production. Under such production the *exchange value* of what a worker produces in a given day exceeds that of his *labor-power*. The capitalist seeks to pay only for the worker's labor-power, thus appropriating for himself a *surplus value* equal to the difference between the exchange value of the labor-power and that of the total product the worker produces in a given day. Out of this surplus value comes the capitalist's profit. This profit is the basis of what Marx calls "expanded capital." Such capital in part will be put back into the productive process. Marx, however, distinguishes two types of advanced capital, that which goes to procure the means of production (tools, machines, raw materials, interest, rent, etc.) and that which goes for procuring labor-power (i.e., that which is advanced for wages). The former is known as *constant capital*, while the later is called *variable capital*.[36]

Only variable capital undergoes the alteration in value during the productive process, for it brings a day's worth of products in exchange for a day's worth of labor-power, assuming wages are equal to the value of labor-power. Only the variable component of capital can grow, yet as Marx later points out, the proportion of variable capital to total capital decreases as the total capital accumulates. This decrease is due to increased use of machinery and technology as a means to raise productivity. As capitalist competition develops each capitalist strives to outproduce and undersell the other, thus revolutionizing the means of production.[37]

Machines, however, do not create new value. Rather "like every other component of constant capital" machinery "yields up its own value to the product it serves to beget."[38] As machines replace workers those replaced are forced to compete with those still employed for a diminishing portion of available capital. According to Marx the increase in the total laboring population is "always moving more rapidly than that of the variable capital or the means of employment."[39] Thus is created the reserve army of labor or relative surplus population. But this "surplus" is what it is solely due to capitalism's dependence on variable capital to put it to work. Without such capital its productive capabilities are of no use, except as a means to pressure those employed to keep their wage demands modest.

The subordination of the so-called surplus population to the demands of capital leads to the inability to see the human population itself as a resource. This inability is a central feature of

Malthusianism, and it is widely adopted by the futurists who seem to analyze every resource but the human. This undialectical approach leads to both sociological and technological distortions. Social statistics are separated from technical capabilities and vice versa. These mechanically separated categories are then projected mathematically to create an abstract model of the future used to stimulate political action in the present. However, the projected model retains little of its roots with living reality. The *costs* of developing new technologies, such as technologies to alleviate pollution and waste, and the *costs* of putting the unemployed to work are *costs* calculated in terms of capitalism and its need to reproduce surplus value through the exploitation of labor-power. Machinery is not seen as a means to shorten the workday and hire more employees, rather it is seen as rendering people superfluous.

An illustration of futurism's modern-day Malthusian approach is provided by the Meadows group's discussion of chromium consumption. Three trends: chromium reserves presently known, usage rates based on present technology, and actual costs based on capitalist economic relations are abstracted and projected mathematically. This results in the prediction of a chromium crisis to occur around 2050. The possibilities of new technologies such as the development of chromium substitutes and new recovery techniques and of newly discovered reserves are also programmed in with little change in the forecast of disaster. What is particularly significant in the Meadows group's data is the view that *costs* rise faster than new technologies can bring them down. What is crucial, however, is that the *costs* referred to here are *capitalist* costs based on the use and expansion of variable capital. The Meadows group concludes:

> Given present resource consumption rates and the projected increase in these rates, the great majority of the currently non-renewable resources will be extremely costly 100 years from now.[40]

Based on the above analysis the authors of *The Limits to Growth* urge the adoption of a global "no-growth" economic system. One is reminded here of a similar urging by Malthus who feared that the more forward-looking capitalists of his time would view the aristocracy as the parasitic class it actually was. Malthus had defended the aristocracy's playing the necessary role of unproductive consumers, consuming the excess goods which the capitalists could not consume themselves and which the working class could not afford to consume because of its need to be thrifty.[41] Marx compares what he calls the "honesty" of the classical economist David Ricardo in recognizing the productive capabilities of capitalism irrespective of their effect on particular classes with the "contemptible" Malthus who draws "only those conclusions which are *acceptable* and useful to the aristocracy as against the bourgeoisie and to both as against the proletariat."[42] Could it be that the "science" of the Meadows group and other futurists is falsified precisely at the point where its conclusions might threaten capitalism or a section of capitalists?

4. Leisure, Labor, and Thermodynamics

As we have noted the development of idealist thinking is not insulated from the progress of science, yet the futurist conception of science and technology takes on a fetishized form in which the inanimate, non-human component of technology is equated with the whole. The fact that science and technology can either liberate or enslave humanity was dramatically noted by Marx:

> In our days everything seems pregnant with its contrary. Machinery, gifted with the wonderful power of shortening and fructifying human labor, we behold starving and overworking it. The newfangled sources of wealth, by some strange, weird spell, are turned into sources of want. . . . Even the pure life of science seems unable to shine but on the dark background of ignorance. All our invention and progress seem to result in endowing material forces with intellectual life, and in stultifying human life into a material force.[43]

Machines, of course, are both made and operated by human beings. If they cannot be operated they cease to be machines. But as humans transform the natural environment to create machines, humans also transform themselves. The development of technology is thus both a physical and social transformation. Yet

Marx shows how this process is misperceived. The expropriation of the products of one's labor obscures the social nature of production; thus humankind's creations stand detached or *estranged* from their creators. The essential interrelation between an individual and what he has created is hidden, or, in Marx's words:

> ... if the product of man' labor, his labor objectified, is for him an *alien*, hostile, powerful object independent of him, then his position towards it is such that someone else is master of this object, someone who is alien, hostile, powerful, and independent of him...[44]

As the products of one's labors become commodities they become fetishized. That which was actually the product of a relation between persons and things is seen as a relation solely between things. There is a second aspect to this fetishism. Technology and machinery are viewed basically as "labor-saving" rather than as "labor-enhancing." This way of viewing labor and technology lies, we believe, at the base of the futurist tendency to project the desirability, if not the inevitability, of a "leisure society." The "good life" is seen as a life of conspicuous consumption rather than one of organized production for human welfare.

As we have already noted, machinery and services do not of themselves produce additional value for the capitalists. As the proportion of variable capital to the total shrinks, and as devices for temporarily overcoming capitalism's contradictions, such as the super-exploitation derived from imperialism, become less available, the "leisure society" becomes less credible. The projection of leisure is replaced by that of austerity.

From the Marxian standpoint, *leisure* and *austerity* are the twin offspring of technology fetishism. Neither concept contains a recognition of the special role of labor, as an essential element in technology or as the key to human fulfillment. In his *1844 Manuscripts* Marx noted a similar opposition of "luxury" and "thrift". He points out that writers like Malthus stressed the need for luxury, the consumption of luxuries being thought necessary to the stimulation of production, while others like Ricardo urged thrift as a stimulus. Marx continues:

> Everything which the political economist

12: The Ideology of Austerity

takes from you in life and humanity, he replaces for you in *money* and in *wealth*; and all things which you cannot do, your money can do.[45]

But money brings things not through the active creative role of the individual but through its power over others. Individuals who flaunt their wealth are "ephemeral" people who can know others and themselves only as individuals who are "sacrificed and empty".[46] Marx contrasts the alienation of individuals in a class-divided society with the full potential of liberated labor:

> The transcendence of private property is therefore the complete *emancipation* of all human senses and qualities, but it is this emancipation precisely because these senses and attributes have become subjectively and objectively *human*. The eye has become a *human* eye just as its *object* has become a social *human* object — an object made by man for man . . .
>
> In the same way the senses and minds of other men have become my *own* appropriation. Besides these direct organs, therefore, social organs develop in the form of society; thus, for instance, activity in direct association with others, etc. has become an organ for *expressing* my own *life*, and a mode for appropriating human life.[47]

Thus for Marx the future is ultimately to be shaped by emancipated human labor, while the fetishized technology of the futurists can offer only the presence or absence of commodities. Just as Malthus saw in the unemployed population only a wasteful surplus, the neo-Malthusians of today see an excess population straining present resources. The tapping of the resource of the population itself is blocked by capitalism's need to extract surplus value.

As evidence of the qualitative role of labor in production, which futurism tends to overlook, the Soviet writer, Arab-Ogly, notes the findings of the French demographer, Alfred Sauvy, and the U.S. economist, Edward Denison, to the effect that the growth of production in the U.S. and other capitalist countries has been due more to *estensive* factors. That is, greater wealth is more a product of better organization and higher skill levels than of increased employment and the growth of fixed capital.[48] An indication that this trend is likely to continue is suggested by the continuing increase in the proportion of the U.S. labor force composed of skilled scientific and technical workers. For example, between 1960 and 1973, while the size of the total U.S. labor force increased 24 percent, the number of professional and technical workers grew 61 percent, increasing from 11 to 14 percent of the total.[49] This qualitative transformation of the work force signals an important change in the forces of production. Technology itself is becoming more and more a direct productive force. This fact provides further evidence of the importance of not overlooking the qualitative side of labor, but most futurists continue to do so. A recent example of this mistake is the work of Barry Commoner.

Commoner's book *The Poverty of Power* contains an eloquent and moving description of economic waste and its human costs. Moreover, Commoner does not shirk from laying the blame for the present environmental and economic crises at the doorstep of monopoly capitalism. Towards the end of his book he calls for socialism.[50]

Although his analysis of socialism is brief and filled with anti-Communist and anti-Soviet innuendos, Commoner does employ the term in a form meaningful enough for Marxists to take seriously if not fully accept. Moreover, he brings to his disucssion a strong scientific background, a fact which adds weight to what he has to say. However, his book defends a number of anti-working class conceptions and, as we shall try to show, falls into the trap of technology fetishism.

It might be objected that Commoner really is not a futurist in the sense we have been employing this term. To be sure, no other major futurist writer has so specifically and persuasively condemned capitalism. Nevertheless, his approach involves the typical futurist method of constructing a conceptualized future and using it as his primary vehicle for thought and action. He achieves this conceptualization by using the Second Law of Thermodynamics to postulate the eventual running out of available energy. Present rates of energy consumption are hastening this catastrophe.

The Second Law of Thermodynamics notes the tendency of energy systems to move towards a state of equilibrium (maximum unavailable energy or *entropy*). A piece of ice, for example, when placed in a cup of warm water melts while cooling down the water. Eventually, the water seems to be a uniform medium temperature. The Law extends this principle to all closed energy systems. Stars, including our sun, are cooling down. On earth, Commoner maintains, available energy in the form of fuel resources is being "irretrievably lost."[51] Commoner goes on to show how the production of many synthetic materials such as plastics uses up large amounts of energy which cannot be retrieved except at the price of using even greater amounts to retrieve them.[52] Because the mass production of plastics is highly profitable, plastics have been substituted for other more energy-efficient materials.

Commoner also claims that highly mechanized production systems expend enormous amounts of energy. While such systems increase the level of productivity per worker, they do so by wasting both energy and capital. In Commoner's view labor too is wasted, for modern production methods require less "participation" of labor than those of earlier periods, thus the ability of the productive system to "regenerate jobs" is weakened.[53]

What then is Commoner's solution? It would appear to be a return to more "capital-efficient" production using less modern technology and less energy. Artificial materials are to be replaced with "natural" ones, thus insuring the creation of jobs through more "participation" of labor in the productive process.

It is hard to see how Commoner can avoid the charge that his recommendations call for the continuation of primitive manual labor as the principal form of production for a good part of the world. Indeed his comments to the effect that certain underdeveloped countries are "particularly suited" to the production of natural fibers would seem to be advocating that they remain the "labor-intensive" centers imperialism and colonialism have made them to be.[54]

Does the Second Law of Thermodynamics have the implications Commoner attributes to it? He believes this principle mandates as "the fate of the universe" a "downhill process" which is "irreversible." He admits that living things can create "islands of order" through the wise use of resources based on understanding the law, but such possibilities do not change the overall result.[55] But does the law mandate such a result? Many scientists do not share Commoner's view. The infinite size of the universe may accomodate entropy-increasing activities as well as those which go the other way. And what precisely does it mean to say entropy is always increasing in an infinite system? Does this mean a running out of energy? J. D. Bernal points out that entropy can be said to increase only in "closed systems." Is the universe such a system?[56]

In his work *Dialectics of Nature* Frederick Engels noted the idealist, pro-creationish implications of what has been called the "thermal death" interpretation of the Second Law.[57] Such an interpretation ignores the infinite organization and richness of both matter and energy. More recently, the Soviet biologist M. M. Kamshilov remarks how organization and interaction are inherent features of matter that can never reach an equilibrium in some maximum entropy state.[58] He notes the tendency to confuse the *purely energetic* with the *informational* aspects of energy, as Commoner does. Doing so overlooks the fact that the decisive anti-entropic aspect of the development of human beings "belongs to the accumulation of information" rather than the expenditure of energy.[59] There is thus no inherent "disorganizing" factor in life as the "thermal death" view would seem to suggest. One sees here an up-to-date formulation of Engels' well-known comments concerning the "spiritual element in production" which the bourgeois economists of his time ignored, and which Commoner also seems to ignore. Labor, Engels maintains, is not merely "sheer labor" that is, physical force. It includes the element of invention, and this element comes free from nature.[60]

The labor-intensive, "organic" style of production favored by Commoner ignores the qualitative dimension of labor. Instead labor is set abstractly against raw materials and the principle of energy-efficiency is applied exclusively to physical resources and brute labor. This view turns much of the human resource into an unusable "surplus" in the tradition of Malthus. Commoner also holds that the U. S. at present is experiencing a capital shortage which hinders setting labor and the means of production to work at full capacity.[61] Victor Perlo has noted that Commoner's claim of such a shortage seems absurd in the light of vast idle capacity and record profits.[62] Yet it seems to us that Commoner is, in part, led to this conclusion by precisely his failure to recognize fully the qualitiative dimension of labor. Humankind is just beginning to tap the energy of the atom. If, as Commoner suggests, we are to be guided by thermodynamic principles, then the waste of the special resource of creative human labor falls under these principles. But futurism does not grow out of real living labor, but is far more a product of detached speculation.

5. The Divisive Effects of Futurism

Malthus was the protector of aristocrats. Whose interests does futurism serve? As we have noted it mainly aims to retain capitalism or, at best, to project an austere form of socialism. Its quasi-scientific rationalizations on behalf of austerity and cutbacks in living standards serve the interests of anti-working-class policies. But there are differences among capitalists and various petit-bourgeois strata. Those tendencies in futurism which hold that we are running out of oil do not see eye to eye with the oil monopolists who calim unlimited supplies provided "incentives" (i.e. super-profits) are granted. It seems to us that much of futurism has a special appeal to certain middle strata, including some of the "smaller" capitalist groupings, presently being squeezed by the giant international monopolies. The Club of Rome which sponsored the Meadows *Limits to Growth* report seems to be composed mainly of European and Japanese but not U.S. monopoly capitalists. Intellectual strata are a particular target of futurism. Persons in this grouping are highly sensitive to the special questions futurism raises while being vulnerable to the pressures created by the present crisis of capitalism.

In the United States, the expanded commitment to education in the early 1960's brought many new students and faculty to the campuses, often from working-class backgrounds. They were profoundly affected by the democratic movements of the time. Patterns of Cold-War thinking and elitism began to give way. The onset of the education crisis has given rise to diverse responses. Many professors are organizing into trade unions at an extremely rapid rate. The American Federation of Teachers which had only 3,000 members at the college level in 1967, now has over 63,000.[63] This unionization brings intellectual strata into closer association with the industrial proletariat and its outlook.

While changes are taking place in the status of the professoriat, similar changes are taking place among intellectual workers as a whole. The U. S. Census Bureau reports that the percentage of all professionals in the self-employed category has dropped from 36.9 in 1950 to 15.3 in 1960 and to 7.4 in 1970.[64] Obviously, such workers are becoming more and more integrated into large-scale enterprises and, with this process, are being transformed into wage workers. This "proletarianization" has the potential to disrupt the traditional role of the professional elite as a bulwark of the status quo.

By the concept of "general guilt" futurism attempts to counter ideologically any militant trends, especially ones of class struggle, which may develop amongst the intelligensia. Instead, it attempts to enlist participation in the austerity crusade. Robert Heilbroner, for example, offers the view of intellectuals being "sentries for society" with the task of preparing "their fellow citizens for the sacrifices that will be required of them" while taking "the lead in seeking to redefine the legitimate boundaries of power and the permissible sanctuaries of freedom . . ."[65]

By exploiting legitimate concerns regarding the utilization of resources and the hope for a rational future, plus the prevailing scepticism regarding traditional institutions, futurism exerts an extremely divisive influence on movements for progressive change. It is an influence dripping with elitism, racism, and hypocrisy. Its cries for austerity are rarely aimed at monopoly corporations or the military which wastes more resources than any other institution. Instead they are aimed at the working class and middle class, and they are aimed in a cynical and manipulative way. Possible future shortages of certain resources like petroleum and natural gas are used as excuses for artificially-created present shortages designed to maximize profits. In December, 1973 in the midst of the famous gasoline shortage, Senator William Proxmire warned his constituents of how the impending energy crisis was everybody's fault because they had blandly shrugged off earlier warnings to conserve fuel. He then cheerfully suggested that perhaps doing with a bit less might be a positive educational experience.[66] Perhaps for some it would, but what lesson is it supposed to teach to persons like the friends and relatives of Eugene J. Kuhn, late of Mansfield, Ohio, who during the bitter winter of 1976-77 froze to death in his home because the Ohio Edison Company shut off his power after he failed to pay a bill of $18.38? A spokesman for the company said it was a "sad thing" that Kuhn died, but confessed that he could not think of any policy which could prevent similar occurences.[67]

Marxists know that there is a solution. The powers of genuine science and learning are on the side of the struggle for prosperity and for socialism. The ideological trap of the obscurantist, anti-technological, and Malthusian notions of the futurists stands in the way of gaining the ideological clarity and political unity to harness those powers.

Notes

1. The term "futurology" as used in this essay seems to have been first used by Ossip Flechteim in 1943. Flechteim sought to inject into the "value-free" positivist conception of science prevailing at the time a sense of ideological commitment with frankly anti-Communist aims in order to counter "Marxist Utopian thinking." See Ossip Flechteim, "Futurology — the New Science of Probability," in Alvin Toffler, ed., *The Futurists* (New York; Random House, 1972), pp. 264-76; also, Ossip Flechteim, *History and Futurology* (Meisenheim am Glan: Hain, 1966).
2. Alvin Toffler, *Future Shock* (New York: Random House, 1970); Marshall McLuhan, *Understanding Media: The Extensions of Man* (New York: McGraw-Hill, 1964, 1966) and *The Medium is the Massage* (New York: Random House, 1967); Paul Ehrlich, *The Population Bomb* (New York: Ballantine Books, 1968), and with Anne Ehrlich, *Population, Resources, Environment: Issues in Human Ecology*, (San Francisco: W. H. Freeman, 1970, 1972); Donella H. Meadows and Dennis L. Meadows, *et. al.*, *The Limits to Growth* (New York: New American Library, 1972, 1974); Barry Commoner, *The Closing Circle* (New York: Knopf, 1971), and *The Poverty of Power* (New York: Knopf, 1976).
3. Above all see Daniel Bell, *The Coming of Post-Industrial Society* (New York: Basic Books, 1973); also Herman Kahn and Anthony J. Wiener, *The Year 2000* (New York and London: Macmillan, 1967).
4. In addition to the work of the Ehrlichs, the Meadows group, and Commoner, one might cite Robert L. Heilbroner, *An Inquiry into the Human Prospect* (New York: Norton, 1974, 1975), for an extremely strident statement of this view.
5. Toffler, *Future Shock*, p. 5. Hegel once observed that the Owl of Minerva "spreads its wings only with the falling of dusk": i.e., serious philosophical analysis requires a rooting in established objective fact. For the futurists, on the other hand, it seems that the Owl is to fly at dawn bumping into the first tree in its path.
6. Marshall McLuhan, "Automation: Learning a Living," in

Toffler, *The Futurists*, p. 65.
7. Alvin Toffler, *The Eco-Spasm Report* (Toronto and New York: Bantam Books, 1975), p. 117.
8. *Wall Street Journal* staff, *Here Comes Tomorrow* (Princeton, N. J.: Dow Jones Books, 1966, 1967).
9. *Ibid.*, p. 13, 16.
10. *Ibid.*, pp. 59-72.
11. *Ibid.*, p. 180.
12. *Ibid.*, p. 152.
13. *Horizon* (Summer, 1965), pp. 109-15. Women exist in Toffler's projections only as mothers who, in their simple ignorance, will not be able to assure their *sons* that they will enter a particular profession.
14. Compare *Future Shock*, p. 7 with Toffler *Horizon* article p. 115.
15. *Ramparts* (March, 1971), p. 58.
16. Toffler, *The Futurists*, p. 3.
17. *Ibid.*, pp. 13-26.
18. Toffler, *The Eco-Spasm Report*, pp. 77, 87. Toffler's "scientific" approach to forecasting is indicated in his preface (p. viii) where he tells us his research on current economic conditions took the form of jetting around the international lecture circuit and conversing with "a prime minister, many cabinet officials, economists, businessmen, union leaders, feminists, students, environmentalists, right wingers, and middle-of-the-roaders." He also "attended rallies and read leaflets."
19. Ehrlich and Ehrlich, *Population, Resources, Environment*, p. 422.
20. *Ibid.*, p. 405.
21. Toffler, *The Eco-spasm Report*, pp. 56-57.
22. Commoner, *The Poverty of Power*, p. 236.
23. *Ibid.*, pp. 195-210.
24. Toffler, *Future Shock*, pp. 420-21.
25. *Ibid.*, p. 421.
26. Karl Marx, "Theses on Feuerbach" in Karl Marx and Frederick Engels, *The German Ideology* (abridged), (New York: International Publishers, 1970), pp. 121-23.
27. See Ernest Nagel, *The Structure of Science* (London: Routledge & Kegan Paul, 1961), p. 6; see also Norman Campbell, *What is Science?* (New York: Dover Publications, 1952), Chapter III.

28. See Jean-Paul Sartre, *Being and Nothingness*, trans. by Hazel E. Barnes (New York: Philosophical Library, 1956), p. xlix and Part III, Chapter 2; see also James Lawler, *The Existentialist Marxism of Jean-Paul Sartre* (Amsterdam: B. R. Gruner Publishing Co., 1976), Chapter 5. For a general Marxist discussion of contemporary bourgeois philosophical trends see F. V. Konstantinov et. al., *The Fundamentals of Marxist-Leninist Philosophy* (Moscow: Progress Publishers, 1974), Chapter XXII, especially pp. 604-24.
29. Meadows and Meadows, p. 129.
30. Frederick Engels, *Ludwig Feuerbach and the Outcome of Classical German Philosophy* (New York, International Publishers, 1941), p. 24.
31. Thomas R. Malthus, *First Essay on Populaton* (New York: A. M. Kelly, Bookseller, 1965).
32. Frederick Engels, "Outlines of a Critique of Political Economy" in Karl Marx, *The Economic and Philosophical Manuscripts of 1844*, ed. by Dirk J. Struik, trans. by Martin Milligan (New York: International Publishers, 1964), pp. 219-222.
33. For a Marxist discussion of this issue see V. Kosolapov, *Mankind and the year 2000* (Moscow: Progress Publishers, 1976).
34. Marx, *Economic and Philosophical Manuscripts*, p. 220.
35. *Ibid*.
36. Karl Marx, *Capital*, Vol. I (New York: International Publishers, 1967), pp. 186-211.
37. *ibid.*, p. 622.
38. *Ibid.*, p. 387.
39. *Ibid.*, p. 630.
40. Meadows and Meadows, p. 75.
41. Thomas R. Malthus, *Principles of Political Economy*, Second Edition (New York, A. M. Kelly, Bookseller, 1964), Book II, Chapter 1, Section IX, see also *Capital* I P. 595.
42. Karl Marx "Malthus as Apologist" (from *Theories of Surplus Value*, Vol. II in *Marx and Engels on the Population Bomb*, ed. by Ronald Meek (Berkeley: Ramparts Press, 1971), pp. 132-37.
43. Karl Marx, "A Speech in London," in Howard Selsam, David Goldway, and Harry Martel, eds., *Dynamics of Social Change* (New York: International Publishers, 1970), p. 335.
44. Marx, *Economic and Philosophical Manuscripts*, p. 116.

45. *Ibid.*, p. 150.
46. *Ibid.*, p. 156.
47. *Ibid.*, pp. 139-40.
48. Eduard Arab-Ogly, *In the Forecasters' Maze*, (Moscow: Progress Publishers, 1975), pp. 205-06. This book contains a general discussion on futurism by a Soviet Marxist.
49. U. S. Dept. of Commerce in *Information Please Almanac, 1964* (New York: Simon and Shuster, 1963) p. 280; and U. S. Bureau of Labor Statistics in *Information Please Almanac, 1975* (New York: Information Please Almanac, 1974), p. 73.
50. Commoner, *The Power of Poverty*, pp. 243-47.
51. *Ibid.*, p. 29.
52. *Ibid.*, pp. 23, 195-210.
53. *Ibid.*, p. 226.
54. *Ibid.*, p. 236.
55. *Ibid.*, pp. 20-24.
56. A number of writers have denied that the Second Law applies to the universe as a whole in the way it applies to a "closed system." See for example J. D. Bernal, *Science in History*, Third Illustrated Edition, Vol. 3 (Cambridge, Mass.: M.I.T. Press, 1971), pp. 903-04 and Jacob Bronowski, *The Ascent of Man* (Boston and Toronto, Little, Brown and Company, 1973), pp. 347-48.
57. Frederick Engels, *Dialectics of Nature*, trans. and ed. by Clemens Dutt (New York, International Publishers, 1940), p. 216.
58. M. M. Kamshilov, *Evolution of the Biosphere* (Moscow: Mir Publishers, 1976), pp. 18-19.
59. *Ibid.*, p. 222.
60. engels, "Outlines . . ." in Marx, *Economic and Philosophical Manuscripts*, discussion of the relation of labor to thermodynamic principles from the standpoint of dialectical materialism, see David Morgan, "Barry Commoner and the Second Law of Thermodynamics" in *Science and Nature*, No. 1 (1978), pp. 15-25.
61. commoner, 1976, p. 230.
62. Victor Perlo, *Book Review*, "The Poverty of Power" in *Political Affairs*, November, 1976, p. 59.
63. Figures for 1967 are from John Pappademos, "Intellectuals and the Working Class" in Gerald Erickson and Harold L. Schwartz, eds., *Social Class in the Contemporary United*

States (Minneapolis: Marxist Educational Press, 1977), p. 78: 1978 figures from *American Teacher* (September, 1978), P. A26.
64. Pappademos, in *Social Class*, p. 78.
65. Heilbroner, *An Inquiry*, p. 137.
66. For this episode and a general Marxist discussion of the 1973 "energy crisis" see Gus Hall, *The Energy Rip-off* (New York: International Publishers, 1974).
67. *Waterloo Courier*, January 14, 1977, p. 2.

SCIENCE & SOCIETY

───── An Independent Journal of Marxism ─────

From Recent Issues

**HISTORY OF MATHAMATICS IN THE AGE OF
  IMPERIALISM** *Beatrice Lumpkin*

**ON MATERIALIST CONTRADICTIONS:
  A CRITICISM** *Morris Colman*

**ON MATERIALIST CONTRADICTIONS:
  A REPLY** *M. Mark Mussachia*

**WORKING WIVES: THEIR EFFECTS ON
  THE STRUCTURE OF THE WORKING
  CLASS** *Gabriel Kolko*

**"THE TRADITION OF AMERICAN
  REVOLUTION LITERATURE":
  THE MONTHLY** *NEW MASSES*, **1926 – 1933**
  David Peck

| Subscription: $10 | Foreign Subscription: $12 |
| Institution: $15 | Foreign Institution: $17 |

SCIENCE & SOCIETY, 445 West 59th Street, New York, New York 10019

gulliver

Deutsch-Englische Jahrbücher / German-English Yearbook

GULLIVER intends to become for German and English-speaking scholars, producers of culture, and representatives of democratic movements a medium of 'horizontal' communication, so that not everything that comes into the Federal Republic will first be filtered through the hierarchies of multinational companies or the 'think-tanks' of the state apparatus. Thus GULLIVER prints articles, conference reports, and reviews in both languages.

No. 1 contained critical essays on Shakespeare, Shelley, industrial folk song, James Connolly, Caudwell, the Left in Britain, progressive American theatre, and Segal's *Love Story*.

No. 2 focussed on cultural studies and had contributions by Raymond Williams, Stuart Hall, Graham Murdock, David Craig, Dieter Herms, H. Gustav Klaus and many others.

No. 3, a special US number, is out now
DIRK HOERDER: Radical Equality or Liberal Rhetoric
PHILIP S. FONER: The Black Workers and Organised Labor in the 70s
KLAUS ENSSLEN: Schwarze Autobiographie in den USA seit 1960
ARNO PAUL: Zum Theater der San Francisco Mime Troupe
RICHARD RUNDELL: Ragtime – Bicentennial Nostalgia
PAUL BATES: The Significance of *Roots*
(English abstracts of German articles are included)

Editorial address: Thomas Metscher
                     Heidland 15
                     2802 OTTERSBERG 2 (W. Germany)

Price: DM 15.50 per issue (DM 12 for students)

Orders from:

Argument-Verlag, Postfach 21 0730, 7500 KARLSRUHE 21 (W.-Germany)

A Journal of Radical Perspectives on the Arts

praxis 4

Democracy must occasionally be bathed in blood.
Junta boss Pinochet speaking on behalf of ITT, CIA, Kennecott Corp., etc.

Robert Sayre, 'Goldmann and Modern Realism: Introduction to the *Balcony* Article'

Lucien Goldmann, 'Genet's *The Balcony*: A Realist Play'

Stefan Morawski, 'Historicism and the Philosophy of Art'

Alan W. Barnett, 'José Hernández Delgadillo: The New Art of the Mexican Revolution'

Marc Zimmerman, 'Exchange and Production: Structuralist and Marxist Approaches to Literary Theory'

Ariel Dorfman, 'The Invisible Chile: Three Years of Cultural Resistance'

Marc Ferro, '*La grande illusion*: Its Divergent Receptions in Europe'

Andrew Turner, '*Ballads Moribundus*' (28 drawings)

William Hartley, '*Lambras*: A Vision of Hell in the Third World'

James Goodwin, 'The Object(ive)s of Cinema: Vertov (Factography) and Eisenstein (Ideography)'

G. L. Ulmen, 'Aesthetics in a "Disenchanted World"'

Louis Aragon, 'John Heartfield and Revolutionary Beauty'

Kenneth Coutts-Smith, 'The Political Art of Klaus Staeck' (with over 60 reproductions)

'The Image as Weapon: Interview with, and Photomontages by, Christer Themptander'

Gregory Renault, 'Over the Rainbow: Dialect and Ideology in *The Wizard of Oz*'

Alberto Asor Rosa, 'Gramsci and Italian Cultural History'

Stefan Heym, 'The Indifferent Man' (short story)

Heinz Brüggemann, 'Bertolt Brecht and Karl Korsch: Questions of Living and Dead Elements Within Marxism'

Richard Albrecht and Matthias Mitzschke, 'Bert Brecht: "Bolshevik Without a Party Book" or *Petit-Bourgeois* Intellectual?'

Thomas McGrath, 'Some Notes on Walter Lowenfels'

'The Spanish Civil War: A Portrait in Verse, with Photographs by Hans Namuth and Georg Reisner'

Plus notes and discussion by Leonard Henny, Edward Baker and Bram Dijkstra; short reviews by *Lee Baxandall, Jonah Raskin, Frank Galassi and David Peck;* poetry by *Yannis Ritsos, Ernesto Cardenal, Denise Levertov, Ricardo Alonso, Margaret Randall, Teresa de Jesus, Vincente Gomez Kemp, Don Gordon, Walter Lowenfels;* drawings by *Rene Castro.*

Single copies: $3.75. Individual subscriptions (*including* outside the U.S.): $7.00 for two issues. Sustaining subscriptions: $25.00. For checks in Canadian dollars please add 10%.

Praxis. P.O. Box 207, Goleta, California 93017 USA

Black Liberation Journal

AN EYE OPENER

BLACK LIBERATION JOURNAL   235 West 23rd Street   New York, New York 10011

$4.00 (U.S. & Canada)
$5.50 (Foreign)

LEFT CURVE

Magazine published by artists on the role of culture in the struggle for liberation.

Issue #7 includes:

- analysis of mural movement
- photography of Lester Balog
- history of Artist's International
- Italy today including photos of daily life
- (Provisional) Art & Language: Auckland 1976
- contemporary appalacian poetry
- practice of architecture - from positivism to dialectics
- video on the left: a critique
- critique of Harvey Swados
- Teamsters Graphic Group
- Radical Elders Oral History Project
- plus reviews, documents, letters, etc.

$2.50/copy Subs. $7 (3 issues)
                $10 Institutions

1230 Grant Ave. Box 302
San Francisco, Ca. 94133

art and revolution

GRAZER PHILOSOPHISCHE STUDIEN

From Recent Issues:

Die Philosophie Franz Brentanos

Edgar Morscher, Brentano and His Place in Austrian Philosophy; *Stephan Korner*, Uber Brentanos Reismus und die extensionale Logik; *Burnham Terrell*, Quantification and Brentano's Logic; *Klaus Hedwig*, Der scholastische Kontext des Intentionalen bei Bretano.

Aufsatze/Articles
Barry Smith, An Essay in Formal Ontology; *Ryszard Zuber*, Analycity and Genericness; *Saul Traiger*, Some Remarks on Lehrer and Richard's "Remembering Without Knowing."

Besprechungen/Review Articles
Karel Berka, Gottlob Frege: Wissinscaftlicher Briefwechsel, Hamburg: Meiner 1976; Christian THIEL (Hrsg.): Frege und die moderne Grundlagenforschung, Meisenheim: Hain 1975; *Joachim Pfarr*, Bernulf Kanitscheider: Vom absoluten Raum zur dynamischen Geometrie, Mannheim Bibliographisches Institut 1976.

Herausgeber/Editor: **Prof. Dr. Rudolf Haller, Philosophisches Instit. Universitat Graz, Heinrichstrabe 26, A-8010 Graz, Osterreich, Austria.**

political affairs

Stimulating Marxist studies and analyses on a wide variety of subjects

- detente and world peace • Middle East conflict • Southern Africa • international solidarity
- Black liberation • liberation of all oppressed peoples • the fight against racism
- rank and file movements • trade union developments
- the economic crisis • inflation • how to combat it
- women's equality
- the anti-monopoly movement • the struggle for socialism

Providing a Marxist approach to burning domestic and international problems, *Political Affairs* is indispensable reading for trade unionists, peace and freedom activists, students of politics and society as well as all those who seek clarity about current issues.

As the monthly theoretical journal of the Communist Party, USA, *Political Affairs* is the most authoritative source on the policies and views of the CPUSA.

One-year subscription $7.50.
Free sample copy will be sent on request.
Order from:

        Political Affairs Publishers
        235 W. 23rd St., Room 500
        New York, NY 10011

THE INSURGENT SOCIOLOGIST

A quarterly review of progressive and marxian thought and enquiry, including major articles, review essays, book reviews, and research notes.

OUR MOST RECENT ISSUE INCLUDED:

Erik Olin Wright's *Intellectuals and the Working Class*

Paul Goldman's *Sociologists and the Study of Bureaucracy: A Critique of Ideology and Practice*

BRAVERMAN SYMPOSIUM:

Jack Sattel's *The Degradation of Labor in the 20th Century: Harry Braverman's Sociology of Work*

Dale Johnson's *Strategic Implications of Recent Social Class Theory*

Al Szymanski's *Braverman as a Neo-Luddite?*

FORTHCOMING:

Special issues focusing on class and class consciousness; Poulantzas, Althusser and French Structuralism; Marxism and Culture; and revolutionary movements, for which we are still seeking materials.

New Directions in Power Structure Research, II
Edited by G. William Domhoff
(Fall, 1979)

Special Issue
Labor & Work

A full-length issue on labor and work, this volume includes essays on the labor process by **Stanley Aronowitz**, **Richard Edwards**, and **David Gartman**; essays on rank-and-file insurgency in the UMW and USW by, respectively, **Paul Nyden** and **Phillip Nyden**; essays on women and the home economics movement and reserve army of labor by, respectively, **Susie Strasser**, and **Margaret Simeral**; a review of labor today by **Sidney Peck**; and, additionally, **Sam Friedman's** "Changes in the Trucking Industry and the Teamster's Union: The Bonapartism of Jimmy Hoffa;" **Peter Drier's** "Newsroom Democracy: A Case Study of an Unsuccessful Attempt at Worker's Control" and **Cynthia Valentine's** "Internal Union Democracy: Does it Help or Hinder the Movement for Industrial Democracy?"